Advances in
Applied Developmental Psychology

Volume 1

edited by

Irving E. Sigel
Educational Testing Service

Ablex Publishing Corporation
Norwood, New Jersey 07648

ISBN: 0–89391–090–2
ISSN: 0748–8572

Ablex Publishing Corporation
355 Chestnut Street
Norwood, New Jersey 07648

Contents

Preface

It gives me great pleasure to introduce the *Advances in Applied Developmental Psychology*. This series will be adjunctive to the *Journal of Applied Developmental Psychology,* and have the same goal: namely, to publish reports of research or conceptual and policy papers dealing with issues related to application of developmental psychology to settings in which knowledge of development is relevant.

Although there is a similarity in overall goals between the two publications, there are some clearly defined differences. Aside from enabling writers to discuss their work in depth and detail, the *Advances* will also provide a forum where space limitations are less likely to constrain the writer from extensive presentations. In addition to the length, the *Advances* will contain reviews of research with special reference to how they bear on application. For example, the article in this volume by McCall poses some interesting issues about the use of research-based knowledge and the media. While not strictly a research issue, it does deal with some important policy questions relevant to the researcher, service persons and the media. This is an issue-oriented article that may have some spin-off in terms of research, but its significance resides in its relevance to how the field of applied developmental psychology should interface with media. The numerous issues that McCall's discussion raises will hopefully inspire much discussion. On the other hand, the other papers deal with different issues with and without a data base. Each of them is a timely and relevant topic in its own way for developmental psychologists interested in application.

The volumes in the *Advances* series will not deliberately be thematic in a substantive sense. Rather, they will present material of various types appropriate for the various settings requiring developmental knowledge. The diversity of the papers will also reflect the status of the field. Applied developmental psychology is a relatively new area; not new in terms of the use of research knowledge in service settings, but new in the sense that psychologists are beginning to see this area as one which will eventually have an identity of its own.

Some academic departments are planning to institute (or have already instituted) graduate programs in applied developmental psychology. In comparison to the clinical field, applied developmental psychology has not reached a state of consensus as to what it is, how students should be educated, and what the relevant substantive disciplines are that are involved. For some it can be identified as a clinical program with a strong research identity. Is applied developmental psychology a special case of applied psychology, a field represented by a journal of its own and a mission; or is it like industrial psychology where the content of the field is essentially service settings dealing with specific industrial issues? It should be made clear, however, that when the term *settings* is used with developmental psychology concerns, the definition is not just in terms of the age groups served but in the purpose and conceptualization of the setting's program. Therefore we refer to service settings of any age group where developmental change is an inherent goal of the program. It could be argued that most service settings involve change, be it a clinical therapeutic situation or an educational setting. There is, of course, truth to this argument. However, chances are that many service personnel do not perceive the change as developmental, but rather as just change. A developmental perspective, however, is different in that it refers to conceptualizing and examining change in terms of process. Just to note that differences between age groups occur is of little scientific, or even practical, value. However, when change is discussed in terms of process, or other constructs which provide explanations for change, our theoretical understandings and a basis for application are enhanced. Successful application, I believe, requires an understanding of the process itself and the context to which it is applied.

The *Advances in Applied Developmental Psychology,* then, is intended to report the new developments in a very broad field. This volume reflects the breadth. There is an article covering developmental psychology and the media, as well as one covering developmental psychology in the preschool. The chapter dealing with changes over time among students identified as handicapped reflects still another legitimate developmental interest. What we shall see is that the field is broad and, at the moment, defies circumscription. As long as we claim that what is involved is the application of human developmental knowledge to the various settings concerned with the human condition, we are entering the domain of applied developmental psychology. Perhaps the time and experience the field of applied developmental psychology will come into its own as a bona fide specialty. The *Advances* series is conceptualized as a service to that end. It is in this spirit that we enter into the inauguration of this new series.

Thanks go to ABLEX Publishers and to Educational Testing Service for helping actualize this new venture. My personal thanks go to Linda Kozelski at ETS for her assistance in helping to bring this series to fruition.

Irving E. Sigel
October, 1983

1

Child Development and Society: A Primer on Disseminating Information to the Public through the Mass Media

Robert B. McCall
Boys Town Center, Boys Town, NE 68010

Perhaps the fastest growing movement in developmental psychology during the last few years is child development and social policy. Initially, this movement consisted mainly of attempts to provide information and to influence legislation and other government policies. More recently, however, the orientation has broadened to other forms of relationship between child development and society. One new interest, for example, is disseminating the fruits of our discipline to the general public through the mass media (Brown & Rubinstein, in press; McCall & Stocking, 1982).

The communications media, for their part, also seem interested in psychologists. One study, for example, showed that 76% of social scientists have some contact with the media at one time or another, and social scientists are 39% more likely to be called than are scientists in other fields (Dunwoody & Scott, 1982). Moreover, talk shows are booming (Carter, Howard, Yang, & Gelman, 1979), and behavioral professionals, in general, and child and family specialists, in particular, are popular guests.

As a result of this mutual interest, developmental professionals are increasingly likely to be involved with the media. But before the horse runs away with the cart, perhaps we ought to ask ourselves if this is a good idea, consider some of the ethical issues involved, and prepare ourselves to be effective when we do participate in media activities.

1

TO GO, OR NOT TO GO, PUBLIC

Despite the current interest in the media by some researchers and clinicians, others are skeptical of the media and of the performance of some of their colleagues who participate. "Going public," after all, can be a nasty business (Goodfield, 1981; McCall & Stocking, 1982). Some would claim you can get burned, it is self-promotion, it can do more harm than good, and it is downright unethical. I consider some of these issues below.

Why Do This in the First Place?

The reasons for communicating with the public can be divided into two broad classes—self-serving and altruistic.

Benefits

On the self-serving side, researchers and service providers need public constituencies, perhaps now more than ever. Researchers need funding to conduct research, and service providers, especially those working in public agencies, need funds to continue to provide those services (McCall, 1983). I believe the best way to develop a constituency is not simply to appeal for their support but to give them something they can use. This shows society what we can contribute, that we do contribute, and that such a contribution is worth maintaining. We can accomplish these goals in part by "giving psychology away" (Miller, 1969).

More altruistically, communicating our knowledge to society might help someone. Although we sometimes become bogged down with perceptions of inadequacy, we do know things that can prevent problems from arising, help people identify problems early, contribute to solutions, and benefit society in general.

Many of us think that we must tell people exactly what to do in a given situation to be successful in the media. While the media do love "how-to's," it is not necessary to be prescriptive to be useful or even to be popular. For example, it is helpful for people to understand the acting-out behaviors of certain adolescents, the consequences to mother and child of an early pregnancy, and the typical stages of development. People can be helped simply by knowing that they are making a good effort, their instincts are sound, and their children are normal.

In fact, in many media situations, it is sufficient just to be interesting. Behavioral scientists and service professionals are blessed with the fact that most of the issues that we confront professionally are fascinating to people. While this is sometimes a liability, it is easier for us to be interesting to the general public than a molecular chemist. And when parents in particular are asked what they want to know, the most typical answer is not how to solve a specific problem but "about the normal process of development" (Clarke-Stuart, 1978). Much of what we know, the public wants to know.

Getting burned

Almost every psychologist who has been the source of at least a handful of newspaper stories can spin yarns about the inaccuracies of one or more of the stories. Scientists feel that the press is generally rather inaccurate, and studies do reveal that accuracy rates for science are worse than for general reporting (Tankard & Ryan, 1974). However, our memories and general impressions are worse than the actual case. For example, when scientists from several fields were asked about the reporting of science in general, 60% said it was "generally accurate." But when the same scientists were asked about a specific story reporting their own research, 95% said it was "generally accurate," (Tichenor, Olien, Harrison, & Donohue, 1970). Moreover, when scientists identified the types of errors in stories about them, most were errors of omission rather than false statements (Tankard & Ryan, 1974).

It seems that scientists remember the errorful stories and forget the accurate articles, and scientists would like a more comprehensive report of their work than is usually the case. So while inaccuracies occur—and reporters and scientists alike wish the rates were lower—it is not as bad as our general impression.

But you can get burned by the media in another way. You can be the object of ridicule or depricating humor. I do not know of any data on this issue. My impression is that it happens, but not often. True, occasionally a scientist's work is trivialized, as in the Golden Fleece Awards, but even those infamies have become infrequent following certain legal proceedings. Also, several letters to the editor of the Los Angeles *Times* criticizing a depricating story on a recent American Psychological Association (APA) convention were followed shortly by the departure of that reporter.

Finally, scientists can be hot-boxed on the air. This is also rare in my experience, but those who are roughly treated often make extreme claims or advocate extreme social or political points of view. If such people were politicians, corporate executives, or military personnel, I would guess that many scientists would applaud the media for aggressively probing a deserving extremist.

Yes, you can get burned, but it is not common and you can do things that will promote accuracy and lessen the likelihood of being roughly treated.

Harming rather than helping

When your words appear in the paper or on the air, you have no control over how people will interpret them and no control over what those people might do as a result. You could be misunderstood, and people could make wrong decisions, perhaps even harmful ones.

True, it could happen. But is it common? No one knows, but I doubt it. Are there many more people helped than harmed? Again, no one knows, but I think so.

No situation is risk free. Would anyone claim that psychotherapy could not be harmful? Would it be more harmful not to communicate and allow the public to muddle through in "blissful" ignorance? The task, for me at least, is to communicate and learn how to do it effectively and carefully. I offer some suggestions later in this paper.

Outcome

How does one know that communicating does any good? It is difficult and costly to evaluate media effectiveness, and we must adjust our expectancies about what can be accomplished through the media. Typically, in research and clinical practice, psychologists expect most participants to change in predictable and observable ways. But the criterion in the media is not the *percentage* of people who change their behavior, but the *absolute number* of people who hear the message or are influenced by it and *the cost per person*. For example, in a television campaign to help people stop smoking in Finland, only 1% of the nation's smokers gave up their habit for at least 6 months as a result of the program. But that amounted to a great many people and each "cure" was achieved at a cost of approximately $1.00 (McAlister, Puska, Koskela, Pallonen, & Maccoby, 1980). Furthermore, when the message is informational rather than prescriptive, no specific behavioral change or action may be predicted. Most people who see a program on child abuse, for example, may never need the information, some may not use it for months or years, and others may only acquire an attitude about services for the abused.

The "effects" of media messages are often difficult to predict or measure, and when evaluation is possible, the process is much different than in psychology. But few argue with the potential of the media to disseminate information to enormous audiences at modest cost, to raise consciousness, to set agendas, and to create or reinforce attitudes (McCombs & Shaw, 1977; McQuail, 1969).

But Is It Ethical?

The ethics of certain "media psychologists" are currently being debated. The American Psychological Association once prohibited psychologists from providing advice or therapy in the media. Now the standards allow advice but not therapy, although the distinction between the two is not clear. A special APA task force is currently working on this and other ethical issues pertaining to psychologists in the media.

Most of the serious ethical concerns revolve around clinicians on radio or television who answer the personal questions of callers (Barthel, 1983; Kalter, 1983). It is not unusual on these programs for people to request help for very serious problems—suicide, homosexuality, divorce, and incest. The typical caller is on the air with a psychologist for approximately 4 minutes and rarely longer than 9 minutes (Feldman, 1982), and the psychologist is expected to bring this problem to some sort of conclusion in this time. While many of the ethical issues pertain specifically to this situation, others have broader applications, even to the situation in which a research child psychologist imparts information to a newspaper reporter. I discuss a few of these ethical issues below.

The information given out in the media must be accurate

This principle seems obvious, even trivial. But when a psychologist functions in the media, it is not so obvious or trivial. Suppose you are asked, "Is it unusual for an infant not to walk or talk at 15-months-of-age?" or "When does a baby first love his or her parent?" Since you are the "expert," you would probably answer these questions, even if you know little about the topic. It is difficult to say "I don't know" when you are live and in color.

Even during an interview with a newspaper reporter, when it seems more acceptable to admit ignorance, it is not unusual for psychologists to make inaccurate statements. I have conducted dozens of tape-recorded interviews with child development specialists across the country, and I have found numerous instances of factual errors even when the professional describes his or her own research. We usually attribute such mistakes to the reporter, but this is not always true.

Even more errors can occur when the professional "gets on a roll," begins to make informational and interpretive pronouncements in the absence of data or experience, or offers social or political prescriptions that appear the next day as having the force of science behind them. We often think better of those statements when we see them in cold type.

Of course, concern for accuracy can go too far. Some conservatives would require that all qualifications on a phenomenon be expressed, all details of each study be described, generalizations be limited to the circumstances of the research, and psychologists refuse to speculate on real situations that have not been studied directly. This approach is scientifically safe, but not very useful. The media would regard us as boring—the deadliest of media sins—and the public would perceive us as arrogant and obfuscatory.

It is difficult, but possible, to provide clear, simple, short, and direct answers that are intellectually honest, useful, and interesting to the audience. Some specific guidelines are offered below. Basically, however, child and family professionals who appear in the media must make a fundamental distinction between the medium and the message. The medium—your performance and style—is very important in the media. It should be conversational, informal, relevant, understandable, relaxed, and sometimes even light. But the medium should not compromise the message. Whatever your style, you must be accurate. Of course, mistakes will be made, but you must always be attentive to what you are saying, restrict yourself to topics that you know something about, label fact from theory or conjecture, and even say "I don't know."

Telling people what to do

Giving advice, diagnosing psychological problems, and prescribing therapeutic action for a specific individual over the air is a major concern of some critics of media psychology. The usual context is a radio or television program hosted by the psychologist that features anonymous calls from members of the audience seeking help with personal problems. While this is the most ethically dangerous context, many of the same issues arise in newspaper and magazine "advice" columns, and when a developmental psychologist is asked questions by a broadcast audience.

Critics of this activity make several points. First, callers usually are given only a few minutes to describe their problems, the psychologist typically asks only a few questions, and the entire episode must be brought to some conclusion within a few minutes (Feldman, 1982). This period of time, critics maintain, is simply too short to accurately diagnose a problem and prescribe an effective solution for a particular individual. Moreover, even if the particular caller is dealt with accurately and responsibly, an untold number of individuals in the listening audience who think they have the same problem may judge the conclusions to be appropriate for them as well as the caller, even though drastic differences may exist between their situations. Also, in personal therapy, mistakes of diagnosis or treatment can be corrected in the course of therapy, something that is nearly impossible in the media. Finally, what about individuals who call but never get on the air? When you go to a therapist, at least you get an interview—being ignored could be the last straw for a depressed individual who feels no one cares.

To deal with these issues, psychologists are sometimes encouraged not to address their on-the-air comments to the specific person but to discuss the problem in general terms. In this way, several circumstances bearing on the problem can be mentioned, alternatives provided, and specific advice or prescriptions avoided. But obviously the appeal of these programs is the personal nature of the activity—a real person with a real problem who gets a real solution. A compromise might be to address the comments directly to the specific person but to *avoid* making a clear diagnosis of the problem. Therefore, do not conclude,

"You are a very hostile woman who probably had a punitive father, and you can't live with your husband or without him." Also avoid drastic prescriptions for change, such as, "I think you should divorce him right away," or "Maybe you should have an affair."

Of course, severe prescriptions are sometimes warranted, such as, suggesting a suicidal person call a hot line or specialized agency, or advising a troubled individual to seek psychotherapy or counseling. But usually one does not have enough information to be confident of the appropriateness of a specific diagnosis or a prescription for drastic action. Ironically, however, state licensing exams often require such conclusions with even less information.

While the examples used above are clinical, research developmental psychologists can be faced with similar questions and issues: "My baby is 15-months-old and does not walk—is something wrong?," "My father has played with me sexually—what should I do?," "What can I do to make my child smarter?"

Should it be done at all?

It is easy to claim that it is impossible to provide accurate, balanced advice and information that is well matched with individual callers, letter writers, readers, and listeners. Some would suggest that psychologists should stay out of the media altogether, and they especially should not respond to individual requests for personal guidance and advice. On the other hand, this is our profession; must we do a perfect job or no job at all? Certainly, individual therapy and research are not perfect—we do the best we can under the circumstances.

In evaluating this issue, it helps to contemplate what might happen if psychologists did not act as sources for stories, appear on talk shows, and host their own programs. For one thing, society would not benefit from our knowledge. One argument made in favor of audience call-in shows, for example, is that without them many callers would not receive any help for their problems.

Second, someone else would perform these functions if psychologists did not. While some nonpsychologists can be quite good at answering personal questions, most lack the training to handle delicate situations. For example, I had the opportunity to listen to a tape of a call-in program hosted jointly by an experienced media psychologist and a nonpsychologist radio personality with 25 years of experience hosting his own call-in program. The topic of the program was sexual problems, and one male caller complained of being embarrassed by frequent erections while talking to women. The radio personality seized the opportunity to make light of the matter by responding with locker-room remarks about "patting it down." A few minutes later, however, it became obvious that the caller was suicidal. The psychologist immediately asserted herself, advised the individual to find someone to be with for the evening, to call a hot line or a suicide prevention service, and to hold the line so that her assistant could continue to talk with him off the air. The contrast between how the psychologist and how the nonpsychologist handled this individual convinced me that at least some psychologists have a much better chance of helping people through a crisis than some very successful radio personalities.

I believe some psychologists have accepted the principle that "bad" psychologists appear in the media so "good" ones should not go there lest they become tainted by association. But even if the premise of this argument were true, the conclusion has the practical effect of keeping the presumed status quo. If "good" psychologists do not accept the responsibility to communicate their knowledge, the situation will not improve and they have little right to complain. Other individuals may tell the public that they can teach their baby to perform mathematics and read at 2 or 3 years of age, or that handicapped children can be cured by a demanding set of exercises. The result may be false hope, guilt, frustration, and sorrow. Is it not just as unethical to be mute in our offices when extreme claims or bad advice are beamed to thousands, or millions, of parents? Is it also not unethical—or at least selfish—to accept public money to do research but to refuse to report the results to the funding public? The communication enterprise may not be perfect, but I believe it is better with us than without us. We should reward those who do it well and do what we can to discourage those who do it poorly.

Assuming some of us are going to communicate through the media, let us do it with skill. Being an effective source, guest, or program host requires abilities in addition to those necessary to be a good psychologist. Some guidelines on how to be effective in the media follow.

A PRACTICAL GUIDE TO PARTICIPATING IN THE MEDIA

Few psychologists will become columnists, writers, hosts, and producers, but the majority will be sources for journalists and guests on interview and talk shows, which may have audience participation. The following guidelines apply to these roles.

Before the Actual Event

A number of factors need to be considered before the actual interview, including knowing whether you have something to say, making the contact with the media, and preparing for the interview.

Do I have something to say?

In my view, the most crucial aspect of disseminating information to the public is not "translating" the terminology of our discipline into common parlance but selecting information that is interesting to parents and citizens. If *what* you say is interesting, *how* you say it becomes less important. As a practical matter, however, the media decide what the public finds interesting by controlling what information is communicated. Unfortunately, in my view, the media have not adapted their criteria for what is newsworthy to fit the realities of behavioral science, but we must adapt to their criterion anyway.

For example, something is newsworthy if it represents a change, if it is different, if it is counterintuitive or surprising, and if it contradicts prevailing thought, beliefs, traditions, or ways of doing things. Can you imagine the headline, "World Trade Towers Still Standing?" (Burrows, 1980). No one expects them to fall, so the fact that they remain is not news. Therefore, just because science has demonstrated that divorce has a negative influence on children does not mean it will make the newspapers if everybody already believes it. This definition of news is also why cute results that have little generality and little importance sometimes make the newspapers—because they are not what we expect, they are surprising. It is also why the extreme positions of some of our colleagues make big news while more restrained views do not. For example, claiming that intellectual and personal characteristics are firmly established by age 3 is more startling, and thus newsworthy, than saying that people change and adapt to changing circumstances throughout much of their lives.

An event—something that happens—is also newsworthy. The need for an event is sometimes reflected in the journalist's penchant for "breakthrough" studies, announcements, or papers at a convention. Similarly, new results are more exciting than a penetrating review of "old" data. Of course, this ignores the fact that scientific truth rarely is made in a single study and usually appears dimly through an integration of entire literatures.

Sometimes, however, you can use the journalist's love of an event as an excuse to provide information on a topic that otherwise would not receive any attention. Valentine's Day gives an excuse for communicating information about human relationships and love; a celebrated crime in which a son kills his abusive father provides a context for communicating information about adolescent abuse; and a court case involving discrimination in testing sets the stage for information on how tests are created, scored, and interpreted. Such events are called "news pegs," and the media will be more interested if what you have to say can be related to an event in the news or a current theme in society.

Another criterion of newsworthiness is that the event or information affects people's lives. Information that is purely "academic" is, by definition, not very interesting. Instead, it should tell people what to do, provide information to assist them in making their own decisions about issues and actions, or help them understand phenomena that are common to their experience. This is why "how-to" articles are so popular, why journalists ask for the implications of your research for the "person on the street," and why they always ask for a concrete, commonplace example.

Controversy is also newsworthy, especially if it is about a topic that affects people's lives. The search for controversy sometimes results in minority viewpoints receiving equal billing with established principles. If a new study says X causes Y, an enterprising reporter might call several professionals for their opinions. If they all agree that X causes Y, the reporter may continue to call professionals until one disagrees. It is not a search for validity but a search for balance. While the article may say that most psychologists feel X causes Y, the dissenter may receive a disproportionate emphasis in the story.

Famous individuals are more newsworthy than unknowns. For example, Walter Sullivan, *The New York Times* science writer, reportedly (Science, technology and the press, 1980) said: "With Linus Pauling, you report it because it's Linus Pauling . . . even if it *is* kooky." Also B. F. Skinner's invited address on aging at the 1982 American Psychological Association convention received tremendous press coverage, and when reporters were asked why they gave it so much emphasis, the single most frequent response was that it was B. F. Skinner (Don Kent, 1983, personal communication).

The task for us, therefore, is to *select* information to present to the media that satisfies these criteria. Otherwise, we run the risk of the media "hyping" material that is less intrinsically interesting to meet these criteria.

Making contact

Most academics and service professionals wait for the media to make contact with them; they are surprised to discover that a substantial number of newsmakers call the media, not the other way around. But typically, the contact is made through an intermediary. Major corporations have public information offices and often highly paid public relations firms whose business it is to issue news releases, encourage reporters to cover activities of the corporation, train executives to interact effectively with the press and talk show hosts, arrange appearances for major executives on radio and television, and generally keep the media interested in the corporation. Psychologists can go to the information offices of their universities or the public information office of the American Psychological Association for help in making contact with the media.

While you do not need to wait for the media to call you, the media are suspicious of individuals who appear as if they are using the media for their own benefit. It is quite reasonable for you to call the local newspaper if a well-known individual is coming to give a public speech, if your organization now provides a new service, or for some other event that is legitimately in the public interest. On the other hand, if you call a reporter because you have discovered 10 easy rules for rearing children or because you have a sure-fire method of pacifying rebellious adolescents, you may be greeted with suspicion. The issue is whether the material is newsworthy, responsible, in the public interest, and whether the public or you will be the primary beneficiary. The media must perform public service, but that is different from granting individuals free publicity.

Should I cooperate?

A good many psychologists are skeptical about the media and wonder if they should cooperate at all (e.g., Rubin, 1980). While I encourage you to cooperate, it is a good idea to know what you are getting into.

For example, if a newspaper reporter or a free-lance writer calls, you should know their position or experience (general assignment reporter, science writer, editor), the newspaper or magazine they write for, the topic and main point of the story, what information you are to provide, and who else the reporter expects to interview. Often the caller will provide this information immediately, but it is certainly reasonable for you to ask politely if they do not. Generally speaking, the larger the publication and the more experienced and specialized the reporter, the more time they will have to work on the story and the more knowledgeable they will be about research and about behavioral development. But there are many fine local and general assignment reporters as well, and local publicity may be more important to you than the glamor of a brief mention in a national publication.

If the caller is from a broadcast medium, determine the nature of the program, the interviewer, the topic and main point of the episode, the program length, the other people who will be on the program with you, the role you are to play, whether the program will be edited, and whether it will have audience participation. If the program is produced in another town and you are concerned about it, call the TV critic of the local newspaper to ask about the program style. Also inquire if your expenses are to be paid (this is not always the case).

Now you need to decide to participate or not. Newpaper interviews have the least pressure, because your thoughts will be transmitted to the public through a reporter, an editor, and a headline writer, not by you directly. On the other hand, something can be gained or lost during the transmission, and you are not likely to be able to check over the article before publication.

If you are invited to be a guest on a radio or television program, other issues arise. Obviously, your ability to speak clearly, simply, briefly, and directly is crucial, and if the program involves audience participation you will need to be able to deal with very practical and sometimes naive questions. You also need to decide whether the program emphasizes controversy and whether you are willing and able to handle that. While you will have no control over the questions, you will have control over the answers—whatever you say is what will be broadcast, since most of these programs, whether live or recorded, are not edited.

You may also be called to participate in a documentary film or television program. These can be very time consuming—it may take several hours of recording and a good deal of waiting around for an appearance of less than 30 seconds in the final product. However, they are almost always edited, you can ask to restate an answer (although you don't get to choose which answer is actually used in the final product), and you may be able to spend a good deal of time with the interviewer before your performance, clarifying what you have to say and what they need.

Finally, the local radio or television news may call. While they deserve your cooperation, they are the most risky of media opportunities, because they are composed so quickly and your appearance is so brief. They are likely to want to tape you the same day they call—perhaps within a few hours. They will know almost nothing about you or what you have to say, the interview itself is disconcerting because the camera is not always taping you (but your voice is always being recorded), and less than 15 seconds of what you say will be included in the episode. If they do call, find out as much as you can about the nature of the story and why they want to interview you. Prepare a statement of less than 20 words (not more than 12–15 seconds) of what you want to say. Make that statement in a conversational style (do not memorize it) immediately after the reporter asks you the main question, and be very mindful of what you say during the remainder of the interview.

For some of you, there still remains a nagging question, ''Will I get roasted?'' For example, what if ''60 Minutes'' calls? ''Hang up,'' is the advice of some insiders. Even one CBS producer reportedly cautioned a prospective ''60 Minutes'' guest that ''at best you'll be raped, at worst, killed'' (Klepper, 1981). If you survive, of course, it is a major triumph. The Adolph Coors Brewery ran enormous newspaper advertisements with the headline, ''The Four Most Dreaded Words in the English Language: 'Mike Wallace Is Here' '' and proceeded to tell readers all the good things Mike Wallace found out about Coors Brewery. At the very least, you need to know if the program thrives on controversy and investigative reporting.

In my experience and that of others (Hilton & Knoblauch, 1980), the vast majority of reporters and interviewers are not out to get you. Their job is to bring information and entertainment (i.e., interesting and useful information or conversation) to the public. There are, however, some danger signs to watch for. If a journalist seems to have his or her mind made up about what the point of the article will be and keeps coming back to certain questions, hoping that you will answer in a certain way, be careful. If your study is not terribly important but represents a cute or odd finding, you risk being cast in the role of trivial entertainment. If the broadcast will have several people with different perspectives participating simultaneously (e.g., the network morning shows, "Nightline"), you need to decide if you are willing and able to handle that situation. Finally, if the program or interviewer thrives on controversy and investigative reporting (e.g., "60 Minutes," "20-20"), be very careful.

But, in my opinion, the most important factor in whether the media will roast you is your own behavior and statements: if you advocate an extreme social or political point of view; if you believe most people are rearing their children the wrong way; if you suggest a simple solution to a complex problem; if you are arrogant, argumentative, self-serving, or have something to sell. The media's job is to be suspicious and investigative. You asked for it.

Preparing background material

If you expect to be dealing with the media, it helps to have prepared a few documents in advance.

For one thing, make up a one-paragraph *biographical sheet* that gives your name, title and affiliation, background specialty, major authorships, years of experience, national consultantships, and so forth. Then add a paragraph entitled "Biographical Details" in which you describe your educational history, a few highlights of your professional career, main articles or books, national offices and consultantships, and so forth. Do not overdo it. Then add a series of one-sentence paragraphs representing topics or issues that you are prepared to discuss. A good model to follow for this section is the promotional material printed on the dust jacket of a book. This information guides an interviewer toward your areas of expertise, but do not write this material in the form of questions that you want to be asked (that style infringes on the interviewer's territory). A hypothetical sample appears in Figure 1.1.

In addition to the biographical sheet, if you have just published a study or literature review that is of public interest and will be made available to the media, you should consider having a press release written.

A press release is a short statement of the information you wish to communicate written in the form of a newspaper story or broadcast announcement. It features the who, what, when, where, why, and how of the information, beginning with the conclusion and implications followed by more minor details.

Most psychologists are ill-equipped to write a professional release, but the staff of a university public information office is quite experienced at it. They will judge whether your research is of public interest, and they may write a news release for you. Occasionally, the APA public information office will also perform this function.

If you do not have access to a public information office, do not try to write a news release that sounds like a newspaper article. Instead, write a short, clear summary of your article or message. This should not be the abstract of your

Name: Barbara R. Smith, Ph.D.

Title: Child Psychologist
Associate Professor of Psychology
State University
College Park, Rhode Island 01473
(773) 424-1732

Background: Research specialist in infant development.

Author of *Infant Development,* a textbook for college students, and *Your Baby,* a book for parents.

Author of more than 45 scholarly articles on infant development.

Biographical Details

Dr. Smith received her doctorate in psychology at Private University in Someplace, Illinois in 1975. Since then, she has published more than 45 articles for scholarly audiences on the growth of attachment and love between parent and infant, the different ways parents and infants play and relate to one another, and the consequences for the baby of a lack of parental involvement. She was named to the Panel on Infant Development of the National Academy of Sciences in 1982, is a frequent consultant to government and private agencies regarding infant development, and lectures at universities from coast to coast. Dr. Smith's recent book, *Your Baby,* provides new parents with the latest research information on the capabilities of infants, how they develop behaviorally, and what parents can do to enjoy their baby more.

Topics of Expertise

An infant can recognize his or her parent as being familiar within the first week of life.

Babies probably do not love you simply because you are their parent but because of what you do together.

Love and attachment is probably *not* cemented into place forever during those great moments of contact in the hospital nursery.

"Responding" to your baby may be just as important—even more important—than "stimulating" your baby.

Continually ignoring a baby may be one of the most devastating psychological experiences for an infant.

FIGURE 1.1.   Sample Biographical Sheet for the Media (Fictional)

journal article but similar to what you would tell a nonpsychologist friend about your paper. Stress the main conclusion of your research or paper and its implications for parents, teachers, or society. Then give a short paragraph describing the research you actually did, and a reference to your paper, book, or presentation. It will also help to provide some background information about how prevalent the problem is, how many people in the United States or your locality are affected by the issue under investigation, and anything else that places it in public context.

News releases, or this brief statement, provide the reporter with the basic facts of what you have to say and improve the accuracy of reporting (Dunwoody, 1982; Tichenor, Olien, Harrison, & Donohue, 1970). Also, preparing these statements helps you focus on what you really have to say. It is far better for you to know your major point in advance than for the reporter to fish around for it. I believe that scientists and other professionals are often less interesting sources and guests than they could be, because the interviewer does not know what the professional has to say, and the professional does not take the initiative to steer the conversation toward the topics of his or her expertise. These statements help both you and the interviewer get to the main point.

Rehearse

Once you know you are going to meet with the media, gather together what factual information you may need, study it, think of questions you may be asked, and jot down notes, catch phrases, and concrete examples on how to answer them. Then get somebody to conduct a mock interview. Do not memorize your responses, but practice answering briefly (two sentences), conversationally (no academic jargon), and concretely (commonplace examples).

The Interview

The media's primary method of data collection is the interview, and none of us is trained to be interviewed. Our profession communicates primarily to itself, not to outsiders, and it does so through a highly specialized form of writing. Even when we do speak, it is usually a lecture to a captive audience. We are not practiced in short-answer, off-the-cuff, practical, or commonplace responses to undisciplined questions from an audience who needs to be kept interested and is primarily concerned with practical matters of childrearing. The media interview is one-draft dictation to an alien audience. Few of us are skilled at dictation, and those few are rarely satisfied with their first drafts.

It is a skill, however, that many of us can learn with a little guidance, preparation, and practice. So go to your interview having selected the information that you feel nonprofessionals would find interesting and useful; know in advance the few points you want to make and how you will express them; come armed with some commonplace, concrete examples to illustrate your points; and be prepared to handle the naive or testy question. Here's how.

Present an attitude of cooperation and respect

Treat the interviewer as a professional skilled in another discipline, and do not tread on his or her responsibilities. For example, do not tell the interviewer what you want to be asked and do not request to see the questions, even if the interviewer has written them out (very unusual). Instead ask politely whether the interviewer wishes you to emphasize point A, B, or C—all of which are acceptable to you.

In the case of a print journalist, remember that you are the subject, not the author of the article. You are the rat in the journalist's experiment (Victor Cohn, cited by Goodfield, 1981). As such, do not expect to be able to review the article before it is published—have you allowed one of *your* subjects to read one of *your* reports recently? Some reporters do check facts with sources, especially magazine writers, but this is unusual (McCall & Stocking, 1982). Journalists feel that checking facts provides news-makers the option of censorship over a free press, because news makers often want to change more than the facts. Frequently there is not time to do it, and often it is a hassle because scientists want to add material that reporters feel is not important (Broberg, 1973; Dunwoody, 1982). But checking does improve accuracy (Tankard & Ryan, 1974; Tichenor et al., 1970), so you can certainly volunteer to do it. If you do review the article, be sure to restrict your comments to errors of fact and important omissions and emphases, leaving the journalist to chose the main theme, most interpretations, and writing style.

Arrogance is probably our worst enemy. Do not, for example, continually refer to your book or to your research, even though that is the main reason you are being interviewed. Sometimes it helps to portray yourself as a fellow parent by being sympathetic with the problems raised by the interviewer or audience. Let the substance and breadth of your information communicate your authoritativeness, not your style.

Be brief. Try to answer questions in two or three sentences. Believe me, it can be done, but it takes practice. So have a person who is not a psychologist help you see the kernel of what you have to say. Then practice that short answer. Otherwise, if you are long-winded, you risk being cut off before you have made your main point, you invite the journalist to select what he or she thinks is important rather than what you think is important, and you encourage the journalist to paraphrase your words rather than to quote you. If your short answer is interesting, you will be asked to elaborate.

Lead with the conclusion. When you are asked a question, begin your answer with the conclusion—the bottom line—and the shorter and more direct the statement, the better. Why? For one thing, the journalist is poised to write down your answer immediately after asking the question. If you give the essence of your answer later, an inexperienced reporter may be writing something else you said and miss the main point. Also, the interviewer may cut you off after a few sentences to change the subject, thus depriving you of completing your point.

Avoid jargon. Be conversational and try to use phraseology that is familiar to the audience.

Use commonplace, concrete examples. Have a bag of short, everyday examples to illustrate your main points—something that is common to the experience of the audience. This is especially difficult for researchers who usually do not have a reservoir of case studies or a great deal of experience with the everyday problems of parents. So ask people where you work if they have ever experienced X or Y and what they did about it, read the parenting articles in national magazines for case study material, and interview a few subjects in your own research to relate their behavior to their experiences.

Use only a few simple statistics. Obviously, *p* values are out, but statistics indicating the frequency of runaways, for example, or the percentage of runaways who are abuse victims can be very persuasive and add credibility to your statements. But use only one statistic per sentence and no more than two per answer.

Call a spade a spade. Make clear what is known as a result of research, what is mainstream clinical practice, what is your personal judgment or opinion, and what is rank speculation. Child professionals are less likely than nonprofessionals to distinguish these different types of statements (Robinson, 1982).

Stay within your competence. It is easy to get carried away and pontificate on something you know little about, especially when a concerned parent asks a very reasonable, practical question, but one outside your expertise. Do not be afraid to say you do not know, even during a live broadcast interview, but explain why you do not know (e.g., "No one has really studied that question," "A physician could answer that more knowledgeably than I"), or say what you do know about the topic (e.g., "I don't know how much TV is too much, but there are some signs you can look for. For example, . . ."). And be certain about your facts and statistics—do not guess or estimate.

Watch your politics. In my experience, many of the psychologists who are most unhappy with the media are also the most political, frequently recommending extreme or unusual social or governmental changes that reporters feature in their articles and headlines, or which interviewers challenge on the air.

Always be "on the record." Make an assumption: No matter what the context, pretend that you are talking to at least 10,000 people representing every point of view imaginable every moment you are with a reporter or an interviewer. Consider yourself always on the record, whether or not the pencil is poised or the red light is on.

Legal issues

Because psychologists are only recently appearing in the media, certain legal issues are ambiguous and unresolved. For example, if a questioner or listener follows the advice of a psychologist given in the media and that advice results in psychological or physical harm or loss to that person, can the psychologist be sued for malpractice? If so, would malpractice insurance cover it? Legally, this is uncharted territory, and the outcome of a given case would be difficult to predict.

A second issue can arise when the interviewer wants to call you a "psychologist." Academic psychologists should be aware of licensing laws in their states that typically prevent people calling themselves by a title that involves any variant of the word "psychologist" unless they have passed a licensing exam or otherwise meet state requirements. Some states permit employees of the government and educational institutions to call themselves psychologists and even deliver services if such services are reasonably considered part of their jobs. Is giving advice to parents in a newspaper column or on a radio or television program part of a professor's job?

If you appear in the media of a state other than your residence, calling yourself a psychologist may not be a problem, because most states have clauses in their licensing laws that exempt nonresidents from compliance for a short period of time. But licensing laws differ from state to state, so be careful if you are not licensed.

Broadcast Interviews and Audience Participation

Live broadcasts, especially those involving questions from the audience, require some additional guidelines.

Practice. Definitely practice some of the points made here with a friend and a tape recorder. You need to think and answer quickly, briefly, conversationally, and politely, and most of us need practice.

Know what to expect. Try to listen to the program you are to be on several times before your appearance.

Be prompt. Be quite clear what time you are to arrive at the studio and when you are to go on the air. Do not be late, even though it is likely you will wait in the lobby until a few minutes before you are to go on.

Appearance. Although you can wear anything for a newspaper or radio appearance, dressing up contributes to a professional image. But for television, proper dress is a necessity. According to Hilton and Knoblauch (1980), men should wear suits or sport jackets; women should wear dresses or suits. Avoid white, light blue, black, herringbone, and loud patterns of any kind. Solids of grey, darker blue, yellow, brown, khaki, and beiges are best, and limit yourself to no more than one muted patterned item. Also avoid bright colors, even solids; they can clash with the set design. Also, while wedding rings and watches are acceptable, bracelets that make noise and chains and necklaces that might brush against a lapel microphone should be removed. Finally, if you ordinarily wear eye glasses, wear them on television. If you have a choice, avoid chrome or shiny frames, and if you can angle the lenses slightly downward without looking odd, this will help to prevent glare.

Makeup. Very large stations will insist that guests be made up, both men and women. Typically, facial makeup is applied into the hairline and down the neck, so plan on a change of shirt or blouse after the program. Smaller stations do not make up guests, so you must deal with the issue yourself. The purpose of television makeup is to prevent the lights from glistening brilliantly off your shiny face. So, if you are a man without makeup, you may simply want to rub your face, especially your forehead, with a clean handkerchief before you go on and during commercials. Or you can muster your courage, visit a cosmetic counter, get the correct shade of pancake makeup, and do it yourself, but have a professional TV makeup artist select the makeup and show you how to apply it. If you are a woman, use your usual makeup, but apply it lightly (otherwise you look chalky) and avoid bright shades of eyeshadow and lipstick (Hilton & Knoblauch, 1980).

Posture. Once on the set, sit erect, feet firmly placed on the floor, with your jacket or suit coat buttoned or around in front with as few folds as possible. Orient yourself comfortably toward your host, perhaps with your forearm resting on the arm of the chair. Crossed legs or crossed ankles give a more relaxed impression, but ask the floor director if they will appear disproportionately large in the picture.

Props. Some people prefer props to keep their hands busy. If you need one, a nonshiny pen or pencil might do. It is sometimes helpful to have notecards (e.g., giving average ages and age ranges for developmental milestones, or statistics on the frequency of certain problems), and these can either be held in your hand or placed out of sight on a table.

Your behavior. Do not fiddle with the microphone or clothing near the microphone, and if you need to sneeze or cough, turn your head away from the microphone and cover it with one hand and your face with the other.

Also, always assume that you are on camera, even when you are not talking, because directors like to vary the pictures and frequently intersperse shots of you listening while the interviewer poses a question or when you are being introduced.

Stylistically, do not act. Try to be natural, honest, sincere, and fairly upbeat. Laugh easily in appropriate places, and sympathize with problems when they are discussed.

Finally, look at the interviewer, not at the camera or the monitor. Of course, it is great to be able to look into the camera's eye and talk to people one-on-one in their living rooms. Some guests are able to do this naturally, without lecturing, and without a rapid turn of the head or eyes toward the lens when the red light goes on. But this often takes practice, so it is safer to look directly at the interviewer rather than to appear to be grandstanding or lecturing to the folks at home.

Establish any ground rules before you go on the air. You won't have much time, but you can indicate to the interviewer issues and points you think are very important and topics you cannot discuss. Phrase these requests in terms of what you can and cannot talk about, rather than what the interviewer can and cannot ask you. For example, you might say, "I think it is very important that people understand that sexual abuse traps everyone—the child, the mother, and the father—in a no-win situation." Or "I am happy to discuss the psychological characteristics of assassins, but I cannot comment on John Hinkley in particular because I don't know him." You can also ask the host what is important to get across, but do not be surprised if he or she does not really know. If that is the case, offer several points that you would be happy talking about. Without these tactful suggestions, you may find that the interview is superficial and off target, you do not get a chance to make the points you came to state, and the audience misses the information that you are uniquely able to provide. Finally, you may want to indicate that while you are willing to talk generally about problems raised by the audience, you cannot diagnose or prescribe treatment for specific individuals.

Relax. Almost everyone gets nervous, even those who are very experienced. You may be even more nervous when you see how casually the whole thing proceeds. For example, you probably will not see the interviewer until a few minutes before air time, there will be little or no discussion of the topic before the program begins, the interviewer is not likely to know much about you or your topic (that is why you should send the biographical sheet and a news release in advance of your appearance), your chair will probably be uncomfortable and you will wonder where to put your hands, the production crew will be bored to death with the whole affair, and the introduction the host provides to the viewer may shock the socks off you (e.g., "Today we are going to learn how to make geniuses out of your babies because our guest is Dr. . . ."). It is amazing TV programs come off as well as they do.

Personal questions. There are several ways of dealing with the personal questions of the audience. First provide information about the topic in general. *Q:* "My baby is 15-months-old and doesn't walk. Is something wrong?" *A:* "Approximately 10–20% of normal infants do not walk by 15 months of age. The vast majority of these babies are perfectly normal."

Second, refer people to specialists: "If your late-walking child is of concern to you, consult your physician" or "That's a good question, but I am not a specialist in nutrition and I cannot tell you whether you should give your baby a vitamin C supplement to prevent colds. I feel you should consult your physician about your infant's diet and certainly about any supplements."

Third, provide alternative courses of action without endorsing one or another: "Some parents deny privileges, place the child in his or her room for a specified period of time, or sit the child in a corner as alternatives to spanking."

Fourth, encourage the callers to solve their own problems. Ask what they have tried, did it work, why not, what other alternatives are open to them, and how do they feel about those options? Teach them to problem solve, and point out pros and cons of various alternatives.

Complex questions. You may have to be brief, but you do not have to be simplistic. Complex questions should be dealt with appropriately: "That is an important question, but it is easier to ask than to answer. It depends on A, B, and C'' or ''We don't really know the answer to that, but some psychologists feel it is caused by X, others by Y, and others by Z.''

Attitude. Try to be sympathetic, understanding, respectful, and hopeful to your questioners. Project a warm, kind, sensitive attitude, even when you disagree with the person. For example, a mother told Phil Donahue how she beat her son with a belt for smoking a cigarette. Instead of accusing her of child abuse, Donahue said something akin to: ''I'm sure you love your son, and I'm pleased that this worked out for you. But not all parents would like that approach. Some might do A, some would prefer B, and others have tried C.'' Also, find something positive even in the most dismal circumstance, and provide people with some sympathy and realistic hope that their problem can be solved.

Fumbling. If you fumble your words, do not go back to correct them unless you have given out incorrect information. Also, do not correct errors made by the interviewer or a caller, but, of course, you should be accurate in your own statements about that topic. If necessary, make the correction to the host during a commercial break.

Special Tactics

Very rarely are interviewers deliberately antagonistic, but TV producers do like to put people with opposing views on the same program. So, if you are asked a question you want to dodge or if you get into an adversarial situation and are attacked by an interviewer or another guest, you may need special strategies (Hilton & Knoblauch, 1980):

Listen. Some of us are so concerned about what we say during a broadcast interview that we forget to listen to what other people are saying. It is embarrassing and arrogant to misunderstand a simple question by a caller or to request that it be repeated; it is death if you are in an adversarial position and have not heard the argument of your antagonist.

Bridging. Sometimes you will not really want to answer a question but you are willing to talk about a related topic. Provide a brief, even superficial, answer to the question, and then shift to the topic of your choice. *Q:* ''When does a baby first love his or her mother?'' *A:* ''One of the first steps in loving someone is being able to recognize them as being familiar. A baby can recognize a parent as being familiar at . . .''

Redefining the question. Sometimes you can avoid answering a question by redefining it in a way that you can answer it. The bridging example given above is one way. Another might be: *Q:* ''What is the single biggest mistake parents make in rearing their children?'' *A:* ''It's easy to criticize. I think most parents are doing the best they can. Child rearing is a difficult job and parents need all the encouragement and support they can get. It would be presumptuous of me to criticize.''

Answering with a question. Sometimes you can avoid answering a question by responding with a question. *Q:* "Should I get a divorce?" *A:* "How do you feel about that prospect?" Sometimes antagonistic questioners can be handled in the same way. *Q:* "For decades specialists have been saying that intelligence is essentially established in the first several years. What makes you think that isn't true?" *A:* "Do you feel your intelligence was determined at age 3?" Be careful with this tactic though, it can make you sound sassy.

The faulty premise. A favorite tactic of antagonistic interviewers is to draw an extreme conclusion based on a faulty premise. Your response is to impugn the premise, not the conclusion. *Q:* "Every child needs a fulltime mother, so shouldn't working mothers feel guilty?" *A:* "Every child needs to develop a loving relationship with a few people early in life, and while that takes some time, it does not require continuous 24-hour contact. It doesn't even require that the person be the child's mother."

The A or B dilemma. Some interviewers, either to get a simple answer or to be antagonistic, force the guest to pick between two simple extremes. *Q:* "Which is more important, heredity or environment?" Obviously, neither alternative is correct, so do not answer the question as posed. But do not insult the interviewer for asking an unanswerable question. In this case you can say, "Both are necessary, just as both natural ability and training are required to be an Olympic athlete."

Off-the-wall questions. Don't get led into unchartered waters by a wild question. Dodge it. *Q:* "What is the single most important thing for a parent to know?" *A:* "We'd all like to know that. Raising children is difficult, and it's different from one family to the next. It cannot be reduced to a simple formula. That is why it is so challenging and potentially rewarding."

Badgering. Very rarely an interviewer or another guest will badger. He or she may constantly interrupt, twist your words, and inaccurately restate your position. Do not respond in kind. The audience will see the antagonist as the villain, especially if, by contrast, you remain very calm, polite, and unruffled. However, allow yourself to be interrupted only twice. On the third time, lean forward, smile, and even touch the person on the arm if you can reach that far and say, "Just a moment please. I wonder if I can finish this point" (Hilton & Knoblauch, 1980).

On Tour

If you write a book for general audiences, the publisher may sponsor a media tour to advertise the book. You may be scheduled to be on several radio and television talk and news programs in several cities all in a few days. It sounds glamorous and it is—for about one day. After that, one television or radio studio is the same as the next, the questions are the same (interviewers read them off the book jacket or your prepared statement), last-minute cancellations can occur because of late-breaking news events, appointments may be scheduled too close together and a delay at one station can make you late for a live broadcast at the next station, and you can come away with the feeling that you have been so much "media meat" talked at by plastic smiling faces. But this is the way popular books are sold these days. If you are bored, try being a bit more interesting in your interviews.

EPILOGUE

Communicating the fruits of our discipline through the mass media is an effective way to build a constituency for developmental psychology and to help people by providing accurate and balanced information they can use. Like any activity, it can be done well or it can be done terribly, even irresponsibly and unethically. Not everyone should communicate, but some should, and those who do it well should be encouraged. It is a responsibility we have ignored too long.

REFERENCES

Barthel, J. (1983, April 26). Hi, you're on the air—What's your problem? *Woman's Day, 81*, 128–133.

Broberg, K. (1973). Scientists' stopping behavior as indicators of writers skill. *Journalism Quarterly, 50*, 763–167.

Burrows, W. E. (1980, April). Science meets the press: Bad chemistry. *The Sciences*, 1980, 15–19.

Carter, B., Howard, L., Yang, J., Gelman, E. Radio's gabfest. (1979, October 29). *Newsweek*, 87.

Clarke-Stuart, A. K. (1978). Popular primers for parents. *American Psychologist, 33*, 359–369.

Dunwoody, S. (1982). A question of accuracy. *IEEE Transactions on Professional Communications, 25*, 196–199.

Dunwoody, S., & Scott, B. T. (1982). Scientists as mass media sources. *Journalism Quarterly, 59*, 52–59.

Feldman, H. R. (1982). Psychology and the media: An exploratory study. Unpublished manuscript.

Goodfield, J. (1981). *Reflections on science and the media*. Washington, DC: American Association for the Advancement of Science.

Hilton, J., & Knoblauch, M. (1980). *On television! A survival guide for media interviews*. New York: AMACOM.

Kalter, J. (1983, June 4). No problem is too intimate for your TV therapist. *TV Guide*, 4–6.

Klepper, M. M. (1981, December 28). A TV interview need not be a lynching. *Wall Street Journal*.

McAlister, A., Puska, P., Koskela, K., Pallonen, J., & Maccoby, N. (1980). Mass communication and community organization for public health education. *American Psychologist, 35*, 375–379.

McCall, R. B. (1983). Family services and the mass media. *Family Relations, 32,* 315–322.

McCall, R. B., & Stocking, S. H. (1982). Between scientists and public: Communicating psychological research through the mass media. *American Psychologist, 37,* 985–995.

McCombs, M., & Shaw, D. (1977). The agenda-setting function of the press. In D. Shaw & M. McCombs (Eds.), *The emergence of American political issues: The agenda-setting function of the press.* St. Paul, MN: West Publishing Co., 1–18.

McQuail, D. (1969). *Towards a sociology of mass communications.* London, England: Collier-Macmillan.

Miller, G. A. (1969). Psychology as a means of promoting human welfare. *American Psychologist, 24,* 1063–1075.

Robinson, B. E. (1982). Family experts on television talk shows: Facts, values, and half-truths. *Family Relations, 31,* 369–378.

Rubin, Z. (1980). My love–hate relationship with the media. *Psychology Today, 13,* 12–13.

Rubinstein, E., & Brown, J.D. (Eds). (in press). *The media, social science and social policy for children: Different paths to a common goal.* Norwood, NJ: Ablex.

Science, technology, and the press: Must the "age of innocence" end? (1980, March/April). *Technology Review,* 46–56.

Tankard, J., & Ryan, M. (1974). News source perceptions of accuracy of science coverage. *Journalism Quarterly, 51,* 219–225, 334.

Tichenor, P., Olien, C., Harrison, A., & Donohue, G. A. (1970). Mass communication systems and communication accuracy in science news reporting. *Journalism Quarterly, 47,* 673–683.

2

Dimensions of Preschool: The Effects of Individual Experience*

Louise B. Miller, Mary B. Bugbee, and Duane W. Hybertson
University of Louisville

INTRODUCTION

Research during the 1960s and 1970s has provided a substantial body of knowledge about early intervention and in particular preschool education and its value for children who are at risk in the educational arena. The following generalizations can be made with some confidence:

---

*This study involved 1 year of planning, 2 years of pilot studies, 1 year of implementation, and 5 years of data reduction, analyses, interpretation, and writing. The only people continuously involved with the project during that entire period were the senior author and the program assistant. But at every stage of the enterprise, we were counseled and instructed by colleagues, students, preschool teachers, and office staff.

A number of graduate students helped design and carry out pilot studies. Diane Hybertson brought our ideas about the observation matrix to fruition and developed the master instrument. She also prepared the training tapes and procedure. Her contributions were of high quality and very valuable. Rondeall Bizzell developed the final version of the instrument and trained the classroom monitors. Her unique combination of creativity and diligence brought her from preschool teacher serving as a subject in a pilot study to full research colleague, and her contributions span an equally wide spectrum. Beverly Bleidt very competently coordinated the testing procedures and was largely responsible for checking of tests and preparation of data for analysis. Kay Proctor trained testers and observed teacher and child behavior in the classrooms throughout the school year while performing secretarial and administrative duties and keeping an eagle eye on all details from classroom and testing materials to significance levels and N in tables. Mary Frances Bettinger continued her exceptional administrative assistance through the first 2 years of the project.

Consultants were invaluable throughout the years. The study was derived from a previous study and planned in collaboration with Jean Dyer, coinvestigator in that study. At various times, she also

Many different programs can have decisive beneficial effects on later measures of school success (Consortium for Longitudinal Studies 1982; Palmer & Anderson, 1978); different programs have different immediate effects (Erickson, McMillan, Bennell, & Callahan, 1969; Karnes, Hodgins, Teska, & Kirk, 1969; Miller & Dyer, 1975); the effects of programs (both preschool and elementary) are related in a general way to program goals and styles of implementation. For example, the effects of academic, didactic programs have typically been manifest in higher IQs or better performance on achievement tests such as language, math, and information, whereas superiority in reasoning involving abstract language, divergent thinking, and nonverbal problem-solving has been shown to result from more open and flexible or nondidactic programs (Miller & Dyer, 1975; Soar & Soar, 1972; Stallings, 1975).

There is little information concerning the means by which preschool programs achieve their effects. In the more "structured" programs children are typically exposed to academic content in greater amounts and for longer periods of time than is the case in less didactic programs. But it has also been shown that different programs result in consistent differences in teacher and child behavior and in the methods used in implementation (Miller & Dyer, 1975; Weikart, Epstein, Schweinhart, & Bond, 1978). This is true for both the molar dimensions, which are similar for all children in a classroom (such as grouping, materials, content, group activities, giving information versus asking for performance, etc.), and also for the more molecular dimensions, which may vary from one child to another (e.g., specific teaching techniques, such as drill and rein-

served as a consultant regarding methodology, in particular statistical problems. Her suggestions regarding the format of the final report probably rescued the readers from an indigestible complexity.

In the early stage, we were greatly helped by advice regarding categories of observation, measures of change, and design problems. Those who consulted with us in these areas were Irving Sigel, Robert Soar, and J. S. Kounin. Lilian Katz enriched our thinking about teachers and their role in the classroom.

To Shirley Moore we are immensely grateful for her thorough and detailed critiquing of the final report. Her comments and questions led us to think through and clarify a number of issues and interpretations. Joanne Nurss also read the report and made some helpful comments.

Thanks are due our eight teachers who faithfully attended their training sessions and conscientiously carried out instructions. We were impressed not only with their sincere desire to learn the program and their concern for the children, but also with their interest in the research. Their names are: Catherine Brittle, Janora Couch, Wilhelmina Gilbert, Bette Payne, Cordelia Porter, Geraldine Redden, Ernestine Reeves, and Willie Sanderson. The teachers' aides also learned the Peabody Program and, despite a lesser amount of contact with the research staff, they worked with enthusiasm and dedication. Aides were: Janet Anderson, Lucy Gordon, Lurlean Love, Mary McKinney, Mary Murrell, Mildred Shumake, Rosa Valentine, and the late Carrie Wigginton.

The staff of the Head Start Program in Louisville, under the direction of Margaret Wright, were cooperative and helpful, as were principals and school personnel.

The study was funded by the National Institute of Child Health and Human Development whose continued support through the years has made possible the kind of field research which could not otherwise be carried out.

forcement). In general, the more didactic techniques are associated with more academic content. Does the superior academic performance produced by such programs result primarily from a larger amount of exposure to their content or from the didactic methods typically used? Do academic programs have less success in developing such skills as flexibility in problem-solving simply because they focus on other things or because the techniques typically used are antithetical to such development?

The establishment of relationships between program dimensions and program outcomes is important for a number of reasons. First, there is little evidence that the superiority produced by highly structured and didactic programs at the pre-kindergarten level will last without continued and similar intervention, and there is some indication of detrimental effects if such programs are not followed by similar ones in succeeding years. For example, we found that disadvantaged children who had the highest IQs and achievement scores after such a program (Bereiter-Engelmann) and then entered a nonacademic kindergarten not only performed much worse on the Metropolitan Readiness Test than children from that same program who had a more academic kindergarten, but also were well below children from other programs (Miller & Dyer, 1975).

Second, we cannot be sure that increasing IQ and academic performance are the most appropriate outcomes for a prekindergarten program. Children who were relatively quite high in achievement and IQ after a 1-year academic prekindergarten have been found to be surpassed in school achievement by children from less didactic programs as late as 8th grade (Miller & Bizzell, 1983).

Psychometric intelligence and other areas of development may not be well differentiated in the preschool years. Such characteristics as curiosity and flexibility are developmentally important in their own right (Kamii, 1975); they may become increasingly essential as the child progresses through school. They may also be propaedeutic to the full development of cognitive ability.

Third, if the relations between program components and program effects could be established, it might be possible to "blend together the 'open' versus 'prescribed' features" of programs (White & Siegel, 1976, p. 43) and maximize development of divergent thinking and logical reasoning in low SES children in addition to the acceleration of IQ and academic skills.

A number of comparisons of intact programs have examined both program dimensions and program effects (Miller & Dyer, 1975; Soar & Soar, 1972; Stallings, 1975; Weikart, et al., 1978). Results of three of these studies suggest that early academic progress is most likely to be affected by specific teaching techniques such as drill (Gordon & Jester, 1973); drill, practice, and praise (Stallings, 1975); and didactic teaching and the ratios of positive to negative reinforcement (Miller & Dyer, 1975). The consistency of these results is very promising, but direct connections between the previously identified teaching techniques and program effects have not yet been established.

The present study was designed to determine the effects of specific teaching techniques and child behaviors in preschool on the development of divergent skills, logical reasoning, and conventionally measured convergent abilities. The problems encountered in using various methodological approaches are discussed in the following section.

RESEARCH STRATEGIES

No research method appears to be entirely satisfactory in attempting to establish the links between program components and program effects. Three that have been widely used are: comparison of intact program models, experimental variation of methods while attempting to hold content constant, and observations of techniques and program components in a number of different classrooms. All of these present serious difficulties.

Program Comparison

Comparison of intact programs has been, and will probably continue to be, useful as a strategy for answering a number of important questions; however, this method presents a number of problems when the research goal is to establish a link between children's classroom experiences and behavior, and the development of various competencies and characteristics.

Confounding of Content, Activities, and Materials with Teaching Techniques

There appears to be a necessary relationship between the goals and content of a program and the teaching techniques used. Some techniques are applicable only to certain tasks. For instance, one can hardly "request elaboration" on the answer to "what number comes after four?" Similarly, since drill involves repetition, a child cannot be drilled in finding alternative solutions. *Drill* as a teaching technique is necessarily embedded in an ecological context, and the whole situation—including the behavior of both teacher and child and the content of the lesson—constitutes a miniature treatment that may be an irreducible unit (MacDonald & Clark, 1973). In a 1968 experiment we compared four programs: Bereiter-Engelmann, a highly structured, academic drill, small-group program; Darcee, an academic, small-group program but less focused and somewhat less didactic; Montessori, a program which used academic material but was highly individualized and nondidactic; and Traditional, a typical "freeplay" nonacademic, nondidactic program. These four programs were implemented for one year in Head Start classes for 4-year-olds. The program components, which were identified by means of video-tape and classroom observations throughout the year, consisted of ecological variables (such as grouping), molar teacher–child contact variables (such as Giving vs. Eliciting),and specific teaching techniques (such as the Ratio of Positive to Negative Reinforcement).[1] Child behavior variables included such activities as manipulation, verbal recitation, conversation, and role playing. Although many differences were found among programs both in their methods and in their effects on such variables as IQ, achievement, curiosity, and divergent thinking, we pointed out that "the fact that most of the dimensions which were identified did discriminate programs, combined with the effectiveness of programs as total treatments, precluded any clear-cut answers to questions about which components were responsible for which outcomes" (Miller & Dyer, 1975, p. 14).

The methodological problem of confounding of program techniques with program content is also clearly seen in two studies of Follow-Through programs. The Soars (1972) made observations and did testing in 70 Follow-Through classrooms and in 14 comparison classes. They found that a factor from the Reciprocal Category System labeled "drill vs. pupil initiation" was negatively correlated with pupil gain scores on six abstract language measures (Gordon & Jester, 1973, p. 200). A factor labeled "flexibility" was positively correlated with the same six measures. However,the Soars found that a factor from the Teacher Practices Observation Record labeled "teacher-directed activity vs. pupil-selected activity" separated the Follow-Through programs decisively, with the Bereiter-Engelmann program falling at one extreme and an approach like the British Infant School model falling at the other (Gordon & Jester, 1973, p. 197). Certain classroom interactions, in other words, were typical of certain programs and those programs were also characterized by other components such as content. Therefore, one could not confidently relate the program effects to the particular techniques used.

Similarly, in Stallings' (1975) study of Follow-Through classrooms, a high rate of drill, practice, and praise contributed to higher reading and math scores, whereas higher scores on a nonverbal problem-solving test of reasoning were related to more open and flexible instructional approaches. Multiple correlations between the means for outcome measures and the observed classroom variables were in the .70s and .80s. Again, however, a number of predictor variables were typical of certain programs, and the degree of similarity between the specified

---

[1]For convenience, in this paper the terms "negative feedback" or "negative reinforcement" are used in their original sense—that is, meaning a negative event utilized to indicate that the preceding behavior was incorrect or unacceptable, rather than in the recent redefinition within the field of learning, which refers to the removal of a noxious stimulus to increase behavior.

program models and the comparison classrooms in other respects (such as materials, ecological format, and content) is not known.

Confounding of Molar Method Dimensions with Teaching Techniques

A second problem in program comparisons has been the confounding of molecular teaching techniques such as reinforcement with more molar method variables that are related to program philosophy and format. Two of the most important molar method variables are group versus individual instruction, and giving information versus requesting performance. These two method dimensions have been widely recognized as being important influences in the classroom, particularly in respect to the child behaviors induced. Most systems for observation in the preschool include some method of assessing the extent to which teachers present to children versus making demands on children to perform in some way (e.g., Katz, 1969). It is sometimes assumed that in preschool there should be a high level of pupil activity in the form of participation (particularly verbalization, e.g., Holt, 1971) with the implication that teachers should do more asking than giving. In the traditional lecture versus question–answer (discussion) research with older children, lecture has generally proved superior when the desired goal was recall of facts. But results have varied when the measures of success required adequate deployment of facts and skills in problem-solving. Not only is this dimension important in itself, but it can be expected to vary among programs. In our 4-program comparison (Miller & Dyer, 1975), the ratios of Elicit to Give ranged from 0.89 (Montessori) to 2.54 (Bereiter-Engelmann).

The Group–Individual dimension has also been shown to be an important contact variable (Katz, 1969). In the field of education, the "individualization" of learning is often stressed. For example, Olson (1972) emphasized individualization as a major criterion in his assessment of "quality" in school classrooms. Individualization of instruction ranges from isolated tutorial sessions to an emphasis on interacting with individual children with a group format. The programs in our comparison (Miller & Dyer, 1975) varied in the extent to which teacher contacts took place primarily with the group or with individual children. The ratios of Group to Individual contacts ranged from 0.53 (Montessori) to 2.64 (Bereiter-Engelmann). Further, though both Darcee and Bereiter-Engelmann were organized in a small-group format, the ratio of Group to Individual contacts was much less in Darcee (0.74) than in Bereiter-Engelmann (2.64).

The two dimensions of Give/Elicit and Group/Individual combine to form four "modes" of instruction: Give/Group, Give/Individual, Elicit/Group, and Elicit/Individual. Studies have shown that these major modes of instruction are important determinants of child behavior. In one study (Ebert, Miller, Bugbee, & Dyer, 1974), it was found that with content controlled, different modes used by the same teacher produced distinctly different child behaviors; in another study (Ebert, 1974), the influence of mode was found to be decisive for the same children with the same teacher across a wide variety of tasks, despite individual differences. For example, the type of off-task behavior was different in different teaching modes. Fidgety, rhythmic, and withdrawal behavior was the predominant form of off-task behavior in the Group modes, while in Elicit/Individual, only a little more than half of the off-task behavior was of this type; the rest consisted of activity involving peers or materials.

When a teacher interacts with an individual child during small-group sessions, the remainder of the children become observers. This situation constitutes a fifth mode of instruction which may be called *nontargeted*. Kounin and Gump (1974) have shown that preschool children's task involvement is lower when "other children are emitters" (p. 560). In Ebert, et al.'s (1974) and Ebert's (1974) studies, children were on-task 90% or more of the time in all modes except nontargeted. Nontargeted children were on-task about 85% of the time. Most task behavior in Give/Group as well as in the nontargeted mode was nonverbal (predominantly looking and listening) while in the Elicit/Group mode about half the task behavior was verbal.

Not only are these molar dimensions of teaching method important determinants of child behavior, but they interact in complex ways with the more molecular teaching techniques. For example, more frequent asking for performance has been found to be associated with more frequent reinforcement (Miller, Bugbee, White, & Dyer, 1974). Biber and Dyer (1972) found that instructional contacts of all kinds were correlated with reinforcement.

Unit of Analysis: Classroom Means Rather than Individual Experience

A third methodological problem in the program comparison approach is the use of the classroom as a unit of analysis. Since teachers are not interchangeable and can only handle a limited number of children, some control for teacher variation, particularly in unmeasured characteristics, is essential in order to compare programs. The usual solution has been the use of a number of classes in each program and either observation of the classroom events across all children or the pooling of observations on individuals.

Although this procedure is useful for the purpose of comparing program effects while controlling for teacher differences, it may not be adequate to the task of determining the relationship between individual children's classroom experiences and their development. Those dimensions that differentiate classrooms are frequently the more easily obtained ecological characteristics, which are similar for all children, such as format. Children's behaviors vary even in response to these. The molecular classroom dimensions such as teaching techniques are not experienced to an equal extent by all children, and with respect to these techniques individual responses have a reciprocal relationship to teacher behavior. There is, in fact, little information available on how individual children function in the classroom (Almy, 1975). As yet, however, studies which have examined the dimensions of preschool programs in relation to their outcomes have done so at the level of classrooms or programs rather than at the level of individual children. In both the Stallings (1975) and the Soars (1972) studies, observational data and outcomes were analyzed only at the level of the classroom, and predictions were not made for individuals. In the Miller and Dyer (1975) study, individual children's scores on classroom behavior were not obtained and only program means on observation data were used.

Experimental Variation of Techniques

The most frequently used experimental strategy has been to train teachers to utilize different techniques with the same lessons. This method permits rigorous control over the variables under study, but it too presents formidable problems.

Content changes with techniques. Although teachers have been able to control specific dimensions of their behavior after appropriate training, it has not been possible in such studies to vary teaching techniques without also modifying content (Francis, 1971; Siegel & Rosenshine, 1973; Wright & Nuthall, 1970). This has been the case even in the most rigorous experiments in which single, discrete variables were isolated (Church, 1971; Hughes, 1971; Miller, Bugbee, & Dyer, 1974; Nuthall & Church, 1973).

Variables combine in actual classes. Another problem with this research method is the fact that the appropriate unit of instruction remains elusive. An analogy to chemistry illuminates the difficulty of selecting specific variables for manipulation in actual classrooms. Though hydrogen and oxygen are both important elements, the mixture of the two creates something quite different. Some single elements of teacher behavior may be influential if present in some threshold amount—for example, negative feedback on the part of the teacher, if frequent enough, might inhibit learning regardless of the teacher's other methods, the nature of the program materials, or the task content; single elements of child behavior, such as complete lack of response in a group situation may result in a child's failure on some outcome measure. On the other hand, some combinations of behaviors may constitute important patterns, which provide effective or ineffective learning situations. For example, the proper ratio of structuring the task to asking questions may be a necessary condition for adequate learning, although the absolute amount of either variable may not be crucial. Some variables may only be of importance in a complex mixture of other components.

Lack of generalizability. If simultaneous control over method and content could be achieved, such experiments would be desirable to determine the "limits of strong structure" (White & Siegel, 1976, p. 430). However, the more carefully teacher behavior is controlled and the more rigidly the roles of teacher and child are prescribed, the less likely it is that the relationships between process and product can be generalized over other situations.

Observational Method

Observational research has the advantage that any pattern obtained may be reasonably assumed to have considerable generality. When the focus is only on identifying behavioral patterns, this method has considerable value. The investigator who makes observations in a large number of settings, which vary in many respects, can use statistical methods to extract patterns of classroom interactions (Prescott, Jones, & Kritchevsky, 1967). It has several disadvantages however, for the purpose under discussion.

Obscures the content–process link. For the purpose of relating process and product, this strategy does not remove the methodological disadvantage that is inherent in a comparison of intact models—it simply makes the link between classroom behavior and other program components harder to specify. Those factors that emerge over the background noise of other variation may be the most common, but are not necessarily the most important dimensions of interaction in terms of the progress of individual children.

Forces a focus on molar variables. Different kinds of classroom situations call for different kinds of observational techniques (Shapiro, 1973). Although this difficulty is practical rather than logical, the enormous variety of activities and interaction among classrooms makes it a serious problem. An observation method sufficiently flexible to accommodate the full range of behavior in preschool programs has not yet been constructed. Some techniques that occur almost continually in one class may never occur in another. Selection of categories may of necessity reduce to the most broad and molar events or to those that are universally present.

Single Program Replication

This method involves a high degree of control but not experimental manipulation, and "reduces the ambiguity that would result from a purely naturalistic study" (Cooley, 1975, pp. 39–40).

Single program replication has occasionally been done by developers interested in examining the effectiveness of preselected techniques on a limited set of program goals. In one such study previously mentioned (Siegel & Rosenshine, 1973), the major components of the programs, such as goals, materials and content, were controlled, observations were made, and product data were collected. However, the Siegel and Rosenshine study centered primarily on classroom processes and outcomes specific to that particular program, observations were made on teachers only, and the unit of analysis was the class.

The major advantage of single program replication is that, if standardization of content and other molar program components is successful, program effects beyond those due to entering characteristics and demographic variables can be attributed with some confidence to the more molecular classroom interactions experienced by the individual children. The difficulty in using this strategy is that most of the program models which are sufficiently structured to allow adequate standardization of molar methods (such as Group/Individual and Give/Elicit) tend to limit severely the range of classroom events that can occur.

The strategy of single program replication appeared to be feasible for studying the influence of process on product, provided several criteria could be met: (a) a program could be found that was structured enough to permit standardization of both lesson content and the molar method variables, but with sufficient variety in types of lesson and learning goals to allow a wide spectrum of techniques and interactions to occur; (b) outcomes were assessed not only in convergent skills but also in divergent skills and logical reasoning; and (c) close monitoring was done of individual children's behaviors as well as their contacts with teachers.

The present study combined intensive observations of individuals with eight replications of a single program.

Summary

Previous results have demonstrated differences among preschool programs in their effects on divergent skills, convergent skills, and abstract language or problem-solving; however, the source of these effects and whether they were due to content or method variables could not be determined. Both content and the molar aspects of teaching method must be controlled in an attempt to relate specific teaching techniques to outcomes for individuals. Previous research to examine the relationships between method and product has been primarily at the level of the classroom rather than at the level of the individual child. No research method is entirely adequate to the task of relating classroom experiences to program effects. The strategy selected for this study was a combination of single program replication and individual observation. The plan involved: (a) the selection of a program structured enough to permit standardization of content and molar method dimensions but varied enough to utilize a variety of techniques; (b) the implementation of this single program model in a number of classrooms; (c) systematic observation of the behavior of individual children and their interactions with teachers; and (d) correlations between obtained classroom process varialbes and outcomes measures.

METHOD

Design

After a 3-week orientation curriculum, a single-program model was implemented in eight Head Start classes. All aspects of the preschool experience were standardized, including the orientation curriculum and the full year curriculum, as well as aspects of the classroom experience not directly related to the basic curriculum. These included materials, equipment, activities, room arrangement, themes, field trips, resource materials, scheduling, pacing, and grouping. Demographic data were obtained and 14 pretests administered to 111 mostly black, low-income, prekindergarten children prior to implementation of the basic curriculum. When the basic curriculum was begun, teacher contacts were monitored once a week for 16 weeks. These data were used for two purposes: to verify program implementation and to obtain scores for individual children's contacts with teachers. During the following 10 weeks, individual children were also monitored for behavior in the context of teacher behavior. Children were post-tested at the end of the year. Individual children's scores on 7 teacher-contact variables and 10 child-behavior variables were entered into multiple regressions to predict outcome measures using pretests, age, absences, and demographic variables as controls.

Procedures

Standardizing the Classrooms

Content and Molar Methods.   Program selection in this study was not based on theoretical considerations nor even on the documented value of the program but on methodological considerations.

The search for a basic curriculum centered on finding a program in which the Give/Elicit and Group/Individual dimensions were reasonably well balanced and in which other program components, such as lessons, were specified in sufficient detail that they could be standardized across classrooms. A number of packaged programs were examined by analyzing lesson guides from the standpoint of the teaching techniques that appeared to be employed. In some program models, it was impossible to determine the balance of teaching modes in advance because of inadequate specification of lesson content and activity; in others, instructions indicated a loosely structured program in which teachers were encouraged to improvise; still other programs were well specified but called for an emphasis on a particular mode (e.g., the Distar Program, if followed correctly, is predominantly Elicit/Group and involves relatively little contact with individual children).

The selection of the Peabody Language Development Program (PLDP), Level P (Dunn 1968), was based on several major considerations:

1. The program appeared to engage the teachers in using the molar dimensions of teaching mode just described with high frequencies and in approximately equal amounts. A task analysis of 18 of the PLDP lessons was made, and an estimate of mode predominance in separate lesson segments was computed by adding together the scores for each mode on each lesson segment. A value of 1.0 was assigned when a given mode was clearly predominant, 0.50 when there was a tie between two modes, and a value of 0.33 when there was a three-way tie. The sums of these assigned weights for the various modes were: Elicit/Individual = 25.8; Elicit/Group = 22.0; Give/Individual = 0.0; and Give/Group = 22.1. This indicated that three of the modes occurred in approximately equal amounts. The Give/Individual mode was never predominant, although it did occur occasionally or could be inferred from the instructions.

2. The PLDP could be standardized across classrooms—all materials are included in the kit (records, color chips, picture posters, stimulus cards, puppets, etc.); the daily lesson guides in the manual are quite thorough. In some lessons the teacher was provided with word-for-word scripting. In other cases, instructions were specific with respect to materials and lesson goals while allowing some flexibility in teaching techniques.

3. The PLDP contained many of the elements of programs previously found by Miller and Dyer (1975) to be effective in different areas. For example, it utilized a wide range of materials to be manipulated by the children—a characteristic of both the Darcee and Montessori programs but completely absent in the Bereiter-Engelmann program. On the other hand, the PLDP provided for a considerable amount of group drill in language use, an element basic in the Bereiter-Engelmann program, but virtually absent in both Darcee and Montessori. Although the specific materials used were different from the Darcee and Montessori materials and the content of the drill was not identical to that used in Bereiter-Engelmann, it could be expected that these components would induce the occurrence of various similar techniques, such as requesting repetition and nonverbal performance.

Due to its comprehensive self-contained set of instructional aids, the PLDP was reportedly quite easy to use for parent aides and nonprofessionals, as well as trained teachers. This program was field-tested and specifically designed for Head Start.

Other Classroom Components.   Implementation of the same content, materials, and methods in all eight classrooms with respect to the 20 minutes of didactic instruction each day was controlled by insuring that the teachers used the prescribed PLDP materials and followed the lesson guides. However, these formal lessons constituted a small portion of the 6 hours of school each day. Variation in whole-group and other activities, as well as available materials, can also produce large differences in learning. Therefore, these other components of the learning environment were also standardized to produce settings which were as nearly as possible identical for the children in all classrooms.

1. *Materials and equipment.* Before school opened, the teachers were asked to clear their rooms of all learning materials and play equipment that were not common to the eight classrooms. With the exception of furniture, some heavy play equipment, and a small assortment of standard learning materials common to the eight classrooms from the outset, the rooms were totally equipped by the project. Included were table games, puzzles, flannel board sets, blocks, dolls, manipulative materials, rhythm instruments, records, housekeeping sets, hand puppets, walking boards, tricycles, and so on—all identical across the eight classrooms. This selection was based on a classroom inventory sheet provided by the Head Start office. The Head Start supervisors made specific suggestions under each category. In all, approximately $800 was allocated for each classroom; this amount included the cost of Peabody Kits.

2. *Room arrangement.* Although the eight classrooms were all in different schools and therefore varied in size and floor plan, they were arranged similarly. Before school opened, the teachers and project staff agreed on the following learning and activity centers: Book Corner (bookshelf, throw rugs); Music Center (records, musical instruments); Science Table (seasonal items, magnifying glass); Housekeeping Corner (kitchen, dolls, dress-up); Block Area (large blocks and play equipment); Art Center (easel, art supplies); Manipulative Area (tables and shelves with games, puzzles, etc.); and Circle Area (open space for circle time and group work).

   In addition, general room "decor" was agreed upon. Bulletin-board displays, art work, seasonal decorations, and charts (weather, helpers, calendar, nutrition, etc.) were standardized throughout the year by group consensus during monthly teacher meetings. Generally, the selection was based on seasonal factors, topical themes, or curriculum-related content.

3. *Themes and field trips*. Related to the standardization of classroom decor, the themes for the year were also identical across classes. The themes served as topics for whole-group discussions each morning as well as a basis for selecting songs and music, art projects, and wall displays. These were selected by the teachers as a group and included such topics as Fall, the weather, Halloween, and the family. In addition, since Head Start provides funding for several field trips during the year, the teachers collaborated on this as well. They all chose to take their children to places like the zoo, a turkey farm, and a children's theatre.

    Where possible, field trips and other special events, such as classroom visitors, were coordinated with the themes, which in turn were often related to current seasons, holidays, or curriculum content.

4. *Other learning experiences*. Song books, records, and rhythm instruments were provided so that the children in all classes would be exposed to similar musical activities. Records, book lists, a Resource Booklet, and other mimeo materials were provided to serve as guidelines for standardization of the following: the Book Corner and story time; and activities related to art, manual dexterity, and gross motor development.

    As with other components of the classroom environment, such as play equipment and table games, the teachers all had access to these same resources and materials, but the precise amount of exposure time given to each area by the teachers in each class was not monitored, and may have varied to some extent.

5. *Daily scheduling, programming, and pacing*. During orientation, the project staff worked in conjunction with the Head Start supervisors to set up a daily schedule and an overall program of activities for the teachers— one that reflected the typical format for classes in the Head Start program locally. The day was divided into five learning periods, each designating a type of activity or experience. For example, the mornings were divided into First Assembly (large group opening discussion, singing, etc.) and Work-Play period. For the "Work" part of this period, the teacher taught the Peabody lesson to half of the children while the assistant supervised art and table activities for the other half. Then, the groups switched and the same procedure was repeated.

    Although school opened the last week of August, the Peabody Program was not introduced until October. During the "pre-PLD Program" period, room arrangement was finalized, children were pretested, and the teachers and assistants participated in intensive weekly training sessions with the project staff. (Teacher training is described in more detail in a subsequent section.) In general, it was the intent of the staff to use this contact with the teachers to impose a great deal of structure on the daily program during the first 6 weeks in order to standardize the learning environment for all eight classes. Step-by-step schedules of activities were provided. When the Peabody Program began in mid-October, many of the goals were dictated by the Peabody lessons, while others were tied to general program areas (large muscle development, music assembly, etc.).

Sequencing was controlled in that the Peabody lessons were systematically scheduled, and teachers were instructed to follow the schedule throughout the year within the general framework of adjusting responses and questions to individual children's "entry" levels for any given lesson.

6. *Grouping and order effects.* The Peabody lessons are intended to be used with groups of about 6–8 children. When school opened, the teachers randomly assigned their children to two learning groups (half of the class in each) for lessons. They were asked to make changes only if by chance one of these groups seemed to be a lot "slower" than the other, or if one turned out to be overloaded with disruptive children. With the exception of dropouts and replacements, no changes were made after the Peabody lessons and weekly observations were begun.

In addition, the teachers were instructed to alternate the order in which they taught the two groups each day. Thus, if one group had the Peabody lesson first on Monday, they were taught second on Tuesday, first again on Wednesday, and so forth. This was done to control for order effect, because it was expected that some of the teachers might improve or extend their teaching in the second session based on practice during the first. Or, they might consistently spend less time in the second session, especially those with early lunch periods (10:00 or 10:30 a.m.).

Teachers

Biographical Characteristics.   Eight teachers, all black, aged 31–53-years (median = 39) were selected by the Director of the Louisville Head Start Program from a pool of 13 who had taught in the Head Start Child Development Center day care programs for 3-year-olds. All had a year or two of college credits, mostly in early childhood education and a minimum of 5 years experience in teaching young children. Their IQ scores (Peabody Picture Vocabulary Test) ranged from 90 to 130, with a mean of 111.13. Eight assistant teachers were available to help slower children and absentees, plan extra projects, supervise alternate groups and teach the Peabody in the teacher's absence.

Training.   A half-day workshop was held in August and the teachers were given an overview of past research as well as an orientation to the current year's project. Following this, the teachers and their assistants attended six weekly, 2½-hour training sessions lasting through mid-October. During that period, the daily program structure for the eight classes was planned, outlined, and scheduled for the teachers by the project's curriculum coordinator. Each week the coordinator familiarized the teachers with the next week's activities, schedule, and instructional material.

In preparation for the Peabody lessons, the greater part of each weekly training session was devoted to familiarizing the teachers and their assistants with the program philosophy and methodology, as well as with all of the materials included in the kits—manual, stimulus cards, puppets, xylophone, color chips, and so on. The teachers learned how to use the kits and implement the daily lessons through a combination of techniques: (a) viewing and discussing videotaped samples of a Head Start teacher teaching the first few Peabody lessons to her children; (b) reading and discussing sections of the manual pertaining to program goals, methods of reinforcement, use of the various types of materials, and so forth; (c) watching "live" demonstrations in which the staff curriculum coordinator taught several lessons to small groups of the teachers who took the role of children; and (d) practicing actually teaching the lessons to each other, with each "micro-teaching" session involving the teachers in several roles: teacher, pupil, evaluator, and observer.

Throughout the remainder of the school year, the teachers attended monthly training sessions that included guidance with respect to scheduling, classroom management, and special strategies for individual children; demonstrations of later lessons, and the use of new instructional materials; and reminders concerning important methodological components of the PLD Program. In several of these sessions, time was reserved for teachers to view their own video-tapes and those of their counterparts, and to discuss the different ways in which each teacher had implemented a given lesson. Viewing the video-tapes provided feedback to each teacher on her own performance as well as the opportunity to learn a number of ways to vary and improve her delivery. Further, whenever it became obvious that most of the teachers were experiencing a common difficulty with particular lessons, the session was used to "retrain" the teachers and provide strategies for overcoming the problem. For example, at one point it was clear that the teachers were not successfully handling errors on the part of their pupils. One session was devoted to this problem, demonstrating and discussing various ways to remedy the difficulty.

In addition to the training and feedback provided by the monthly sessions, each teacher received in-class feedback weekly on the basis of her teaching performance during a Peabody lesson. The monitors were provided with a checklist and instructed to briefly discuss strengths and weaknesses of lesson implementation. During the first month, the monitors actually "modeled" the lesson for the teacher with one of her groups and then observed the teacher doing the lesson with the second group.

In all, the teachers attended 15 training sessions (including the August orientation).

Children

There were 111 children in the study with males ($N = 55$) and females ($N = 56$) about equally represented. Their mean age at the start of the 1974–1975 school year was 4.2 years. They were mostly from low-income families (mean annual income was $4,850), and parents' education averaged between 11 and 12 years of formal schooling. The mean on Hollingshead's Two-Factor Index of Socioeconomic Status (1957) was 52, falling in the second lowest social class. Thirty-eight percent of the children's fathers and 93% of the mothers lived in the home. Unemployment was rather high: 57% of the fathers and 33% of the mothers were employed. Approximately 90% of the children were black. All were registered for the local Head Start program.

Site

All eight of the classes were part of the Head Start program in Louisville, Kentucky. The classes were located in eight different schools in the west and central areas of the city (poverty areas).

Program

The Peabody Language Development Program is a small-group program designed primarily to foster language development, with Level P intended specifically for Head Start and kindergarten classes. This level emphasizes grammar and sentence patterns, predicated on the hypothesis that mastery of the structure of language is prerequisite to cognitive development. The processes to be stimulated are: reception (auditory, visual, and tactual); conceptualization (divergent thinking, convergent thinking, and associative thinking); and expression (vocal and motor). The first year of Level P heavily stresses auditory reception and vocal expression. Sentence patterns and a variety of cognitive skills are introduced. A skill-content analysis of the lessons scheduled for the first half of the year showed that the major skill components include: (a) identification and positioning of body parts; (b) discriminating objects as groups by size, shape, color, and/or number; (c) discriminating and associating animal sounds; and (d) naming animals, fruits and vegetables, body parts, shapes, colors, and so on.

Probably the most stimulating aspect of the Peabody Language Development Program is the wide variety of attractive materials included in the kits, ranging from a xylophone and story records to 10 sets of colorful picture-stimulus cards (393 in all). Most lessons contain at least one exercise of the following type, using objects or stimulus cards from the kit: The children take turns simply naming things ("This is an apple. These are apples."), identifying their color ("This apple is red."), or classifying them ("This fruit is an apple."). Another type of lesson uses story records and corresponding picture cards. The children listen to the story, look at the pictures, and then answer simple recall questions or retell the story by picking out and describing the picture cards in sequence.

The lively nature of each lesson can be greatly enhanced by the use of hand-puppets—such as "Mr. P. Mooney," "Elbert the Elephant," and "Gasless Goose"—which are employed to give directions and lead the children in songs or learning games. There are some lessons (though not many in Level P of the program) where children are asked to "brainstorm," speculate, or draw conclusions. An example of this is a lesson in which the children are asked to guess (before hearing a story about it) how Mr. P. Mooney got his magic stick; then they tell what they would do if they could use the magic stick themselves. Sometimes the children are asked to pantomime different kinds of animals or modes of transportation.

In addition to the puppets, the kit contains all sorts of other colorful materials the children manipulate while they are learning: magnetic geometric shapes; plastic color chips that can be counted, sorted, matched to other objects, or linked together to form color-pattern chains; plastic fruits and vegetables; a manikin with magnetic backing disassembled into 19 component parts (arms, legs, ears, etc.), a boy and girl manikin each with an entire wardrobe of vinyl clothes; a color-coded xylophone and stick; a "P. Mooney" bag for collecting or hiding objects; several sets of 7 × 9 in. picture-stimulus cards including animals, clothing, food, number concepts, people, transportation, and story cards to go along with the story records.

A good many of the exercises require that the children directly manipulate or respond to the stimulus material. Almost without exception, the material consists of an assortment of objects, a poster, a set of picture cards, a story record, or a puppet that stimulates their activity. The sentence patterns, songs, rhymes, games, stories and "brainstorming," sessions are nearly all centered around or built upon one or another of these materials. In short, the materials and equipment provided in the Level P kits not only teach but also animate each exercise and greatly enhance the teacher's job of making the lessons appealing and fun.

Instruments-Tests

Description.   At the end of the 3-week orientation period, all children were given a battery of tests. The Illinois Test of Psycholinguistic Abilities (ITPA)

(Kirk, 1969) was used to assess program goals which were primarily convergent in nature. The ITPA comprises 10 subtests, 4 at the automatic level, and 6 at the representational level. The 6 tests at the representational level include the receptive, organizing, and expressive processes through the visual, auditory, and vocal and manual channels. At the automatic level, the three processes of decoding, organizing, and encoding are combined, with two auditory and two visual tests involving closure and sequential memory. Raw scores are transformed into scaled scores such that at each age and for each of the subtests the mean performance of the referral group is equal to a score of 36 with a standard deviation of 6. It is possible to group the subtests in several ways depending on which dimension on the model is used—process, channel, or level. Descriptions of the subtests according to the nature of the tasks presented to the child follow:

Auditory reception: Deriving meaning from verbally presented material. Responses consist of simple "yes" or "no" answers to 50 such items as "Do dogs eat?," "Do dials yawn?" Vocabulary becomes increasingly difficult. This is a test of the receptive process at the representational level in the auditory modality.

Visual reception: Deriving meaning from visual symbols. Response consists of pointing to one of four pictures conceptually or structurally most similar to a stimulus picture. This is a test of the receptive process at the representational level in the visual modality and consists of 40 items.

Auditory association: Relating concepts presented orally. There are 42 analogies such as "I cut with a saw; I pound with a _____." "A dog has hair; a fish has _____." This is a test of the organizing process at the representational level through the auditory channel.

Visual association: Relating visual concepts. There are 20 choices to "what goes with" a stimulus picture (e.g., a sock with a shoe or a hammer with a nail), and 22 visual analogies of the type, "If this goes with this, then what goes with this?" This is a test of the organizing process in the visual modality.

Verbal expression: Ability to present concepts verbally. The child is shown four familiar objects one at a time (ball, block, envelope, and button) and is asked to "Tell me all about this." This is a test of the expressive process at the representational level in the verbal modality. The score is the number of discrete, relevant, and factual concepts expressed.

Manual expression: Ability to express ideas manually. The child is shown 15 pictures of common objects and asked to "Show me what we do with a _____." Required response is pantomime such as dialing a telephone or playing a guitar. This is a test of the expressive process at the representational level.

Grammatical closure: Ability to make use of redundancies of language in acquiring automatic habits. There are 33 items presented orally, accompanied by pictures, each consisting of one incomplete sentence to be finished by the child. For example, "Here is a dog; here are two _____." The automatic level is tapped with no distinction among receptive, organizing, and expressive processes.

Visual closure: Ability to identify common objects from incomplete representations. Four scenes are shown, each containing 14 to 15 examples of an object, such as a saw; the time limit is 30 seconds. This test is similar to Grammatical Closure in that all processes are involved at the automatic level.

Auditory memory: This is similar to the usual short-term memory task of repeating digits, but digits are presented more swiftly at the rate of two per second and a second trial is allowed each time. Twenty-eight sequences are included, with digits increasing from two to eight.

Visual memory: Ability to reproduce nonmeaningful figures from memory. Twenty-five sequences are shown for 5 seconds each, and the child is asked to place corresponding chips in the same order; two trials are allowed.

Four additional tests were given to assess nonconvergent or more personal tendencies:

The Dog and Bone Test (D&B): According to the author (Banta, 1970), this is a test of the "tendency to generate alternative solutions to problems." The Dog and Bone was considered a measure of divergent thinking. The materials consist of a small board with four wooden houses, one at each corner, a small dog at one end, and a bone at the other. The task is to devise a variety of paths over which the dog can travel in order to reach its bone. The score is based on the number and quality of different paths the child is able to produce in each of 10 trials; the ceiling is 30.

The Curiosity Box (CUR): The Curiosity Box was designed to assess the "tendency to explore, manipulate, investigate, and discover in relation to novel stimuli" (Banta, 1970, p. 426). This test consists of a box containing a variety of items, inside and outside, which the child can manipulate or look at. Two scores were obtained—a score for verbalization regarding the box and a score for actual exploration (activity). Tallies were made during every ½-minute for a 5-minute period. The ceiling was 20 for verbalization and 50 for activity.

The Early Childhood Embedded Figures Test (EFT): EFT is described as a test of "perceptual field independence," which is defined as "the tendency to separate an item from the field or context of which it is a part" (Banta, 1970, p. 426). The child's task is to locate a cone embedded in 14 line drawings, some geometric and some realistic. The child covers the cone with a duplicate cut-out. The ceiling is 14.

Basic Concept Inventory—Part I (BCI-Logic): BCI-Logic consists of 51 items from the Basic Concept Inventory, a diagnostic test developed for use in the program designed by Carl Bereiter and Sigfried Engelmann. Part I was selected because seven of the items appeared to assess deductive skills. Three of these seven items test deduction when sufficient information is given; the other four require the child to recognize that there is insufficient information for making an inference. Only the seven logic items are of interest to this study. The first logic item consists of a picture of two boxes. The child was told that there was a ball in one of the boxes. Then the examiner pointed to one of the two boxes saying, "The ball is not in this box. Do you *know* which box the ball is in?" The second item involves three boxes (insufficient information). The third item is a picture showing only the feet and legs of four individuals standing behind a large truck. Three are male, as indicated by shoe and sock style, and one is female. The child was asked to indicate whether he *knew:* (a) how many children there were; (b) which boy is tallest; (c) which child is *not* a brother; (d) which child is named Tom; and (e) which boys are brothers. Items (a) and (c) could be deduced; for (b), (d), and (e), there was insufficient information and the correct answer was "No," or "I don't know." Each correct item provided one point for a total score of 7.

Recruitment and Training of Testers.   The tests were divided into two batteries. The first battery consisted of the Dog and Bone, Curiosity Box, Embedded Figures, and the logic items from the Basic Concept Inventory—Part I. The second battery consisted of the 10 subtests of the ITPA.

The nine ITPA testers consisted of advanced graduate students or professional psychologists who were trained and experienced in the administration of the ITPA to young children. They were given an orientation of approximately 1 hour to acquaint them with standard instructional procedures and the research design. Six of these testers gave the pretests. Two of that group, plus five others, did the retesting in the Spring.

For the other tests, recruitment was done through local community service organizations. Two of these testers were similar in demographic characteristics to the children to be tested: black, similar SES, and residents of the same neighborhoods. The other four were white and middle class. All were female. Training for these individuals consisted of approximately 8 hours of seminars dealing with general testing procedures, a brief orientation to the particular research project, and detailed instructions concerning the administration of the tests chosen for this research study. All testers were required to give "practice tests" to at least three children enrolled in Head Start classes rather than the eight experimental classes, in addition to attending the seminars. Five of these testers were available for retesting in the Spring.

Test Administration.   In order to begin the Peabody Program as soon as possible, pretesting began early in September. The children had been in school for approximately 2 weeks at that time. All children enrolled in the eight experimental classes were tested, with the exception of three children who were repeatedly absent.

The first battery was given in the following prescribed order: BCI–Part I, Embedded Figures, Curiosity Box, and Dog and Bone. The tests were administered individually and total testing time per child was approximately 30 to 40 minutes.

When an entire class had been given the above tests, ITPA testing began. Test completion dates for each class varied by only a few days. The majority of the children were given all tests within 3 weeks. Due to absences on the part of the children, testers occasionally had to return to one school several times to pick up one or two children. The last child was tested by the second week of October.

To reduce the effects of tester bias, an attempt was made to schedule as many testers as possible into a class. Five classes were tested by four testers, two classes by three testers, and one class by two testers. Strict counter-balancing was not possible because of the variation in the schedules of the testers. Some were available every day while others tested only on a parttime basis; consequently, some tested more children than others.

Instruments-Observation

In general, it was desirable that the predictors generated by these instruments (a) differentiate among children in terms of their contacts with the teachers, for example, children who were drilled a lot, those who received relatively more negative than positive reinforcement, and so forth; and (b) represent meaningful differences among children in respect to their styles of participation in the program, for example, the quiet onlooker, the active volunteer, the nonattentive, and so forth.

Teacher–Child Interactions (PIMS)

Technique. For monitoring teacher behavior and teacher–child interactions, the Peabody Implementation Monitoring System (PIMS, Table 2.1) was derived from a previously developed tally sheet (Miller, 1970). Row categories represented the *target* of the instructional act (Group, Child 1, Child 2, Child 3, etc.) and the 13 columns indicated the type of instructional act.

The authors of the PLDP stressed the importance of positively reinforcing the children and ignoring failure, repeating questions to maximize opportunities for students to practice, participating in group drill to provide a model, and correcting errors without direct negative feedback.[1] It was also of interest to know whether teachers who exhibited a high rate of positive reinforcement and omitted negative reinforcement simply allowed the children to practice errors, or whether they provided immediate corrective feedback through supplying the answer themselves. A further distinction was made between task-related feedback and behavior management (nontask). Also, since task feedback contains additional information if the teacher elaborates on the simple "That's right," or "No," the categories of "Confirmation" and "Disconfirmation" were added. These categories constituted elaborated reinforcement in contrast to "−R" and "+R",

TABLE 2.1. Peabody Implementation Monitoring System (PIMS)

Observer_____ Date_____ Lesson #_____ Part_____ Session #_____

	Elicit		Give		Feedback							
					Brief				Elaborated			
					Task		Nontask					
	Information	Repetition	Participation	Information	+	−	+	−	Confirmation	Disconfirmation	Supplying	Structuring
Group	1-A	2-A	3-A	4-A	5-A	6-A	7-A	8-A	9-A	10-A	11-A	12-A
Individual[a]	1-B	2-B	3-B	4-B	5-B	6-B	7-B	8-B	9-B	10-B	11-B	12-B
Child a												
Child b												
Child c												
Child d	1i	2i	3i	4i	5i	6i	7i	8i	9i	10i	11i	12i
Child e												
. . .												
Child j												

Teacher_____ School_____ Group_____ Total Time_____

[a]Individual = Sum of children a through j.

which collected brief reinforcement conveying the correctness or incorrectness of a response. The molar dimension of "Give" was defined as any act intended to inform, reinforce, explain, and so on, when no response is being elicited. "Elicit" collected all acts intended to elicit performance from the child, whether requests or commands.

By combining across the subheadings under Give and under Elicit, the percentages of these molar dimensions could be obtained. The instrument also provided for separation of teacher contacts to the group versus contacts with each child individually. Total contact to individuals was available by summing over contacts with all 111 children.

The PIMS was constructed not only to include categories which would permit verification of implementation of the Peabody program, but also to enable the recovery of a number of the teaching techniques that occurred in the four programs compared earlier. For example, "Drill" is defined as a combination of giving with participation and requesting repetition.

Four monitors (two regular and two alternates) were trained using both in-class observation and video-taped samples of a Head Start teacher (not involved in this project) teaching Peabody lessons to small groups. Observations with PIMS began as soon as the Peabody lessons were initiated and were made once a week in all eight classes. In a 2-week period, each class was observed twice, once by each of the two monitors. Order was randomized so that no teacher would always be observed on the same day of the week. Monitoring was continual, and tallying was done act-by-act throughout the entire 15- to 20-minute lesson. Each act was tallied in only one cell. PIMS observations were continued over 16 weeks at which point a trend analysis using five periods of 3 weeks each indicated that teacher behavior had stabilized.

Reliability. Early in the observation period, video tapes of Peabody sessions from a previous study were used to obtain reliability data. The four tapes were of two lessons, each taught to two groups of children. Each of the four monitors was compared to each of the others on viewing Time 1 and Time 2, yielding 12 coefficients of observer agreement. The median coefficient of observer agreement was .94, with a range of .90 to .98; the median intraobserver coefficient of stability was .97, ranging from .89 to .98 over the four monitors.

After the monitors had been observing in the classrooms for two months, a second reliability and stability study was done. Monitors viewed four tapes of different Peabody lessons, each taught by a different teacher. Each observer viewed the tapes twice, at intervals ranging from 7 to 10 days in order to measure observer stability and to ascertain whether the high reliability and stability coefficients were due to similarities in the lessons and/or to the teaching style of the individual teacher viewed in the first study. The median coefficient of observer agreement in this study was again .94, ranging from .89 to .96, while the median intraobserver coefficient of stability was again .97, ranging from .95 to .98. These results indicated satisfactory reliability across teachers and across lessons.

Children's Behavior (MOBIC)

Technique. For monitoring each child's behavior the Matrix for the Observation of Behavior In Context (MOBIC; Table 2.2) was constructed. MOBIC is a low inference, multiple-coding category system (Rosenshine & Furst, 1973). All behaviors occurring during a fixed time interval were coded in the classification hierarchy.

In designing this instrument, the focus was on developing a logical conceptual base independent of any particular set of acts and useful in a variety of situations.

The most important characteristic of the system is the fact that all behaviors of the observed individual are recorded in some context. It is increasingly obvious that context is influential in determining behavior (e.g., Rose, Blank, & Spalter, 1975) and that differences among individuals cannot be accepted as valid unless the context is taken into account. As noted earlier, research has demonstrated that the major modes of the didactic situation, such as Give/Group and Elicit/Individual,[2] produced different child behaviors. Consequently, individual differences can be affected by the relative frequency of occurrence of these modes curing observation periods on different children.

The row categories of the tally sheet matrix concern the context in which the child behavior is observed. "Context" is distinct from "stimulus condition." The sequence of activity in an interpersonal interaction does not necessarily permit designation of a specific, single stimulus producing behavior. In the classroom, therefore, a specific teacher behavior may not be the stimulus condition that calls for the child's behavior. For example, a teacher never intentionally attempts to "cause" nontask behaviors. Context was therefore determined independently of the child's behavior.

Since the instrument was used in this study to examine didactic instruction, the context was defined largely in terms of teacher behavior. The major contextual dimension was "targetness." This dimension defined how the teacher was targeting the child during the didactic exchange, that is, whether the teacher was interacting with the child's group, the child as an individual, or a peer. The context of peer behavior was added since certain types of interaction patterns may tend to encourage interpeer on-task behaviors.

The second major aspect of MOBIC is the division of child behavior according to its direction. Since MOBIC was intended for use in this study during small-group instruction, direction included "to teacher," "to peer," or "to self" as column categories. "Direction" was defined in terms of the child's general orientation. It was most distinct during interpersonal interaction or when the child was involved in some type of didactic exchange.

The content of child behaviors was collected primarily under the columns representing children's giving to the teacher. The category "Facts or Descrip-

---

[2]Throughout the report the terms "Elicit" and "Ask" are used interchangeably to mean a request.

TABLE 2.2. Matrix for Observation of Behavior in Context (MOBIC)

Child's Name _____ Sex _____ #Samples _____ Teacher _____ Date _____

Context in Which Child Is Behaving	To Teacher — Give					To Teacher — Elicit		Other	Monitor — To Peer — Give		Monitor — To Peer — Elicit		To Self
	Facts or Description	Opinion Comment	Logic	Divergent	Fantasy	Low	High		Low	High	Low	High	
Targeted by Teacher as a Group Member													
Give	1-A	2-A	3-A	4-A	5-A	6-A	7-A	8-A	9-A	10-A	11-A	12-A	13-A
Elicit	1-B	2-B	3-B	4-B	5-B	6-B	7-B	8-B	9-B	10-B	11-B	12-B	13-B
Targeted by Teacher as Individual													
Give	1-C	2-C	3-C	4-C	5-C	6-C	7-C	8-C	9-C	10-C	11-C	12-C	13-C
Elicit	1-D	2-D	3-D	4-D	5-D	6-D	7-D	8-D	9-D	10-D	11-D	12-D	13-D
Targeted by Peer													
Give	1-E	2-E	3-E	4-E	5-E	6-E	7-E	8-E	9-E	10-E	11-E	12-E	13-E
Elicit	1-F	2-F	3-F	4-F	5-F	6-F	7-F	8-F	9-F	10-F	11-F	12-F	13-F
Nontargeted	1-G	2-G	3-G	4-G	5-G	6-G	7-G	8-G	9-G	10-G	11-G	12-G	13-G

Direction

tion'' was intended to collect convergent performance, which was expected to predominate in the Peabody program. The other four categories (Opinion, Logic, Divergent, and Fantasy) were included as representing other types of behavior possibly related to divergent skills.

A third major consideration in the design of MOBIC was to provide a reasonably inclusive set of low-inference behavioral categories that could be combined in various ways to recover more meaningful classes of events. Low-inference categories have the advantage of yielding high reliabilities but may not be particularly useful as indicators of a child's response to classroom events. For example, the number of task-related responses a child gives is easily determined, but it may be more important to know whether the child was an active participant or responded only when requested to do so. It was partly for this reason that the ''Give'' versus ''Elicit'' nature of the child's behavior was also included. ''Volunteering,'' for example, is behavior given by the child in some other context than when elicited.

All columns on MOBIC represented task-related behavior except for ''self,'' which was by definition nontask. ''Self'' was also assumed to be emitted rather than elicited.

Finally, MOBIC was constructed to provide monitors with a system that could be learned easily and would allow rapid tallying of a child's behavior during the ongoing process of instruction.

Content categories were defined as follows:

- *Facts or Description:* conveys information, expresses clarification or confirmation, or repeats previous stimulus.
- *Opinion or Comment:* expresses feelings or comments upon a stimulus in such a way as to differ from the expected response; for example, ''This is fun'' or ''My mother has a red dress, too.''
- *Logic:* expresses evaluation of a problem, analysis, or logical processes. Responses to ''If . . . then,'' ''Why?'' or causality questions, or statements expressing these, were tallied under Logic.
- *Divergent Thinking:* expresses suggestions for problem solving, alternative solutions, or a response to open-ended questions that have more than one right answer; for example, ''What's bigger than a penny?''
- *Fantasy:* behavior that requires the use of the child's imaginative abilities; for example, ''turning into'' someone or something, talking to a puppet, or pretending to take an imaginary trip.

Elicit Teacher, Give to Peer, and *Elicit Peer* were subdivided into low or high interactions, according to the qualitative nature of the interactional content. These were defined as follows:

- *Low:* concerning procedure or orientation, information, repetition, clarification or confirmation.

- *High:* concerning opinion, feelings, analysis, alternative solutions, problem solving, logical processes, fantasy, and evaluation.

The remaining subcategories, *Other* (under "to teacher") and *Self,* were undivided and defined as follows: *Other:* any behavior directed towards the teacher, which was not tallied elsewhere. These behaviors were usually nonverbal responses to procedural instructions by the teacher. *Self:* any off-task behavior. These included withdrawal, rhythmical behaviors, personal behaviors, such as hair-twisting or scratching, off-task talking to peers, or disruptive behaviors. Verbal behaviors were designated by tallies (/) and nonverbal behavior by circles (◯).

Although the 8 × 14 in. tally sheet contained 91 cells, only a few decisions were necessary for the location of the appropriate cell for any act. Cells are identified in Table 2.2 by numbers (representing columns) and letters (representing rows). The monitor first noted context—whether the child was targeted by the teacher as a member of the group or individually, by a peer as a member of a group or as an individual, or was not being targeted (another child was being targeted individually). The second decision concerned the nature of the interaction if the child was targeted—whether the teacher or peer was giving information or eliciting some response. Once context was noted, child behavior was categorized. First the direction was noted; next, whether the child was giving or eliciting; then the specific context of the child's behavior. The act was then tallied according to verbal or nonverbal. Since each of the decisions made prior to tallying eliminated large portions of the matrix, monitors were able to tally quite rapidly.

Four monitors were trained on MOBIC using video-taped samples of teacher–child interactions from a prior study. For 10 weeks, from mid-March through May, MOBIC was used for weekly observations on each child. The schedule was the same as that used for PIMS. Monitors tallied each child for one minute, then returned to the first child and tallied another minute on each. At first, children were observed in random order and all children were observed. Later, random order was maintained but children who had not been pretested in the Fall were omitted in order to obtain an equal amount of observation time for each child on whom complete tests were available.

Reliability. The four monitors observed three different children during a class session. The median interobserver coefficient of agreement was .91. As a later check on consistency, the observers independently viewed a video-tape twice with approximately a 1-week interval between. Median observer agreement and stability were both .98.

Verification of Implementation

Teacher Behavior. Completion of the target number of lessons, time per lesson, and content were recorded. To examine method variables, the profile originally generated from a number of lesson plans was used to approximate the "ideal" distribution of teacher behaviors in terms of all Elicit, all Give, all Positive Task Reinforcement, all Other Feedback, and Structuring. These five categories were replicated for Group and Individual contacts, making a total of 10. Predicted percentages are shown by the dotted lines in Figures 2.1 and 2.2. Giving of information to individuals could not be predicted, and this point is omitted for that reason on Figure 2.2.

The number of lessons observed for each teacher ranged from 20 to 25, with a total of 181 lessons observed. The average time per lesson was 19.4 minutes, close to the 20-minute target. All teachers completed 85 to 90 lessons. Since monitors were observing in the classes once a week throughout the year at

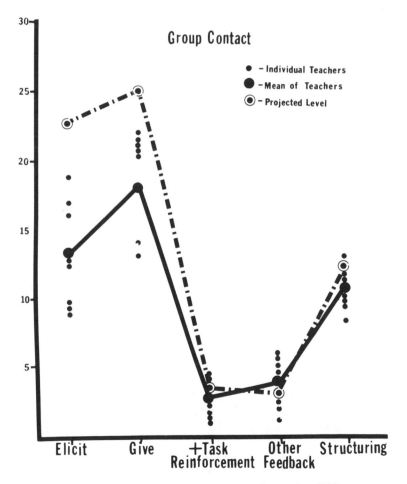

FIGURE 2.1.   Profiles of projected (dotted line) and actual (solid line) percentages of group contacts in various categories.

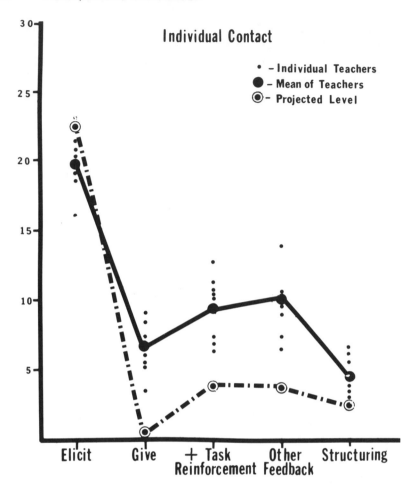

FIGURE 2.2. Profiles of projected (dotted line) and actual (solid line) percentages of individual contacts in various categories.

unspecified times, there was little doubt that teachers used the materials and followed the lessons in the appropriate order. Actual percentages based on 37,267 tallies are shown in Figures 2.1 and 2.2 by solid lines. Overall, teachers approached the model profile, except that they spent more time Giving Information and Feedback to Individuals and somewhat less time Eliciting from the Group than was expected. The relative percentages were quite similar for all teachers, and the program was judged to be a satisfactory implementation.

Child Progress.   All children's scores were included in an examination of overall effects of the program. Separate MANOVA's were performed on pretests and posttests using sex as a contrast. All *F*s were small, with probabilities greater than .10, indicating no sex differences on any of these tests. Pretest scaled scores for the ITPA were below normal (36) on all tests except Grammatical Closure, and on four subtests postprogram scores exceeded the norm. The distribution of raw score gains in pretest standard deviation units indicated that a majority of children gained on all the tests, most frequently between one and two standard deviations. Large losses occurred most often on Curiosity Box and Dog and Bone, but very few scores decreased more than .5 standard deviations (28 on Curiosity Box and 23 on Dog and Bone).

The scores of this experimental group were also compared with those of the entire local Head Start population (of which the eight Head Start classes were a part) on two measures administered by the schools—the Preschool Inventory (Caldwell, 1968) and the Caine-Levine Social Competency Scale (Cain, Levine, & Elzey, 1977). There was no difference on the Preschool Inventory, and on the Social Competency Scale, the difference was in favor of the Peabody classes ($t_{110} = 5.25$, $p < .001$). This difference may be underestimated because the Peabody classes were lower in the Fall, and because no correction was made for inclusion of these classes in the larger sample obtained from the Head Start program.

The gains made in both academic and nonacademic skills indicated that this implementation of the Peabody curriculum was moderately successful, similar in its effects to various other Head Start programs in the community.

ANALYSES AND RESULTS

Examination of the results consisted of the following steps: (a) comparison of the eight classes on the PIMS and MOBIC categories and on the outcome variables to determine whether scores for all children could be combined, (b) construction of a small number of derived variables, (c) examination of classroom patterns, and (d) prediction of outcome measures for individual children using the derived process variables as predictors. The last step defined the major goal of the study. In all cases, statistical significance was determined by $p = .01$. The data-reduction and statistical methods used are explained preceding each of these sections.

Class Comparisons

Since our purpose was to use the classroom process variables to predict outcomes for individuals, it was desirable to use the scores for all 111 children without regard to classes. It appeared unlikely, even though all eight teachers were implementing the same program, that there would be no differences among classes with respect to the frequencies of the various categories of interest. However, such differences would compromise the procedure only if class differences also occurred on the outcome measures. In the latter case, children's scores would need to be adjusted to class means. If classes did not differ in outcome measures, the comparison of classes in observation categories and the differences in teacher style were of interest in themselves as an estimate of the variability obtained with continual control over implementation of a structured program and the extent to which such variability did exist without affecting class means on the outcome measures selected.

Child Behavior (MOBIC)

Absolute frequencies in each column of MOBIC were obtained for each child. These frequencies were adjusted for the number of observations on each child, which for most children was 15 minutes (15, 1-minute observations). These frequencies are shown in Table 2.3 by class. As shown in Table 2.3, nonverbal behavior was very infrequent except under "Facts." Verbal and nonverbal were therefore combined across all columns, but total verbalization was used as a category. Low frequencies under "peer" required that elicit and give be combined. "Logic" occurred too infrequently to be used.

Analyses of variance of column frequencies on MOBIC using individual variance within classes as error revealed that significant class differences occurred for Facts (nonverbal), Opinion, Self, To-Teacher Total, Other, and Total Nonverbal. Class 8 had the lowest number of Facts per child (19.2) and Class 5 the highest (46.9). Class 8 also had the highest number of Self Behaviors (40.9).

Teacher–Child Interactions—PIMS

For the purpose of comparing classes on children's contacts with teachers, the mean for each child was obtained, combined across all sessions observed, and for all children in a class. These frequencies differ from those used in the verification of implementation in two respects: (a) They do not include teacher contacts with the group; and (b) they are more molecular variables represented by separate columns on the PIMS rather than the molar combinations such as Group/Individual and Give/Elicit, which were used to verify program implementation. The frequencies on PIMS columns by class are shown in Table 2.4. All PIMS categories were used. The total of Individual contacts in each class was also analyzed.

Differences among classes with respect to these means were quite large. ANOVA showed that classes differed significantly on Repetition, Give-Other, Positive Task Reinforcement, Negative Nontask Reinforcement, Confirmation, Structuring and Total Individual Contacts. The amounts of Repetition were particularly different.

TABLE 2.3. Frequencies of Child Behavior, Verbal and Nonverbal, in Columns of MOBIC by Class

Class	Facts & Description		Opinion		Logic		Divergent		Fantasy		Ask		Other		Peer		Self		Total	
	V	NV	V	NV	V	NV	V	NV	V	NV	V	NV	V	NV	V	NV	V	NV	V	NV
1	408	168	13	0	2	0	27	3	9	3	8	0	13	166	4	1	27	186	511	527
2	345	53	62	11	2	0	15	0	1	18	12	4	6	120	11	0	71	123	525	329
3	214	68	26	8	2	0	20	0	6	15	5	0	2	126	6	1	35	134	317	352
4	304	150	33	2	2	0	7	0	9	17	15	1	8	158	12	0	83	191	473	519
5	404	252	18	3	0	0	4	0	1	11	7	8	6	176	5	1	56	141	501	592
6	246	137	19	1	1	0	11	0	12	2	6	3	9	133	16	0	166	374	486	650
7	279	117	28	13	1	0	8	0	13	8	5	0	6	217	12	0	67	172	419	527
8	191	59	20	3	1	0	8	0	11	7	16	3	14	123	24	1	217	315	502	511

TABLE 2.4. Frequencies of Child Behavior in Columns of PIMS by Class

| | Elicit | | Give | | Reinforcement | | | | | | | |
| | | | | | Task | | Nontask | | | | | |
Class	Repetition	Information	Participation	Other	+	−	+	−	Confirmation	Disconfirmation	Supplying	Structuring
1	20	1013	6	169	372	49	5	178	156	31	27	151
2	3	715	28	262	313	8	9	119	202	51	39	258
3	3	572	33	154	320	19	2	83	133	35	17	157
4	16	850	38	180	508	14	0	79	229	36	15	127
5	79	871	48	340	346	10	3	103	71	24	63	152
6	7	772	11	345	405	20	2	128	215	47	15	143
7	9	650	12	182	383	19	1	124	148	20	11	96
8	16	804	12	250	470	25	6	294	202	27	30	257

Teacher Style

Beller (1973, p. 583) has distinguished between teacher style and teacher technique. *Technique* refers to "strategies and methods employed" such as amounts of reward or criticism, factual information, or questioning. *Style* refers to "belief systems, attitudes and other personality characteristics which are not planned components of her role functioning." The distinction between these two aspects of teacher functioning is somewhat difficult to make in terms of classroom behavior.

In this study, the teacher behaviors that could be predicted from analysis of lesson plans were considered technique variables and were used to verify program implementation. A few other behaviors, which could be quantified but were not specified by the program, were considered style variables. Two of these were mean-time per lesson and pace—a relationship between frequency of acts and total time per lesson. The mean-time per lesson varied considerably. Teacher 3 averaged 15.5 minutes per lesson and Teacher 8 averaged 22.1 minutes, with the others falling between these values. Differences among teachers on average number of behaviors per session approximated these differences in mean-time per lesson, but there were some discrepancies indicating that there were differences in teaching pace. Figure 2.3 provides a comparison of mean-frequency of behavior, mean-amount of time per lesson, and teaching pace for each teacher. Teachers for whom the discrepancy between the frequency bar and the time bar is large have a fast pace relative to the mean for the eight teachers, while a small discrepancy reflects a slower pace.

In addition to these quantifiable aspects of style, descriptions were obtained from the monitors. Monitors typically arrived in the classrooms early in the morning and thus had an opportunity to observe the teachers in whole-group activities prior to the Peabody lessons. The descriptions were obtained as follows: The two regular monitors were instructed to write independently a page or two on each teacher in enough detail that a person who did not know the teachers could recognize them when visiting the classroom. The project director then combined the two reports on each teacher. In four cases, both the comments and the general tone of the reports were congruent. In the other four, there was agreement on facts, but some behaviors were interpreted differently by the two monitors.

Teacher 1 was the teacher to whom the monitors reacted most differently. They did agree that her room was extensively decorated, that she was talkative and energetic, that she conducted the class at a fast pace, she was very productive, and was concerned about her performance. Their interpretation of these facts differed greatly—for example, one mentioned being "bombarded with colorfulness," the other called the room "cluttered with decorations." One said the teacher was "talkative, smiled a lot, and kept things moving." The other spoke of "constant motion, mechanized presentation, and constant talking."

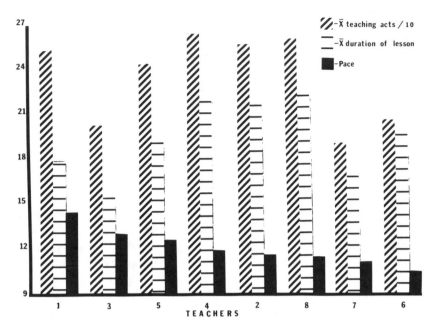

FIGURE 2.3.   Relative teaching pace (solid bars) of the eight teachers as defined
by (1/10) mean teaching acts per minute. Numbers on the ordinate
represent: 1/10 of the mean number of teaching acts per minute
(e.g., 25 = 250 acts per minute); the same numbers indicate the
mean duration of lessons (e.g., 25 = 25 minutes); for pace, the
numbers of the ordinate represent units indicating the ratio of
teaching acts to length of lesson.

One monitor said the teacher was insecure about her performance. The other
simply stated that she was concerned about her performance and asked many
questions for guidance and improvement. There was real disagreement over this
teacher's relationship to the children. One monitor said the children enjoyed the
lessons, and noted that the teacher was physically very affectionate; the other did
not believe the teacher was sensitive to the children's emotional needs. One
commented on the children's ability and noted their creative contributions; the
other was skeptical as to whether the children's learning was commensurate with
the amount of teaching going on.

    Teacher 2 was described by both monitors as having a strict and authoritarian
classroom manner. Towards children she was somewhat distant and impersonal,
but not punitive. She was conscientious and thorough in presenting the lessons.
Apparently, she was determined to maintain her authority in the classroom. This
was described in a positive tone by one monitor as a ''strong sense of justice''
and ''militancy.'' The other monitor commented that Teacher 2 resented nega-

tive feedback and was "defensive." The children were described (by only one monitor) as quiet and well behaved.

Teacher 3 had some difficulty relating to the monitors. However, towards the children she was fun-loving, laughing and joking with them, and clearly enjoyed her teaching. She was concerned about slower children and was especially good in the small-group situation." Her style was to remain stationary most of the time.

Teacher 4 appeared to have a low energy level. She tended to avoid interaction with the children and depended very much on her assistant. However, when she was in contact with the children, her attitude was supportive. She responded with amusement to their comments and was more vivacious when she was telling them stories than in the didactic lessons, which one monitor felt she was not entirely comfortable with.

Teacher 5 was described as calm, patient, good-humored, and warm. She stayed close to the children both physically and emotionally, enjoyed them, and seemed interested in their problems. She was reliable, taking her teaching responsibility seriously and conscientiously.

Teacher 6 was enthusiastic and warm but soft spoken. On these characteristics, both monitors agreed. They also agreed that she was nondirective, asking children for opinions and ideas, letting them choose topics for discussion when possible, and in general allowing a great deal of spontaneity and fun. The class was somewhat noisy, but this was interpreted by one monitor as a disorganized situation in which the teacher "never had good control over the children." The other saw the teacher as "refreshingly permissive" and indicated that she maintained just the right amount of respect and control.

Teacher 7 was described as good-humored, easygoing, and lively. It was agreed that she enjoyed entering into role-playing with the children in various games and dances. Also agreed upon was her sensitivity to children's emotional needs. In two areas again interpretation of the facts differed: According to one monitor, this teacher was always making excuses for herself; according to the other, she could usually "make the best of a bad situation." One saw her as "too lax" in discipline; the other indicated she had a "high tolerance for problem behavior." Finally one monitor commented that this teacher "had difficulty holding the children's attention," while the other noted the teacher did not demand "absolute and unwavering attention."

Teacher 8 was motivated and concerned about her teaching, recognizing that she was unable to handle the lessons or the children in a really adequate fashion. Both monitors agreed that this teacher sometimes had difficulty controlling the children. She tended to resort to threats and a loud voice. Children tended to model her behavior, which escalated the noise level. Although one monitor felt these difficulties were interfering with the children's progress, the other commented that they seemed to be learning, despite the teacher's problems.

Child Progress

Despite the marked differences among classes with respect to child behavior, interaction of individuals with teachers, and in teacher style characteristics, there were no differences among class means on the dependent variables. Means for the eight classes on each dependent variable were examined by means of AN-COVA using the pretest score for each test, SES, absences, and sex as covariates for the posttest. These analyses were done for the entire sample. ANCOVA's were also performed for males and females separately. Using the .01 level of confidence, the F for class was significant for only one test (Verbal Expression) and only for girls. Our conclusion was that classes did not differ on posttests.

The differences among the teachers did not appear to be trivial. The research staff had experienced a considerable amount of concern regarding the value of the program in some classes. It was reassuring to discover that the continual control over implementation combined with the integration of materials and lessons in the program had resulted in similar progress for all eight classes.

Construction of Derived Variables

The two observation instruments yielded a very large number of noninferential categories. Factor analysis has been frequently used with observation instruments to reduce the number of variables or identify meaningful combinations of first-order categories. In the present study, the use of this technique was contraindicated for that purpose, since both of the observation instruments were constructed on the basis of previous research or prior information which guided the selection of categories.

PIMS, the instrument used to observe teacher interactions with individual children, contained subsets of teaching techniques prescribed by the Peabody Program and previously observed in other programs. These categories could be combined to constitute the expected patterns (e.g., didactic teaching).

MOBIC, the instrument for observing individual children's behavior, was a matrix in which the context of teaching mode was included as a basis for deriving hypothesized behavioral categories. These teaching contexts (rows of the matrix) have been shown to be important determiners of child behavior (Miller et al., 1974). Therefore, factor analysis of the cells of MOBIC could be expected to produce factors that would primarily reflect the influence of these modes rather than individual differences in classroom behavior. The inclusion of context permitted the construction of larger categories which would reflect styles of participation in the program.

The method used was logical rather than empirical. Seventeen derived variables were constructed consisting mostly of proportions or ratios of various

TABLE 2.5. Means and Standard Deviations for Demographic Variables, Derived Teacher-Contact Variables, and Derived Child-Behavior Variables

Name of Variable	How Obtained	Males		Females		Total	
		$\bar{X}$	SD	$\bar{X}$	SD	$\bar{X}$	SD
Demographic							
Age		51.42	3.15	49.36	3.47	50.38	3.46
Absences		17.53	11.72	17.68	14.90	17.60	13.35
SES		37.42	11.42	37.18	9.31	37.30	10.39
Derived Teacher Contact	PIMS						
Give/Ask	$100(3i + 4i + 12\,i)/(1i + 2i)$	55.11	25.13	56.39	23.65	55.76	24.29
Didactic Teaching	$100(1i + 4i)/(1i + \ldots 12i)$	50.71	8.85	51.29	7.89	51.00	8.34
Drill	$100(2i + 3i)/(1i + 2i + 3i + 4i)$	2.78	3.30	4.38	4.85	3.59	4.21
$-R/+R$	$100(6i + 8i + 10i)/(5i + 7i + 9i)$	38.42	26.29	33.64	28.37	36.00	27.34
B/E Feedback	$100(5i + 6i + 7i + 8i)/(9i + 10i + 11i)$	262.29	129.57	278.00	150.97	270.22	140.35
Validation	$100(5i + 9i)/(1i + 2i)$	74.18	26.52	74.05	30.06	74.12	28.23
Error Correction	$100(6i + 10i)/(1i + 2i)$	7.13	4.63	6.23	5.86	6.68	5.28
Derived Child Behavior	MOBIC						
Volunteering	$100[A + C + E + G](1,2,3,4,5)/[B + D + F](1,2,3,4,5)$	21.09	22.26	16.36	31.53	18.70	27.27
Group Participation	$20[A + B + G](1,2,3,4,5)/[C + D](1,2,3,4,5)$	72.25	77.95	75.23	76.09	73.72	76.67
Group Disinterest	$100[A + B + C + D](13)/[G](13)$	48.07	48.80	50.29	40.09	49.19	44.43
Peripheral Participation	$100[A + B + C + D](8)/[A + B + C + D](1,2,3,4,5,8)$	20.76	10.41	17.63	9.75	19.18	10.16
Verbalization	All Verbal/(Verbal + Nonverbal)	47.11	13.64	46.89	14.22	47.00	13.87
Opinion	$[A + B + \ldots + G](2)$	2.62	2.90	2.07	2.94	2.34	2.92
Divergent	$[A + B + \ldots + G](4)$	0.93	1.39	0.93	1.51	0.93	1.44
Fantasy	$[A + B + \ldots + G](5)$	1.47	1.92	1.13	1.98	1.30	1.95
Ask Teacher	$[A + B + \ldots + G](6,7)$	0.80	1.08	0.88	1.45	0.84	1.28
To Peer	$[A + B + \ldots + G](9,10,11,12)$	0.68	1.24	0.98	1.64	0.83	1.45

categories of the tally sheets. Seven of these were derived from PIMS, 10 from MOBIC. Table 2.5 presents the means and standard deviations of the demographic variables (age, absences, and SES), the derived teacher-contact variables from PIMS and the derived child-behavior variables from MOBIC. "How obtained" refers to columns and rows on the observation instruments shown in Tables 2.1 and 2.2. Age was calculated for each child in months through December, 1971. Absences consisted of the total number of days absent for each child. The socioeconomic status variable consisted of the education and occupation of the mother. The variables are defined below:

Teacher—Child Contacts (PIMS)

Give/Elicit. The numerator was the total number of all teacher behavior (excluding reinforcement) that consisted of presenting, informing, participating, or structuring with the individual child; the denominator of the ratio was all behavior consisting of requests for performance from that child. This ratio would be low for the child who was "called on" excessively.

Didactic Teaching. This variable was the proportion of all teacher contacts with the child that were requests for performance or the giving of information.

Drill. This was the proportion of Eliciting and Giving that consisted of asking for repetition and participating in the child's response.

Negative Reinforcement/Positive Reinforcement $(-R/+R)$. The ratio of all negative feedback to all positive feedback comprised this variable, which represented the overall preponderance of negative or positive responses by the teacher to the child, whether induced by incorrect responses or improper behavior.

Brief/Elaborated Feedback (B/E Feedback). The numerator of this ratio was the total of task feedback that consisted simply of such comments as "Yes," "Okay," "That's right," and so on. The denominator was the total of confirmation, disconfirmation, and supply of the answer, all of which involved elaboration on the child's answer, such as "That is a square," or "That is not a triangle."

Validation. This ratio of positive reinforcement to elicit indicated how frequently the child was positively reinforced when asked to perform, regardless of how often the child was elicited.

Error Correction. This ratio of negative task feedback to elicit indicated how frequently the child was negatively reinforced when asked to perform.

Child-Behavior Variables (MOBIC)

The derived child-behavior variables obtained from MOBIC were constructed to present behavioral patterns that were expected to be present in the classroom but were not directly assessed by columns, row, or cells of the observational instrument.

Volunteering. There are individual differences in the extent to which children tend to volunteer facts, comments, and so on, during periods when the teacher is presenting to the group. This variable, called Volunteering, was a ratio. The numerator consisted of all substantive task behavior produced in such modes, that is, when the teacher was giving information to the group or to the targeted child, when the teacher was interacting with another child, or when the targeted child was being contacted by a peer; the denominator consisted of all active, substantive task behavior in modes in which the child was being asked to produce such contributions. This ratio was not expected to exceed 1.0, and in fact it was anticipated that in most cases it would be considerably less, since in a structured program there is relatively little opportunity for voluntary contributions, and conversely there are numerous demands for performance on all children. Most of the opportunities for voluntary contribution occurred, of course, in the Give/Group and Nontargeted modes. It should be noted that the nature of the behavior represented in the numerator, although it was all task related, could vary in an evaluative sense from welcomed contributions to unwanted interruptions, depending upon a number of things such as teacher's attitude, the frequency of occurrence from a single child, teacher's estimate of the relevance of the remarks, and so on. Consequently, the optimum ratio for this variable would be difficult to specify and would probably occur somewhere between the extremes of 0 and 1. For this reason the nonevaluative term "Volunteering" was used.

Group Participation. This variable consisted of all substantive task contributions in the Group and Nontargeted modes divided by those contributions elicited directly from the individual child. Because of the frequency of small-group elicitation by the teachers, this ratio was expected to be typically greater than one. Additionally, where group work takes place to any substantive extent, any individual child has fewer opportunities for being individually contacted. Previous studies have indicated that failures to respond when individually contacted are rare among 4-year-olds in small-group situations. Observers have also noted that in small-group programs, teachers tend to watch for nonparticipating children or those who are giving incorrect or inadequate answers and as a consequence, work with these children more often individually within the small-group format. Since the numerator of this ratio included both spontaneous contributions and responses to group elicitation, as well as contributions made when other children were being targeted, a high ratio appeared to represent adequately a tendency to participate fully during group work, whether this involved being directly asked to perform or simply being on-task when the teacher was working with other individuals. Consequently, the term "Group Participation" was intended to represent this comfortable match between the child and the small-group milieu.

Group Disinterest. This variable represents the total off-task behavior when the child was being targeted, divided by off-task behavior when the teacher was working with another child (Nontargeted). In the targeted context, there is more pressure on the child to attend, and most off-task behavior in the small-group format occurs when the teacher is working with another individual child; for this reason the modal ratio was expected to be less than one. A lower ratio was hypothesized to indicate a tendency to stay on task mainly under those conditions most likely to hold the child's interest, that is, when that particular child was being targeted. It should be noted that this variable does not represent an overall high frequency of being off-task, such as might be indicated by the ratio of self to total behavior, but rather the extent to which off-task behavior occurred with higher relative frequencies in group contexts than when not targeted. Since any individual child was most frequently targeted as a member of the group, a higher ratio of off-task behavior when targeted than when not targeted was interpreted as representing a definite failure of the group situation to engage the child's interest and keep the child focused on the task. Hence the name "Group Disinterest."

Peripheral Participation. This variable consists of the percentage of total on-task behavior which consisted of procedural acts relevant to the task but not substantive, such as listening, watching, placing oneself or materials appropriately, and otherwise following instructions. Total task behavior included, in addition to the preceeding, the total substantive participation, such as Giving of Facts, Opinions, and so forth. Both of these indices include only behavior oriented *toward the teacher.* In short, this is the ratio representing the proportion of the total task behavior to the teacher that consisted simply of compliant behavior. This variable was intended to represent the extent to which the child's total task-related behavior was merely passive. The child with a high ratio could be described as a true "on-looker." The nature of the ratio determined that the scores would fall between 1 and 0, and it was expected that they would not exceed .50 since most of the behavior occurring in this particular program consisted of active task contributions. This variable was hypothesized to represent the extent to which a child's response to program demands consisted primarily of formal compliance, in contrast to active and substantive participation; hence, the name "Peripheral Participation."

Verbalization. Verbalization was the simple ratio of the total verbal behavior to the total behavior of all kinds, and provided an index of the extent to which the child was verbal in the classroom, regardless of the type of verbal behavior.

The last five variables on the list in Table 2.6 were not ratios but combinations of frequencies in columns or cells of MOBIC.

Opinion. This was the total of all behavior in this category, regardless of context.

Divergent + Fantasy. For the purpose of prediction, the two columns were combined and the variable represented total frequency of both types of behavior.

TABLE 2.6.   Intercorrelations Among Derived Teacher Variables[a]

	Give/Elicit	Didactic Teaching	Drill	−R/+R	B/E Feedback	Validation	Error Correction
Give/Elicit		−.44**	−.03	.24	.01	.32*	.15
Didactic Teaching	−.41**		−.01	−.40**	−.36*	−.75**	−.13
Drill	.06	−.05		−.33*	.03	.05	−.24
−R/+R	.37**	−.44**	−.01		.49**	−.11	.37**
B/E Feedback	.27*	−.21	.30*	.48**		.18	−.25
Validation	.20	−.73**	−.18	−.11	−.06		−.10
Error Correction	−.04	−.03	−.13	.20	−.31*	−.07	

[a]Males above the diagonal; females below the diagonal.
*$p < .05$
**$p < .01$

Elicit Teacher. The total frequency of all attempts by the child to elicit something from the teacher comprised this variable. Some of these tallies represent questions, others were nonverbal demands for attention.

To Peer. The total of all contacts with peers that were on-task or task-related comprised this variable. Some of these were initiated by the child; some were responses to peers.

Patterns of Behavior

In order to interpret the relationships between observation variables and outcome measures, it was necessary to examine first the patterns of classroom behavior (correlations among observation variables), and the correlations between pretests and teacher- and child-behavior variables. Correlations among the teacher-contact variables are shown in Table 2.6, among the child-behavior variables in Table 2.7, and between teacher and child observations in Table 2.8. Correlations were also obtained between these variables and the pretests (Tables 2.9 and 2.10), among pretests (Table 2.11), and between all variables and the demographic variables (age, absences, and SES). The correlations were obtained for the entire sample and separately for the two sexes. A correlation of .37 in absolute value was required for significance at the .01 level for the 50 to 53 degrees of freedom available; .27 was significant at the .05 level. Emphasis is on the derived variables shown in the tables. However, correlations involving some of the original cell and column variables were consulted as an aid in interpretation.

No direct connection could be made between behavior obtained from the PIMS (such as Reinforcement) and those obtained from MOBIC (such as Opinion). It could not be established, for example, that those child behaviors associated with Reinforcement were the same behaviors which were being reinforced.

TABLE 2.7. Intercorrelations Among Derived Child Variables and Child Column Variables[a]

	Volunteer	Group Participation	Group Disinterest	Peripheral Participation	Verbal	Opinion	Divergent	Fantasy	Elicit Teacher	To Peer
Volunteering		.02	.01	.12	.20	.38**	-.21	.16	.29*	.30*
Group Participation	.13		.32*	.05	-.03	-.10	-.15	.07	-.05	-.05
Group Disinterest	.14	.07		.10	-.21	-.16	-.01	.18	-.05	.08
Peripheral Participation	-.11	.04	.25		-.41**	-.18	.02	-.04	-.16	.05
Verbalization	.47**	-.02	-.10	-.51**		.39**	-.18	.02	.21	.11
Opinion	.51**	.11	-.03	-.15	.49**		-.13	.23	.32*	.09
Divergent	.19	-.25	-.01	-.16	.28*	.27*		.07	-.20	-.32*
Fantasy	.12	.11	-.20	-.26	.05	-.05	-.09		.15	.17
Elicit Teacher	.33*	-.07	.17	-.12	.40**	.27*	-.06	-.04		.09
To Peer	.16	-.10	-.12	-.05	.22	.01	-.08	.38**	.10	

[a]Males above the diagonal; females below the diagonal.
*p < .05
**p < .01

TABLE 2.8. Correlations Between Derived Teacher Variables, and Derived Child and Child Column Variables for Males and Females

	Give/Elicit	Didactic Teaching	Drill	−R/+R	B/E Feedback	Validation	Error Correction
Males							
Volunteering	.01	−.28*	.00	.19	.22	.28*	.02
Group Participation	−.08	.30*	.04	−.12	.06	−.19	−.30*
Group Disinterest	−.31*	.40**	−.00	−.06	−.05	−.34*	−.26
Peripheral Participation	−.12	−.01	−.02	.22	.21	−.05	.01
Verbalization	.16	−.37**	.17	.03	.03	.21	−.14
Opinion	.24	−.36*	.05	−.05	.12	.30*	−.05
Divergent	−.00	.11	.10	−.03	.17	−.11	−.15
Fantasy	−.13	−.05	.10	−.22	.11	.15	−.11
Elicit Teacher	.26	−.12	.10	.09	.06	.02	.04
To Peer	.02	−.17	.00	−.00	−.07	.18	−.08
Females							
Volunteering	.38**	−.28*	.15	.33	.15	.19	−.00
Group Participation	.15	−.06	.11	−.02	−.04	−.06	−.26
Group Disinterest	.25	.04	−.05	.19	.39**	−.16	−.15
Peripheral Participation	.02	−.07	−.18	.14	.25	.03	−.21
Verbalization	.17	−.28*	−.01	.22	.01	.23	.12
Opinion	.21	−.20	−.00	.16	−.00	−.13	.03
Divergent	−.02	.02	−.04	.02	.05	−.02	.23
Fantasy	−.03	−.25	.15	−.14	−.05	.22	−.03
Elicit Teacher	.29*	−.35*	.25	.29*	.27*	.14	−.07
To Peer	.17	−.39**	.01	−.07	.03	.58**	−.06

$*p < .05$
$**p < .01$

TABLE 2.9. Correlations Between Pretest Measures and Derived Teacher Contact Variables for Males

	Give/Elicit	Didactic Teaching	Drill	-R/+R	B/E Feedback	Validation	Error Correction
BCI-Logic	.15	-.35*	.26	-.20	.10	.53**	-.18
Embedded Figures	-.05	-.15	.10	-.08	.02	.22	-.17
Curiosity Box	-.00	-.22	.06	.17	.34*	.01	-.05
Dog & Bone	.11	-.23	.00	.11	.25	.25	-.17
Auditory Reception	-.15	-.20	-.07	-.12	.07	.29	-.31*
Auditory Association	-.03	-.16	.13	-.32*	.10	.50**	-.36*
Verbal Expression	.08	-.45**	.12	.05	.18	.37**	-.11
Visual Reception	.00	-.11	-.01	-.21	-.05	.24	-.40**
Visual Association	-.13	-.12	.06	-.27*	-.22	.20	-.01
Manual Expression	.14	-.33*	.06	.02	.07	.34*	.01
Auditory Memory	.08	-.10	-.04	-.20	.11	.18	-.32*
Grammatical Closure	.07	-.21	-.02	-.15	.15	.45**	-.30*
Visual Memory	-.12	.05	.07	-.30*	-.19	.17	-.14
Visual Closure	-.00	-.18	.06	-.12	-.04	.20	-.07

*$p < .05$
**$p < .01$

TABLE 2.10. Correlations Between Pretest Measures and Derived Teacher Contact Variables for Females

	Give/Elicit	Didactic Teaching	Drill	$-R/+R$	B/E Feedback	Validation	Error Correction
BIC-Logic	−.06	−.35*	.10	−.08	−.07	.40**	−.02
Embedded Figures	−.20	.12	.01	−.24	−.11	.15	−.02
Curiosity Box	.16	−.14	.04	.08	−.04	.17	.11
Dog & Bone	.35	−.19	.00	.23	.18	.16	.06
Auditory Reception	−.16	−.15	−.06	−.16	.01	.34*	.10
Auditory Association	−.26	−.16	−.08	−.31*	−.14	.39**	.12
Verbal Expression	.03	−.08	−.01	−.11	−.05	.17	.06
Visual Reception	.14	−.26	−.02	.11	.14	.30*	−.03
Visual Association	−.07	−.09	−.07	−.04	−.01	.12	.09
Manual Expression	−.10	−.39**	−.01	−.13	−.12	.48**	.05
Auditory Memory	−.11	.10	−.02	−.22	.12	.13	−.14
Grammatical Closure	−.21	−.27*	−.13	−.24	−.14	.48**	−.04
Visual Memory	−.25	.06	.19	−.10	−.01	−.02	−.02
Visual Closure	−.07	−.12	−.01	.02	.21	.20	−.15

*$p < .05$
**$p < .01$

71

TABLE 2.11. Intercorrelations Among Pretests for Males and Females[a]

	BCI	EFT	Curiosity Box	Dog & Bone	Auditory Reception	Auditory Association	Verbal Expression	Visual Reception	Visual Association	Manual Expression	Auditory Memory	Grammatical Closure	Visual Memory	Visual Closure
BCI-Logic		.14	.15	.49**	.39**	.62**	.50**	.14	.23	.38**	.31**	.45**	.32*	.10
Embedded Figures	.19	.05	.00	.09	.13	.07	.15	.26	.39**	.21	.23	.06	.28*	.18
Curiosity Box	.50*	.03	.31*	.18	.18	.01	.34**	.13	-.03	.37**	.16	-.07	-.11	.28*
Dog & Bone	.27	.11	.19		.42**	.37**	.47**	.23	.17	.21	.23	.14	.17	.09
Auditory Reception	.48**	.19	.26	.14		.61**	.45**	.43**	.31*	.41**	.31	.38**	.12	.29*
Auditory Association	.52**	.32*	.29*	.13	.59**		.42**	.25	.20	.28*	.23	.70**	.24	.00
Verbal Expression	.59**	.16	.40**	.12	.43**	.52**		.23	.22	.48**	.30*	.36*	.05	.18
Visual Reception	.38**	.23	.13	.19	.40**	.40**	.52**		.33*	.29*	.21	.30*	.03	.25
Visual Association	.21	.08	.19	.17	.43**	.33*	.35*	.41**		.26	.34*	.16	.32	.21
Manual Expression	.52**	.06	.13	.12	.54**	.49**	.46**	.47**	.28*		.36*	.25	.18	.37**
Auditory Memory	.36*	.31*	.13	-.01	.37**	.29*	.29*	.14	.04	.13		.14	.11	.28*
Grammatical Closure	.50**	.24	.20	.17	.48**	.74**	.42**	.36*	.23	.46**	.23		-.02	-.09
Visual Memory	.31*	.13	.12	.20	.45**	.54**	.44**	.34*	.23	.22	.20	.53**		.03
Visual Closure	.27*	-.08	.06	.07	.41**	.26	.44**	.50**	.22	.49**	.35*	.35*	.41**	

[a]Males above the diagonal; females below the diagonal.

*p < .05

**p < .01

Causal relationships could only have been firmly established by sequential observations of children early and again late in the year. But by making certain assumptions, it was possible to achieve a considerable degree of clarification. The chronological order of events was: pretests, observations of teacher contacts with individual children using PIMS, observations of individual child behavior in the context of teacher techniques using MOBIC, and posttests. The assumptions (which must be viewed as tentative) were as follows:

1. If a particular child behavior was related to pretests or to other child behaviors that were related to pretests, it was assumed to have been present initially and throughout the year; if teacher behavior was related to it, the assumption was that the teacher had responded to the child's behavior rather than produced it. This assumption could be made with some confidence.

2. If a pattern of child behavior *was not* related to pretests or other child behaviors which were, but *was* related to teacher behavior, it was assumed these child behaviors may have been responsive to the teacher's contacts. Such child behaviors could have been present initially, of course, but not related to those tests that were administered. Thus, this assumption is more tentative. However, it has been shown that children's behavior does alter in response to variations in teacher behavior (Smothergill, Olson, & Moore, 1971).

Only two correlations between child behavior and pretests were significant. Males who had higher Manual Expression or Higher Verbal Expression scores did more Verbalizing in class; females who had higher pretest scores on Curiosity Box did more Volunteering.

Teachers were not apprised of children's scores on pretests; however, some correlations between teacher behavior and pretest scores existed, indicating that children's behavior in class at the beginning of the program was in part a function of their entering abilities, and that teachers responded to these differences. Males who had higher pretest scores on Auditory Association, Verbal Expression, or Grammatical Closure received more Validation, suggesting that these children were more often correct. Females who scored higher initially on Auditory Association, Manual Expression, or Grammatical Closure received more Validation. Higher pretest scores on Manual Expression were related to less Didactic Teaching for both females and males. Higher pretest scores on Verbal Expression were related to less Didactic Teaching only for males. Clearly, teachers focused their efforts on those children they perceived as most in need of individual attention.

There were patterns for both sexes that seemed to reflect the behavior of well socialized, outgoing children who participated quite actively in the program. Teachers evidently thought they needed less individual attention. There were interesting differences, however, in the behavior patterns for the two sexes, and what took the place of didactic instruction was quite different for males and females. As shown in Table 2.12 for males there were three child-behavior variables related to less Didactic Teaching: Volunteering, Verbalization, and Opinion. Both Volunteering and Opinion were also correlated with higher Validation scores (+R/Elicit). For females (Table 2.13) four child-behavior variables were related to less Didactic Teaching: Volunteering, Verbalization, Elicit Teacher, and To Peer. Only the peer interactions were correlated with more Validation. Volunteering and Elicit Teacher were both related to higher ratios of $-R/+R$. In short, females who volunteered more and asked more questions received relatively more negative than positive reinforcement. This was not the case for males. A closer examination of the Volunteering scores revealed that males did significantly more Volunteering than females, but for females most of the Volunteering was verbal which, as previously mentioned, was not the case for males. When the positive relationship for females between pretest Curiosity Box scores and Volunteering is considered, a picture emerges of a behavior pattern that was probably viewed as disruptive by the teachers, despite the fact that it was composed of task-related behavior. The standard deviation for Volunteering was much higher for females than for males, suggesting that there were perhaps a few females who were excessively eager to express themselves, and that these were also the most talkative generally. Since classroom verbalization was not related to pretest Verbal Expression scores for females, perhaps there were some females who were not especially capable, but who exhibited a "little teacher" syndrome—offering opinions, asking the teacher questions, and generally doing more talking. Another possibility is that there was simply a difference in the quality of opinions or questions offered by the two sexes. The amount of total Verbalization in class was almost exactly the same for the two sexes. But there were no data available to determine whether the Volunteering by males was more appropriate than that of females or whether teachers were more receptive to it.

A finding of different teacher behavior toward the two sexes is certainly not uncommon. It may be that, to some extent, teachers were responding differently to similar behaviors from the two sexes and using teaching techniques in different ways for males and females, perhaps because of different goals and expectations. The relationship between these child-behavior variables and the reinforcement pattern of teachers is similar in certain respects to the findings of an observational study of 4th- and 5th-grade children by Dweck, Davidson, Nelson, and Enna (1978). In this study, it was shown that there were significant differences in the nature of the feedback given to males and females. Specifically, a higher percentage of the positive reinforcement for task-related behavior given to females was for "intellectually irrelevant aspects, such as neatness" (p. 272) than was the case for males; a higher percentage of the negative task feedback was given for intellectual inadequacy in females than was true for males.

Another interesting sex difference between the child-behavior patterns and

TABLE 2.12. Correlations Between Derived Teacher Variables, and Derived Child and Child-Column Variables for Males

	Give/Elicit	Didactic Teaching	Drill	−R/+R	B/E Feedback	Validation	Error Correction
Volunteering	.01	−.28*	.00	.19	.22	.28*	.02
Group Participation	−.08	.30*	.04	−.12	.06	−.19	−.30*
Group Disinterest	−.31*	.40**	−.00	−.06	−.05	−.34*	−.26
Peripheral Participation	−.12	−.01	−.02	.22	.21	−.05	.01
Verbalization	.16	−.37**	.17	.03	.03	.21	−.14
Opinion	.24	−.36*	.05	−.05	.12	.30*	−.05
Divergent	−.00	.11	.10	−.03	.17	−.11	−.15
Fantasy	−.13	−.05	.10	−.22	.11	.15	−.11
Elicit Teacher	.26	−.12	.10	.09	.06	.02	.04
To Peer	.02	−.17	.00	−.00	−.07	.18	−.08

*$p < .05$
**$p < .01$

TABLE 2.13. Correlations Between Derived Teacher Variables, and Derived Child and Child-Column Variables for Females

	Give/Elicit	Didactic Teaching	Drill	−R/+R	B/E Feedback	Validation	Error Correction
Volunteering	.38**	−.28*	.15	.33*	.15	.19	−.00
Group Participation	.15	−.06	.11	−.02	−.04	−.06	−.26
Group Disinterest	.25	.04	−.05	.19	.39**	−.16	−.15
Peripheral Participation	.02	−.07	−.18	.14	.25	.03	−.21
Verbalization	.17	−.28*	−.01	.22	.01	.23	.12
Opinion	.21	−.20	−.00	.16	−.00	−.13	.03
Divergent	−.02	.02	−.04	.02	.05	−.02	.23
Fantasy	−.03	−.25	.15	−.14	−.05	.22	.23
Elicit Teacher	.29*	−.35*	.25	.29*	.27*	.14	−.03
To Peer	.17	−.39**	.01	−.07	.03	.58**	−.06

*p < .05
**p < .01

teachers' responses to them can be seen in respect to the Group Participation and Group Disinterest variables. For males, Group Participation (involving task-related behavior) and Group Disinterest (involving off-task behavior) were positively correlated. This probably reflects the fact that many 4-year-old boys, even though they are interested and willing to participate in group work, are unable to remain focused on the task even when being targeted as a group member. Males who were high on these variables received more Didactic Teaching individually. On the other hand, Group Participation by females was unrelated to any other child behavior variable or to teacher interactions, and Group Disinterest was related only to a higher ratio of B/E feedback. A good bit of the Brief Feedback was nontask while the Elaborated feedback was all task related. Correlations among the original observation frequencies revealed that off-task behavior in the group modes for females was significantly related to negative nontask reinforcement. This was not the case for males. A reasonable interpretation of these patterns is that males who were off-task during group work were more often contacted for individual instruction; females who were off-task in the same situations were reprimanded.

Drill may also have been used differently for males and females. In absolute terms, females received twice as much Drill as males. Drill was not related to any child behavior for either sex. However, there was a difference in the Drill received by the two sexes in that Drill was positively correlated with the ratio of $-R/+R$ for males but not for females. For females, Drill was correlated with higher ratios of B/E Feedback. Drill was a subset of Didactic Teaching. It consisted of asking for repetition and the participation of the teacher in the response. When Drill occurred, the child was typically required to give several responses before being reinforced. In this way, responses were often shaped and a correct response occurred through modeling after one or more incorrect responses. Therefore, a positive relationship between Drill and $-R/+R$ would be expected. The reason for its failure to occur for females is obscure unless the teacher often failed to provide negative feedback to the females when they were incorrect. In the study by Dweck, et al. (1978), the authors commented that "on a number of occasions when girls have clearly incorrect answers, they received no feedback about the correctness of the answer, but instead were *praised* for intellectually irrelevant aspects of the response" (emphasis in original, p. 274). The authors suggest that "positive evaluation is less indicative of ability for girls than for boys and negative evaluation is less indicative of ability for boys" (p. 274).

Predictions of Outcomes

The two sets of variables (teacher-contact and child-behavior) were entered into separate stepwise regressions for each outcome measure. For each analysis, the first step was to force into the equation four control variables: pretest scores, age, absences, and SES score. Each succeeding step followed the normal stepwise procedure of adding the most significant predictor to the set and deleting a predictor if it fell below significance, with the restriction that the control variables remained in the equation regardless of their significance. The criterion used for deciding significance was a p value of .05. The process terminated when all predictors in the equation were significant and none of the variables left out of the set would add significantly to the explained variance. This sometimes occurred at Step 1, that is, none of the potential predictors were significant when added to the set of control variables.

For several reasons the decision was made to attempt prediction for each outcome measure separately: First, the 10 subtests of the ITPA were designed to measure relatively independent aspects of linguistic functioning; although correlations among them were typically in the 40s and 50s, Level P of the program focuses on the receptive skills and it was of interest to examine ITPA tests separately; second, the four additional tests given were chosen to measure competencies not assessed by the ITPA; finally, the study was partly based on the hypothesis that similar process variables would have different effects on measures of convergent, divergent, and logical process measures.

The first set of potential predictors consisted of the 7 derived variables based on the data from observations of teacher contacts using the PIMS. The second set consisted of the 10 derived variables from MOBIC data on children. As a check on these multiple correlations, a number of cell variables were also tested as predictors. However, since these cells were included in the derived variables, results were not reported in detail.

Results from the stepwise multiple regressions are shown in Tables 2.14 and 2.15, which list all positive and negative predictors for both sexes. The order of listing of criterion variables is arbitrary except that the ITPA subtests are grouped; significant predictors are listed for each outcome measure in the order in which they entered the equation. Several things are immediately apparent from examination of these tables. (a) Every outcome measure was predicted by at least one process variable for one sex or the other. However, the behavior variables typically predicted different outcome measures for the two sexes. (b) All but 2 of the 7 derived teacher variables and all 10 of the derived child-behavior variables were predictive of at least one criterion measure. (c) There were more than twice as many predictors for males (12) as for females (5). Eight of the 10 potential child-behavior predictors were significantly related to outcome measures for males. Only 2 of the child-behavior variables for females were significant. Of the 7 teacher-contact variables, 4 were predictive for males, 3 for females. (d) On most tests, the control variables (pretest, SES, age, and absences) accounted for more of the variance in posttest scores for males than was the case for females. (e) Despite the greater influence of the control variables for males, the classroom behavior variables were also more important, accounting for as much as 20% of the remaining variance in four posttests. For females, the classroom variables accounted for as much as an additional 10% of the variance in only one test (BCI-Logic). (f) Considering the positive versus negative relationship of observation variables to outcomes, it is apparent that of the 11 instances of relationships between teacher variables and outcome measures, 6 were negative—4 out of 7 for males and 2 out of 4 for females. (g) The most influential teacher variable was $-R/+R$, the ratio of negative to positive reinforcement, which was significantly correlated with 4 outcome measures—3 for males and 2 for females. B/E Feedback was also important, predicting 1 outcome for males and 2 for females. Group Participation proved most influential among the child-behavior variables.

Males

From Table 2.14 it appears that on four of the ITPA tests, Visual Reception, Visual Association, Auditory Association, and Grammatical Closure, higher scores were earned by the males who were more outgoing—volunteering, giving opinions or asking questions. Didactic teaching or drill combined with a higher ratio of $-R/+R$ apparently was negatively related to the receptive skills, both auditory and visual, but was positively related to Verbal Expression.

On the group of tests reflecting skills in the visual modality, lower scores were earned by males who were nonverbal, peripheral participants, asking fewer questions. Auditory Memory (digits) was higher for males who had more Divergent and Fantasy responses.

Among the tests of divergent skills, the Dog and Bone was well predicted by Divergent and Fantasy behavior combined with Group Participation. Males who were higher in Group Disinterest had lower posttest BCI-Logic scores.

Females

Table 2.15 shows that for females only the two ITPA subtests at the organizing level were predicted positively by the teacher variables. Higher Validation ($+R/Elicit$) predicted higher posttest scores on Auditory Association and higher ratios of $-R/+R$ predicted higher scores on Visual Association. Two tests were negatively related to a teacher-contact variable: B/E Feedback was associated with lower scores on both Auditory Reception and Visual Memory. Only one child behavior was predictive for females on an ITPA test: Females who verbalized more had higher posttest scores on Visual Association.

The most interesting result for females involved Curiosity and BCI-Logic scores both of which were *lower* for girls who had higher scores on Group Participation.

TABLE 2.14. Predictions of Posttest Scores for Males Using Classroom-Observation Variables

Criterion	Multiple r Control	F(4,45)	Predictors	Multiple r Controls & Predictors Child	Teacher	Multiple r^2 Controls & Predictors	% Increase in Variance	F
Divergent								
BCI-Logic	.37	1.74[a]	Group Disinterest[b]	.48		.23	9%	4.90* (df = 1,42)
Embedded Figures	.42	2.35						
Curiosity Box	.41	2.34						
Dog & Bone	.33	1.41	{ Group Participation / Divergent + Fantasy }	.67		.45	34%	12.88** (df = 2,41)
Convergent (ITPA)								
Auditory Reception	.59	6.15	{ −R/+R[b] / Didactic[b] }		.74	.55	20%	9.32** (df = 2,43)
Auditory Association	.69	10.00**	{ Group Disinterest[b] / To Peer }	.67		.45	10%	3.67* (df = 2,41)
			Opinion	.73		.53	6%	4.96* (df = 1,42)
Verbal Expression	.41	2.25	{ −R/+R / Didactic }		.61	.38	20%	7.31** (df = 2,43)

Criterion variable		F	Predictors				%	F
Visual Reception	.27	0.91	−R/+R Drill[b]; { Peripheral Participation[b], Volunteering, Elicit Teacher[b] }	.57	.46	.21	14%	3.76* (*df* = 2,43)
Visual Association		9.53**	{ Peripheral Participation[b], Elicit Teacher }	.78		.32	25%	4.90** (*df* = 3,40)
Manual Expression	.52	4.22**				.60	15%	7.30** (*df* = 2,41)
Auditory Memory	.67	8.97**	Divergent + Fantasy	.70		.50	4%	4.38* (*df* = 1,42)
Grammatical Closure	.65	8.24**	Volunteering	.70		.49	7%	5.41* (*df* = 1,42)
Visual Memory	.35	1.60						
Visual Closure	.29	1.07	B/E Feedback		.41	.17	8%	4.45* (*df* = 1,44)

[a]*df*'s associated with BCI-Logic were 4,44.
[b]Variable was negatively correlated with criterion.
*$p < .05$
**$p < .01$

TABLE 2.15. Predictions of Posttest Scores for Females Using Classroom-Observation Variables

Criterion	Multiple r Control	F(4,44)	Predictors	Multiple r Controls & Predictors Child	Multiple r Controls & Predictors Teacher	Multiple r^2 Controls & Predictors	% Increase in Variance	F
Divergent								
BCI-Logic	.02	<1.0						
Embedded Figures	.38	1.82	Group Participation[a]	.35		.12	11%	4.79* (df = 1,39)
Curiosity Box	.39	1.93	Group Participation[a]	.48		.23	8%	4.05[b] (df = 1,39)
Dog & Bone	.31	1.18						
Convergent (ITPA)								
Auditory Reception	.58	5.66**	B/E Feedback[a]		.64	.41	7%	4.88* (df = 1,43)
Auditory Association	.69	9.96**	Validation		.73	.53	6%	5.20* (df = 1,43)
Verbal Expression	.46	2.89*						
Visual Reception	.47	3.12*						
Visual Association	.32	1.27	{ Verbalization / −R/+R }	.44	.42	.19 / .18	8%	4.39* / 4.03[b] (df = 1,43) (df = 1,39)
Manual Expression	.56	5.13**						
Auditory Memory	.43	2.44						
Grammatical Closure	.51	3.91**						
Visual Memory	.32	1.28	B/E Feedback		.46	.21	11%	5.74* (df = 1,43)
Visual Closure	.40	2.14						

[a]Variable was negatively correlated with criterion.
[b]$p = .06$
*$p < .05$
**$p < .01$

Although there were not many derived variables that were predictive for females, a very large number of the absolute cell frequencies (not shown in Table 2.15) were predictive. Some combinations of cell frequencies added as much as 34% to the variance accounted for. This suggests that the *context* of the teacher behavior in which the females' behavior occurred was crucial for the meaning of the child's behavior. There may be other derived variables that would reflect the complex combinations of cell frequencies predictive for females. Those derived variables that were hypothesized prior to this study were reasonably successful for males but less so for females.

In general, males who entered the program with more developed verbal expressive skills, and who participated actively, volunteering or offering opinions, evidently benefited from the group work, in terms of the receptive and associative areas of the ITPA, even though they received less attention from the teachers in the form of individual didactic teaching. It is probable that the materials and activities of the program were responsible for these successes. Males who participated more in the group work and who produced more divergent responses had higher Dog and Bone scores. Since the program did not involve many lessons empasizing divergent thinking, it may be that the teachers were responsible for eliciting such responses during group work. Males who were able to stay on task in group work had higher posttest scores on BCI-Logic, suggesting that the group activities did help develop their reasoning abilities. The teachers evidently did succeed in developing verbal expressive skills in those males with whom they worked more often individually. The relationships between Didactic Teaching and the other measures, however, were mostly negative, indicating a lack of success in those areas with the boys most in need of instruction.

One pattern occurred only for males and described a group of boys who did little talking and participated only in a compliant way. Peripheral Participation defines a ''quiet on-looker'' syndrome. This variable was not related to pretests or to any other child behavior variable except negatively to Verbalization. Since no teacher behavior was correlated with Peripheral Participation, it is likely that this variable represents a general level of immaturity. These males had lower posttest scores on Visual Reception and Visual Association. The Visual Receptive skills, according to the ITPA model, are chronologically basic. There was no evidence that participation in the group or individual teaching had a positive effect on these tests for males.

There was no relation between Didactic Teaching and outcome variables for females. Although a few specific teacher or child variables were significantly related to test results, in general they added very little to the variance accounted for by the control variables. The negative relationship between B/E Feedback and Auditory Reception and Visual Memory may be due to the fact that B/E Feedback was positively correlated with Group Disinterest. In the stepwise procedure, one or the other of these correlated variables was likely to be forced out of the equation.

The most interesting result was the negative relationship between Group Participation and BCI-Logic and Curiosity Box scores. Since Group Participation was unrelated to any other child behavior or to any teacher behavior for females, this result is difficult to interpret. The correlation between Group Participation and Divergent responses was negative, and almost significant at the .05 level. Most of the Divergent and Fantasy responses that males gave occurred in the Elicit/Group context. Females, on the other hand, gave most of their Divergent and Fantasy responses in the Elicit/Individual mode. Thus, it is tempting to speculate that group work was more beneficial for males than for females so far as the divergent skills are concerned, possibly because females produced fewer divergent responses in the Group context. What is missing is more detailed information about the nature and quality of those Divergent and Fantasy responses. Also, BCI-Logic and Curiosity Box are quite different in their demands and it is hard to hypothesize the nature of the linkage between Group Participation and both of these tests.

In summary, there were only two significant sex differences in the absolute amounts of classroom behavior: Males volunteered more and females received more individual Drill. More frequent instructional contacts to females has also been found by Biber, Miller, and Dyer (1972) and Fagot (1973). Relationships between the different child-behavior variables and between teacher contacts and child behaviors, however, were quite different for the two sexes; for example, Volunteering and Negative Reinforcement were correlated for females but not for males—Group Disinterest and Didactic Teaching were correlated for males, but not females. Classroom variables in general were better predictors for boys, and when process variables did predict for girls, they did not relate to the same outcome measures. Results suggested that the didactic methods used by the teachers benefited boys only, and only in respect to Verbal Expression; they appeared to have negative effects on the receptive skills. Group Participation was beneficial to boys in developing divergent thinking and logic, but seemed to have negative effects on girls in respect to lower logic and curiosity scores.

DISCUSSION

The Peabody Language Development Program was well implemented in this study. This program provides a sequenced set of lessons designed on the basis of a theoretical approach to early childhood education; it includes a carefully selected set of materials to engage the child's interest and elicit specific behaviors. The program activities induce practice in verbal skills, and the production of information, classification, and other content appropriate for 4-year-olds. It is probably for these reasons that it was possible to control for content and other factors and obtain clear and significant relationships between teaching techniques and outcome measures. The structured nature of the Peabody Program probably also accounted for the fact that elements of teacher style and even competence on which the eight teachers differed dramatically did not result in any significant variation among class means on outcome measures. In a different, more loosely organized program with less specification in regard to the curriculum, the effects of teacher style might have been much more pronounced in the comparison of progress in different classes. This lack of differences among class means emphasizes the problems of using them in comparing programs that vary in their demands on teachers; though program effects may be found, they can only be attributed to the programs as a whole and cannot be specifically related to teaching methods or style within particular programs.

With regard to the efficacy of didactic methods, the hypothesis that Didactic Teaching and/or Drill would have detrimental effects on the test of divergent thinking (Dog and Bone) was not supported by observations of these techniques in the Peabody Program. Nor was the hypothesis that the Dog and Bone would be affected by the ratios of Negative to Positive Reinforcement supported. The finding by Miller and Dyer (1975) of lower scores on the Dog and Bone in the most and least didactic programs may have been due to the absence of elicited divergent responses—in Bereiter-Engelmann because of completely prescribed instructions focusing on academic skills and in Traditional because of a low level of teacher elicitation of any type. Whether there were more divergent and fantasy responses elicited in the Montessori and Darcee programs in that study is not known.

Although Drill, Didactic Instruction, and higher ratios of Negative to Positive Reinforcement did not operate in the Peabody Program to reduce divergent skills, they did appear to have adverse effects on the receptive skills for boys. The wisdom of using these techniques for the sole purpose of increasing verbal expression, therefore, should certainly be questioned. There are probably ways of improving verbal expression which would not have adverse effects, and the receptive skills are surely too important at the prekindergarten level to be sacrificed for the sake of more skillful overt expression.

In general, the examination of process–product relationships in this study indicated that the child-behavior variables were more frequently and more influentially related to outcome measures than were the teacher-contact variables. This result suggests that more attention should be paid to the nature and content of children's responses to a preschool program than to the prescribed behavior of teachers. There are undoubtedly several different ways to induce divergent and fantasy behavior, to insure practice in various skills, or to keep children on task. Focusing on children rather than on teachers would provide much greater scope for generalization across various types of programs; this emphasis might also be informative with respect to the important question of selecting appropriate outcome measures for preschool programs in relation to their long-term goals—a question to which there are as yet no satisfactory answers.

The observation of individual children is quite time consuming but may be cost-effective in the long run. Although MOBIC observations were conducted only during the latter part of the year in this study, at least two sets of observations with this same instrument—one at the beginning of the year and one toward the end—would be much more informative. Many questions regarding the source of child behavior and the amount of change during a program could be answered by this method—questions about which we could only speculate as a result of having one set of observations late in the year after long exposure to the program. Prior to the introduction of a particular curriculum, a baseline for behavior of individual children should be obtained during a series of varied contexts in order to identify those behaviors that represent individual differences rather than the influence of certain materials or activities (Zimiles, 1970).

As previously mentioned, since the Peabody is a tightly structured program and was well implemented in all eight classrooms, the amount of exposure to activities and materials as well as content did not differ significantly among children. Yet there were large individual differences in children's behavior during the lessons. Although in part these variations may have been present prior to the preschool experience, many of the differences in behavior were probably the results of their contacts with the teachers. Changes in children's classroom behavior have been shown to result from experimental manipulation of teacher responses (Endsley & Clarey, 1975; Smothergill, Olson, & Moore, 1971). In the present study, the replication of a single program model and the observation of teacher contacts with individual children permitted an examination of the effects of both specific teaching techniques and child behaviors on outcomes. Indirect evidence in the form of correlations was obtained concerning the relationships between teacher behavior and child behavior. Additional studies will be required to establish the chain of causal relationships leading to different behaviors and subsequently to different degrees of success for individual children. The inferences regarding causal sequences made from the results of regressions in this study must be viewed only as suggestive.

Once the relevant child behaviors leading to various outcomes have been identified, it may be possible, as Wittrock and Lumsdaine (1977) have suggested, to test models and theories "which specify how the learners transfer the nominal stimuli of instruction into functional stimuli which predict and explain their behavior" (p.445). Teacher techniques are important primarily because of what they induce children to do. But the relationships between changes in child behavior and changes in posttest performance indicating different amounts of learning must then be established. Smothergill, Olson, and Moore (1971), for example, found that children modeled their teachers' behavior (verbal elaboration and nonelaboration) but these group differences were reflected in posttest performance only on two verbal tasks (story telling and similarities).

Similar methods cannot be expected to be effective with all children. Individualization of instruction need not mean tutoring each child separately, but at least it should mean assessment of each child's behavioral proclivities and responses to various techniques of instruction. Although aptitude-treatment interactions have proved difficult to demonstrate, this may be due to the fact that ''our generally used aptitude constructs are not productive dimensions for measuring those individual differences that interact with different ways of learning'' (Glaser, 1972, p. 8). Some of the most relevant individual difference dimensions have been shown here to be behavioral responses to the demands of the educational situation.

Finally, our results showed clearly that teachers interacted differently with the two sexes, and that boys and girls emitted different patterns of behavior. The monitors felt that often the participation of the girls was rather routine, suggesting that they were bored, but compliant. If this was the case,the group activity would not have been particularly beneficial and the girls might have been better off engaging in individual activity or peer interactions. The pretests, demographic variables, teacher contacts (PIMS columns), and child behaviors (MOBIC columns) were subjected to factor analyses as a check on the interpretation of correlation matrices. One interesting result of these analyses was the fact that there was a distinct factor for boys involving off-task behavior; however, no such factor emerged for girls. Off-task (Self) behaviors for girls were distributed across several factors in approximately equal proportions. This tends to confirm our impression that there was more variability among girls in their preferences for, and responses to, different modes of instruction. The fact that the derived variables were less predictive for girls than the cell frequencies (reflecting behavior in a specific context of teacher behavior) also lends support to this interpretation. While some types of group instruction may be beneficial for some girls, these may not be the same kinds of instruction which are helpful to most boys of the same age.

In view of these striking differences between boys and girls, the differences in the relationship between classroom behavior and outcomes for the two sexes, and the results of other studies (e.g., Rubin, 1970), it would be tempting to conclude that the formal instructional portion of the prekindergarten day should be conducted separately for the two sexes. However, as suggested by Moore (1980, personal communication), some of these sex differences may be created by teachers and other adults; and to separate the sexes might confound such tendencies. In any case, sex groupings would not necessarily make the adjustment to individual differences any easier.

An alternative to separation of the sexes would be to alert teachers to differences in the reactions of the two sexes and their potential effects on program outcomes. Unfortunately, the demands of group work make adjustments difficult, even though the teachers understand that the sexes require differential treatment. The most appropriate bases for grouping are yet to be determined, but this is a researchable question using observations of initial behavior to determine children's responses to the classroom situation.

Some of the derived child-behavior variables identified in this study predicted well for boys; more investigation is needed to identify the nature of the behavioral variables predictive for girls. The observation schedule used provides a flexible instrument that can be modified to observe numerous types and levels of content in children's contributions and behavior. More refined distinctions among the types of divergent and fantasy responses, and a more detailed examination of the nature of volunteer behavior are two areas that appear particularly promising for further study. We have found that the type of prekindergarten program offered to 4-year-olds can make a difference in their academic performance as late as 8th grade (Miller & Bizzell, 1983); we have found in this study that individual children's behavior in the same type of prekindergarten classroom is a significant predictor of what they learn. What remains to be determined are the connections between program components and the behavior of individual children, and the connections between their behavior and/or early outcome measures and later performance.

REFERENCES

Almy, M. (1975). *The Early Childhood Educator at Work*. New York: McGraw-Hill.

Banta, T. J. (1970). Tests for evaluation of early childhood education: The Cincinnati Autonomy Test Battery (CATB). In J. Hellmuth (Ed.), *Cognitive Studies, Volume 1*. New York: Brunner/Mazel, Inc.

Beller, E. K. (1973). Research on organized programs of early education. In R. M. W. Travers (Ed.), *Second Handbook of Research on Teaching*. Chicago, IL: Rand McNally College Publishing Co.

Biber, H., Miller, L. B., & Dyer, J. L. (1972). Femininization in preschool. *Developmental Psychology, 7*(1)86.

Cain, L. F., Levine, S., & Elzey, F. F. (1977). *Manual for the Cain-Levine Social Competency Scale*. Palo Alto, CA: Consulting Psychologists Press.

Caldwell, B. M. (1968). *Preschool Inventory Experimental Edition, 1968. Administration Manual*. Princeton, NJ: Educational Testing Service.

Church, R. J. (1971). The effects of systematic changes in Standard Four Science lessons. *Educational Research Newsletter, 4*, 15–30.

Consortium for Longitudinal Studies. (1982). Lasting effects after preschool education: A report from the Consortium for Longitudinal Studies. *Monographs of the Society for Research in Child Development, 47*(2–3), Serial No. 195.

Cooley, W. W. (1975). Evaluation of educational programs. In R. A. Weinberg & S. G. Moore (Eds.), *Evaluation of Educational Programs for Young Children*. Washington, DC: Child Development Associate Consortium.

Dunn, Lloyd M., Horton, Kathryn B., & Smith, James O. (1968). *Peabody Language Development Kits Manual for Level #P*. Circle Pines, MN: American Guidance Service, Inc.

Dweck, C. S., Davidson, W., Nelson, S., & Enna, B. (1978). Sex differences in learned helplessness: II. The contingencies of evaluative feedback in the classroom and III. An experimental analysis. *Developmental Psychology, 14*(3), 268–276.

Ebert, D. (1974). Observational classification of preschool children's behavior as a function of teaching mode and individual differences. Unpublished manuscript, University of Louisville, KY.

Ebert, D., Miller, L., Bugbee, M., & Dyer, J. (1974). Behavior of preschool children as a function of mode of teaching in the same task. Unpublished manuscript, University of Louisville, KY.

Endsley, R. C., & Clarey, S. A. (1975). Answering young children's questions as a determinant of their subsequent question-asking behavior. *Developmental Psychology, 11*(6), 863.

Erickson, E. L., McMillan, J., Bennell, J., &Callahan, O. D. (1969). *Experiments in Head Start and Early Education: Curriculum Structures and Teacher Attitudes.* Washington, DC: Office of Economic Opportunity, Project Head Start.

Fagot, B. (1973). Influence of teacher behavior in the Preschool. *Developmental Psychology, 9,* 198–206.

Francis, K. A. E. (1971). A study of the effect of teacher intention and class level on teaching behavior and pupil thinking and learning in the classroom. Unpublished Master's Thesis, University of Canterbury, England.

Glaser, R. (1972). Individuals and learning: The new aptitudes. *Educational Researcher, 1*(6), 5–13.

Gordon, I. A., & Jester, R. E. (1973). Techniques of observing teaching in early childhood and outcomes of particular procedures. In R. M. W. Travers (Ed.), *Second Handbook of Research on Teaching.* Chicago, IL: Rand McNally College Publishing Co.

Hollingshead, A. B. (1957). Two-factor index of social position. Unpublished manuscript, 1957.

Holt, J. (1971). Big Bird, meet Dick and Jane: A critique of Sesame Street. Atlantic Monthly, *227,* 72–78.

Hughes, D. C. (1971). Effects of certain conditions of pupil participation and teacher reacting on the achievement of Form 2 pupils. *Educational Research Newsletter, 4,* 12–14.

Kamii, C. (1975). One intelligence indivisible. *Young Children, 30*(4), 228–238.

Karnes, M. B., Hodgins, A. S., Teska, J. A., & Kirk, S. A. (1969). *Investigations of Classroom and At-Home Interventions. Research & Development Program on Preschool Disadvantaged Children. 1.* Washington, DC: Office of Education.

Katz, L. (1969). *Verbal behavior of preschool teachers: A very preliminary report.* University of Illinois at Urbana, IL. (ED 034 577)

Kirk, Samuel A., McCarthy, James J., & Kirk, Winifred D. (1968). *Examiner's Manual: Illinois Test of Psycholinguistic Abilities.* Urbana, IL: University of Illinois Press.

Kounin, J. S., & Gump, P. V. (1974). Signal systems of lesson settings and the task-related behavior of preschool children. *Journal of Educational Psychology, 66*(4), 554–562.

MacDonald, J., & Clark, D. F. (1973). Critical value questions and the analysis of objectives and curricula. In R. M. W. Travers (Ed.), *Second Handbook of Research on Teaching.* Chicago, IL: Rand McNally College Publishing Company.

Miller, L. B. (1970). Manual for DATA-TAPE. Unpublished manuscript, University of Louisville, KY.

Miller, L. B., & Bizzell, R. P. (1983). Long-term effects of four preschool programs: 6th, 7th, and 8th grades. *Child Development, 54,* 725–741.

Miller, L. B., & Bizzell, R. P. (1983). The Louisville Experiment: A Comparison of Four Programs. In Consortium for Longitudinal Study (Ed.) *As the Twig is Bent: Lasting Effects of Preschool Programs.* Hillsdale, NJ: Lawrence Erlbaum & Associates Publishing Co.

Miller, L. B., Bugbee, M., & Dyer, J. L. (1974). *Experimental shifting of teaching modes in preschool.* Louisville, KY: University of Louisville. (ED 096 014)

Miller, L. B., Bugbee, M., White, S. A., & Dyer, J. L. (1974). Producing various teaching techniques in Preschool. *Classroom Interaction Newsletter, 9*(2), 42–54.

Miller, L. B., & Dyer, J. L. (1975). Four preschool programs: Their dimensions and effects. *Monographs of the Society for Research in Child Development, 40*(5–6), Serial No. 162.

Nuthall, G., & Church, J. (1973). Experimental studies of teaching behavior. In G. Chanan (Ed.), *Towards a Science of Teaching*. Slough, Bucks, England: National Foundation for Educational Research.

Olson, D. R. (1972). On a theory of instruction: Why different forms of instruction result in similar knowledge. *Interchange, 3*(1), 9–24.

Palmer, F. H., & Anderson, L. W. (1978). Early intervention treatments which have been tried, documented and assessed. Paper presented for the Conference on the Prevention of Retarded Development in Psychosocially Disadvantaged Children, Madison, WI.

Prescott, E., Jones, E., & Kritchevsky, S. (1967). *Group day care as a child-rearing environment.* Report to Children's Bureau. Pasadena, CA: Pacific Oaks College. (ED 024 453)

Rose, S. A., Blank, M., & Spalter, I. (1975). Situational specificity of behavior in young children. *Child Development, 46*(3), 464–469.

Rosenshine, B., & Furst, N. (1973). The use of direct observation to study teaching. In R. M. W. Travers (Ed.), *Second Handbook of Research on Teaching*. Chicago, IL: Rand McNally & Co.

Rubin, R. (1970). *Sex Differences in Effects of Kindergarten Attendance on Development of School Readiness and Language Skills*. Research Report #10. (ED 082 840)

Shapiro, E. (1973). Educational evaluation: Rethinking the criteria of competence. *School Review, 8*(4), 523–549.

Siegel, M. A., & Rosenshine, B. (1973). Teacher behavior and student achievement in the DISTAR program. *Chicago Principals Reporter, 62,* 24–28.

Smothergill, N. L., Olson, F., & Moore, S. G. (1971). The effects of manipulation of teacher communication style in the preschool. *Child Development, 42,* 1229–1239.

Soar, R. S., & Soar, R. M. (1972). An empirical analysis of selected Follow Through programs: An example of a process approach to evaluation in early childhood education. In I. Gordon (Ed.), *71st Yearbook of the National Society for the Study of Education: Part II*. Chicago, IL: University of Chicago Press.

Stallings, J. (1975). Implementation and child effects of teaching practices in Follow-Through classrooms. *Monographs of the Society for Research in Child Development, 40*(7–8), Serial No. 163.

Weikart, D. P., Epstein, A. S., Schweinhart, L., & Bond, J. T. (1978). The Ypsilanti Preschool Curriculum Demonstration Project: Preschool years and longitudinal results. *Monographs of the High/Scope Educational Research Foundation,* (Serial No. 4).

White, S. H., & Siegel, A. W. (1976). Cognitive development: The new inquiry. *Young Children, 31*(6), 425–436.

Wittrock, M. E., & Lumsdaine, A. A. (1977). Instructional psychology. In M. R. Rosenzweig & L. W. Porter (Eds.), *Annual review of psychology*. Volume 28. Palo Alto, CA: Annual Reviews, Inc.

Wright, C., & Nuthall, G. (1970). Relationship between teacher behavior and pupil achievement in three experimental elementary science lessons. *American Educational Research Journal, 7,* 477–491.

Zimiles, H. (1970). Has evaluation failed compensatory education? In J. Hellmuth (Ed.), *The Disadvantaged Child, 3.* Compensatory Education—A National Debate. New York: Brunner/Mazel.

3

The Adult Functioning of Children with Specific Learning Disabilities: A Follow-up Study*

Margaret Bruck
McGill-MCH Learning Centre

INTRODUCTION

The term *specific learning disabilities* (LD) refers to a heterogeneous group of children who, along with many clearly intact abilities, show significant deficits in some areas of academic achievement. Although the predominant symptom is usually learning to read, this may be accompanied by other difficulties such as physical awkwardness, directional disorientation, and the more familiar problems of spelling, math, and written work. The persistent difficulties of these children cannot be attributed to mental retardation, emotional disturbance, sensory or neurological impairment, cultural disadvantage or lack of instruction. Estimates of the prevalence of specific learning disabilities range from 3 to 40% of the school population (cf., Belmont, 1980; Farnham-Diggory, 1978).

*This study was supported by the National Health and Welfare Research and Development Program through a project grant (# 6605-1508-44) and through a National Health Research Scholar award to Margaret Bruck.

I would like to thank Sharon Horner for her important contributions from the development through to the coding stage, and to Elizabeth Prorok, Janet Takefman, Harriet Gellis, and Linda Chaim for conducting the majority of the interviews.

I am deeply indebted to the staff of the Learning Centre for their assistance in coding the data and interpreting the results, and for their general support, which was crucial for the initiation and completion of the study.

I will always be grateful to the late Sam Rabinovitch who was not only responsible for the initial idea to conduct a follow-up study but who also devoted his time to establishing a centre where thousands of learning-disabled children could receive the necessary support required for healthy development. It is in his memory that this project is dedicated.

Although there has been a proliferation of clinical, psychological, and educational research on children with learning disabilities, our knowledge of the natural history and long-term effects of the syndrome beyond childhood is limited. Some studies have examined the reading and writing skills of high school students who had been diagnosed as learning-disabled in elementary school (Balow, 1965; Dykman, Peters & Ackerman, 1973; Gottesman, Belmont & Kaminer, 1975; Koppitz, 1971; Muehl & Forell, 1973–1974; Trites & Fiedorowicz, 1976). These data indicate that learning disabilities persist into adolescence; the subjects continued to experience difficulties and to perform below grade level on measures of reading and writing skills.

Other studies have examined the status of late adolescents and young adults who had been diagnosed as learning-disabled during childhood. In the majority of these studies, the average age at follow-up was 17-years and older, and many of the subjects no longer attended high school. The conclusions of the long-term studies are not consistent. Some researchers report optimistic outcomes, while others present a bleak picture of the status and functioning of the adult with diagnosed childhood learning disabilities.

The results of five studies clearly indicate that learning-disabled children function adequately as adults. Rawson (1968) presents a most optimistic picture of the status of 20 LD subjects who attended a private boarding school. As adults these subjects were as academically and occupationally successful as control classmates without reading or writing problems. Most of the LD subjects had completed college and most were employed in prestigious occupations. Despite these accomplishments, the subjects reported that they continued to experience difficulties with reading and spelling. Silver and Hagin (1964) administered a battery of neuropsychological and reading tests to 24 subjects who were diagnosed as learning-disabled during childhood and who at the time of follow-up averaged 19-years-of-age. The subjects continued to display many of the same neuropsychological symptoms that were noted in childhood. In terms of reading skills however, the subjects fared better. Only 9 of the 24 subjects were considered to be inadequate readers. However, most of the inadequate readers showed evidence of a structural organic defect when they were initially diagnosed in childhood. In contrast most of the subjects who were free of neurological symptoms during childhood, and hence considered pure cases of learning disabilities, were adequate readers at follow-up. In a third study of 44 former reading-clinic clients, Robinson and Smith (1962) reported that most of these subjects had graduated from high school and had continued onto college. Only 1 subject was unemployed. Balow and Blomquist (1965) interviewed by phone 32 former reading-clinic patients, 9 of whom agreed to come into the laboratory for more extensive testing. The interview data indicated that most of the subjects had finished high school and one third had continued their education after high school. Occupationally, the subjects held a variety of jobs, less than half of which were classified as semi- or unskilled. The test results from the subsample of 9 subjects indicated that they were reading at a 10th-grade level and that they showed a negative and defeatist attitude (as assessed by a paper and pencil test). Finally on the basis of telephone interviews with 50 former reading-clinic clients, Preston and Yarrington (1967) concluded that, while learning-disabled individuals required more time to complete their education than was required by the average learner, nevertheless their levels of educational and occupational accomplishments were comparable to those reported in national statistics.

In contrast to the above studies, other investigators have concluded that there are many negative, long-term consequences of childhood learning disabilities. For example, the results of one study of 35 former reading-clinic patients (Carter, 1964) indicate that the learning-disabled individual is at risk for high school dropout, low occupational status and poor social adjustment (as assessed by an 11-item scale). In a second study, a group of poor readers were followed-up between the ages of 29 and 35 (Howden, 1967). These subjects were less educated than a control group of good readers, however there were no differences in terms of the two groups' social participations and interactions. Hardy (1968) found that former reading-clinic patients showed poor levels of educational and occupational achievements at follow-up. However, most were satisfied with their jobs and showed good social adjustment. Recently, Spreen (1982) has examined the outcome of three groups of learning-handicapped subjects: those with neurological impairment, those with suspected neurological impairment, and those with no neurological impairment. At the time of follow-up the learning-disabled subjects ranged in age from 13- to 25-years. All three groups of subjects with learning disabilities had poorer educational outcomes and showed more social and personality problems than a group of controls. However the learning-disabled subjects and controls were similar in terms of occupational levels and delinquency rates. The presence of personality problems was associated with degree of neurological impairment. Learning-disabled subjects without any neurological involvement had the best social and emotional adjustments of the three groups and were most comparable to the controls.

The existing studies do not present consistent results concerning the adult outcomes of the learning-disabled child and for a number of reasons the findings are difficult to interpret. First, small sample sizes and inadequate control groups restrict generalization for most of the studies.

Second, because the areas of investigation are mainly limited to academic and occupational achievement or to the acquisition of literacy skills, little is known about adjustment in social and emotional domains. No study has presented a complete description of the learning-disabled adult's educational, literacy, occupational, social, and emotional functioning and status. Given current speculations about the relationship among learning disabilities, juvenile delinquency and unemployment (e.g., Mauser, 1974; Schenck, Fitzsimmons, Bullard, Taylor, & Satz, 1980), it seems particularly important to provide some empirical data to validate these current beliefs. Furthermore, because the frequency of social and emotional problems of LD children has been the focus of recent research (reviewed in Bryan & Bryan, 1978), it is important to determine whether these problems are specific to the childhood years or whether they persist over many years.

A third problem involves the age of the subjects at follow-up. In many studies, because follow-up occurred when subjects were in their early adolescent years, these data reflect the performance of LD subjects still in secondary school and do not indicate the adjustment of individuals who are making the transition to adulthood. When older subjects have been studied the data on their performance have been combined with those of younger subjects, obscuring any developmental trends.

Fourth, in none of the studies in the literature is the nature of treatment services controlled for or examined. Fifth, in many studies the original criteria for the diagnosis of a learning disability in childhood are often missing or questionable. As a result, it is often not clear whether subjects truly had primary learning disabilities or whether they were mentally retarded, emotionally disturbed, socially disadvantaged or organically impaired. The lack of control groups coupled with the questionable criteria of classifying follow-up subjects as learning-disabled present a primary problem for the interpretation and generalizability of the results of most of the follow-up studies. That is, an examination of the characteristics of these LD subjects indicates that in many cases the individuals who have been classified as learning-disabled have low or borderline IQs, are from lower class backgrounds, have a number of psychiatric symptoms or have neurological impairment. While, it is possible that children sharing such symptoms may in addition have a specific learning disability, the presence of secondary symptoms complicates the outcome picture. That is in some studies, the poorer outcomes of the LD sample may be simply associated with low social status or neurological impairment rather than with a learning disability as such. At this stage of investigation, it is particularly important to examine the long-term consequences of a learning disability for children who strictly meet the definition of a learning disability and who demonstrate no other complicating factors. Only after the status of these subjects is determined, should one begin to investigate the outcomes of learning-disabled children with other symptomotology (e.g. as was done in Spreens's 1982 study).

A sixth issue concerns the variability of baseline skills or the severity of learning disability within the sample selected for study. It appears that in many studies, the children with the most severe learning disabilities were the focus of study. Subjects were former clients of a reading clinic or attended a special school for learning-disabled children. It seems logical that in most instances, children who receive special assistance for their learning problems are also the children with the most severe learning problems. There are however, many children with learning disabilities with varying degrees of severity. The fates of these children are of interest to practitioners and parents; however, the current data may not be applicable to this larger group as they focus mainly on the very disabled child. Therefore it is important to include in a follow-up study, subjects who vary in terms of the severity of their learning disabilities and to examine the effects of severity upon outcome status.

To summarize, while results of existing studies suggest that learning disabilities persist throughout adolescence and adulthood, these data do not yield a comprehensive picture of the specific long-term consequences of learning disabilities, of the long-term effects of various treatment programs, and of the types of children who, as adults, will suffer the most long-term handicaps. Based on these concerns, the present study was designed to address the following issues: (a) Do LD children become LD adults? (b) What are the long-term consequences of a childhood learning disability on academic, occupational, social, and emotional adjustment? (c) What is the relationship between childhood remediation and adult measures of academic, social, occupational, and personal adjustment? (d) What combination of characteristics or events best predicts the type of adjustment that children with learning disabilities will make in late adolescence or in young adulthood?

This chapter focuses on the first two issues (for full details of all aspects of the project, see Bruck, 1981). It examines the literacy, educational, occupational, and psychosocial functioning of 101 late adolescents and young adults who had been diagnosed as learning-disabled in early childhood.

METHOD

Design

A learning-disabled group consisted of 101 subjects who had been diagnosed as learning-disabled during their early elementary school years at a specialized hospital clinic and, who at the time of follow-up, were between the ages of 17- and 29-years. Fifty nonlearning-disabled subjects (matched for age, sex and social class) comprised a peer control group, and 51 nonlearning-disabled siblings of the LD subjects (matched for age, sex and social class) comprised a sibling control group. Each of the LD and peer control subjects and at least one of their parents were interviewed individually to obtain detailed histories of past and present functioning in a variety of areas. Each LD and peer control subject was given a battery of academic achievement tests to measure reading, spelling, and math skills.

To determine the long-term consequences and permanence of learning disabilities, the LD subjects' status at follow-up was compared to that of the tested peer control group and to that of the untested normal sibling control group whose status was determined from the interview data.

Clinic Setting

The research setting, the McGill–Montreal Children's Hospital Learning Centre, was established over 22 years ago by Dr. Sam Rabinovitch to provide diagnostic, remedial and counseling services to LD children, their parents, and teachers.

All referred children are assessed by an experienced psychologist or remedial teacher. As a supplement to their normal school activities, some children receive an individualized, clinic remedial program designed to give each child the necessary support and skills to achieve positive experiences in both academic and nonacademic settings. The program includes: teaching the basic skills required for reading, writing, and math; consulting with the child's classroom teacher and other school personnel to explain the nature of the child's problem and to suggest suitable classroom modifications; counseling parents to explain the nature of the child's problem, to give assurance that poor school performance does not reflect retardation or emotional disturbance, and to suggest activities to share with the child who is often in need of intellectual and social stimulation; and counseling the child in dealing with problems of poor self-esteem and frustration, which may be concommitants of school failure.

Those children who are assessed but not accepted for treatment receive some of the consultative services. This involves several contacts with the school and family shortly after the assessment, and when further assistance is required, the Centre's staff responds to the request of parents and teachers. When possible, a tutor (who is not on the clinic staff) will be found for the child.

Subjects

Learning Disabled Group

Pertinent background information on 5,000 children, diagnosed as learning-disabled by the clinic staff, were coded on to a 217 item checklist[1] and then stored on to a computer file. A list of 259 names of potential cases for follow-up were generated from the file. These subjects satisfied the following criteria: between the ages of 5 and 10 upon first clinic contact and assessment; IQ score of at least 90 on either the WISC Verbal Scale, WISC Performance Scale, or the Stanford–Binet; no primary behavioral or emotional disturbances; no major neurological abnormalities (e.g., epilepsy, cerebral palsy); no other physical disabilities that might explain learning problems (e.g., hearing loss); complete assessments of the presenting problem at intake available in the clinic file includ-

---

[1]Copies of the background checklist can be obtained from the author.

ing a reading score; between the ages of 17 and 29 at the time of follow-up and no longer attending high school; and confirmation of the initial diagnosis of specific learning disabilities by a staff psychologist who reviewed the patient file information after computer identification.

Of the 259 subjects, 199 (78%) subjects and their parents were located after an average interval of 13 years between initial clinic assessment and follow-up. Of those located, 156 (78%) families agreed to participate in the study (i.e., the subject and at least one parent),[2] and 101 families selected from the sample pool on the basis of age, treatment history,[3] and availability for testing were included in the study.

Peer Control Group

The LD subjects were asked after the interview to name a cousin or an old friend, of the same sex and age, who to their knowledge had no school difficulties and who might be willing to participate in the study.

The nominated peers and their families were contacted and explained the nature of the project. Peer control families were included in the study if (a) both the nominated peer and one parent agreed to be interviewed; and (b) upon initial contact by the research team, the subject and his parents concurred that the subject had not had a learning disability, had never repeated a grade, or had never received extra tutoring for school problems.

Fifty peer control subjects who met these criteria and one of their parents were interviewed for the study.

Sibling Control Group

After all the data had been collected, it became clear that the peer control group comprised a very select group of subjects who were atypically achievement-oriented and successful in both academic and occupational domains (see pages 113, 114, 118 for detailed discussion). Therefore to obtain a more representative estimate of the academic and occupational status of a nondisabled sample, a

---

[2]Families refusing to participate (either because the subject or the two parents, or both the subject and parents were unwilling) were interviewed briefly by telephone to determine the representativeness of the tested LD group. They were asked why they did not wish to participate, how far they got in school, whether or not they were working, and whether there were any serious social or emotional problems (see Bruck, 1981, for details).

[3]Although the data are not discussed in the present study, half the subjects had received clinic treatment for at least 1½ years and half had received no remedial treatment services. For the purposes of the present paper, all LD subjects regardless of treatment histories will be pooled into one group (cf. Bruck, 1981, for treatment effects).

second control group was selected. These subjects were siblings of the LD subjects.

During the interview parents were asked to state the age, sex, educational status, and occupational status of each family member. As well, they were to name all family members who may have had any learning problems and give the basis for their answers. After all the interviews had been completed, the names of all siblings (of LD subjects) between the ages of 17 and 29 who were no longer attending high school and who had no known history of learning difficulties were listed. A group of 51 sibling controls were matched with the LD subjects on the basis of age, sex, and socioeconomic status.

Procedures

Interviews

Each of the LD and peer control subjects and one or both parents were interviewed individually to obtain detailed descriptions of the subject's childhood and current specific learning disabilities, treatment services, academic and occupational achievements, social, and emotional adjustments.[4] The average length of each interview was 2½ hours. Each interview was audiotaped and then transcribed.

The subjects and their parent(s) were informed before the interview that they would be interviewed separately by a different interviewer, and that all of the information they gave would be kept confidential. There were six trained interviewers on the project team.

When possible both the mother and father of the LD subjects were interviewed. In 35% of the cases only one parent was interviewed. In most of these cases there was only one parent alive or in contact with the subject. In the case of the control subjects, only one parent was interviewed and in all but four cases, it was the mother. Most interviews were conducted in Montreal at the clinic.

Tests

Several days after the interview all LD and control subjects were individually administered the following battery of tests to measure oral reading, reading comprehension, spelling, and math skills: Gray Oral Reading Test, Form A; Reading Comprehension and Reading Rate Subtests of Stanford Diagnostic

---

[4]Copies of the interview can be obtained from the author.

Reading Test, (SDRT) Blue or Brown Level;[5] Reading, Spelling, and Math Subtests of Wide Range Achievement Test (WRAT), Level 1.

Background Data

In order to obtain additional information about the educational history, severity of learning disability, treatment history, social, and emotional adjustments of the LD subjects during childhood, the relevant information in their original hospital clinic files was coded. For some of the control and LD subjects additional information on their educational histories was obtained from past school records, which were released to the research project upon the subject's request.

Coding

The variables coded for the present analyses are classified as antecedent (childhood) measures, or as follow-up measures (for complete details on all coded variables, see Bruck, 1981).

Antecedent Variables

Because the coding of antecedent measures was based primarily on childhood clinic file information, these variables were coded for the LD group only. The first two measures represent childhood cognitive and learning skills, and the last three reflect childhood social and psychological adjustments.

Full scale IQ score at the time of initial clinic contact and assessment was taken from the clinic file.

Severity of learning disability represented a global rating of the severity of each LD subject's learning disability during childhood. Individual profiles were constructed on the basis of clinic file information collected during initial clinic assessments and contacts. In order that the profiles contained similar information for all 101 subjects, the following data were extracted from each file and rewritten in a standard form for rating purposes: age at intake; grade at intake; grade(s) repeated; presenting problems and strengths (e.g., reading comprehension, de-

---

[5]Scores on the Gray Oral Reading Test were used to determine the level of the SDRT given the subjects. If the Gray Oral score was below the Grade 5.0 level, the SDRT Brown level was administered; if the Gray Oral score was equal to or above 5.0, the SDRT Blue level was administered. Because of the SDRT standardization procedures, standard scores on both levels are comparable.

coding, auditory processing, motor coordination); test results (e.g., full scale and subtest IQ scores, visual perception test scores, language test scores, reading test scores).

The 101 profiles were then grouped according to the subject's grade at initial assessment, resulting in eight groups of approximately 13 subjects per group. Each profile was assigned a number to preserve the subject's anonymity.

Three clinicians independently rated the profiles by group, using a 5-point rating scale (1 = least severe, 5 = most severe). Reliability of interjudge rating was generally high. When interjudge ratings differed by only 1 point on the scale, the mean of the judges' ratings was used as an index of severity of childhood learning disability. When the discrepancy among interjudge ratings was larger than 1 point the judges discussed all the cases in that specific group and then independently rerated the profiles. After rerating, reliability improved ($r = .90$), and the mean of the judges' ratings was used as an index of severity of childhood learning disability.

For the purposes of some analyses, subjects were assigned to one of three groups on the basis of severity of disability rating: mild (ratings of 1.0, 1.5, or 2.0), moderate (ratings of 2.5, 3.0, or 3.5), and severe (ratings of 4.0, 4.5, or 5.0). It should be noted that subjects in the mild and moderate groups did have significant disabilities in that they were functioning below grade level in specific academic areas, and they were finding it difficult to function in their classroom. Their problems however were not as serious as those in the severe group. The problems of subjects with mild and moderate disabilities are similar to those of many children who are seen in learning-disability clinics.

Childhood Social and Psychological Problems.   While it is too complex to detail the process of coding childhood social and psychological problems, the following general guidelines were followed. Because of the difficulties of relying on retrospective interview information, which has been criticized in terms of reliability, accuracy of recall, and systematic distortion of events (Yarrow, 1963), a problem was coded if there were clinic file documentation of it, or if in the follow-up interview two members of the family independently described the presence and type of a similar problem. If the data were too sparse or ambiguous, the subject was not assigned a rating. Because of the general lack of detailed information from the clinic files and from the interviews concerning childhood social and psychological adjustments, the codings do not reflect severity of problems or degree of adjustment, but rather the presence or absence of significant problems.

Using these general guidelines, each subject's adjustment in the area of family, peer, and psychological functioning was coded cojointly by two members of the research team (a clinical psychologist and a family therapist). A psychiatric social worker independently made similar judgments. The few interjudge discrepancies (4% of all judgements) were resolved by further review and discussion of the cases.

Family relationships were coded as "poor" if there were problems not centered around poor school work, and if these problems were specific to the target subject. For example, if it were reported that there was a great deal of friction between the target subject and his parents, but that there was also friction between the parents and other siblings, which was caused by the parents' general personality style, this was not coded as a problem. Family relationships were coded as average either when the file information stated that the parents reported good or normal interactions with their child or when during the follow-up interview two members of the family concurred that the parents enjoyed the childhood years with the subject (e.g., "he was a delight" "I always enjoyed him as a child and felt very close to him").

Peer relationships were coded as "poor" when the subject had significant difficulty making and keeping friends. They were coded as average when either the file information explicitly stated that there were no problems along these dimensions, or when during the follow-up interview, two members of the family stated that there were no problems.

Psychological adjustment was classified into one of four categories: "withdrawn" (anxiety, internalizing affective problems); "acting-out" (externalizing, conduct problems); "mixed" (both withdrawn and acting-out behaviors noted throughout childhood); "no problems" (see Achenbach & Edelbrock, 1978, and Quay, 1979, for a description of these dimensions of childhood behavioral deviations). For the purposes of the present analyses "withdrawn," "acting-out," and "mixed" problems were collapsed into one category of "poor" psychological adjustment.

Follow-Up Status

All variables in this section were coded for the LD and peer control subjects. When the information was available, some of the measures were also coded for the sibling controls. The measures are all based upon the follow-up interview and test data. The following variables were coded to describe the general characteristics of the subjects at follow-up.

Family socioeconomic status (SES). The parent's occupation at follow-up was converted into an SES index by use of the Blishen Scale (Blishen & McRoberts, 1976). The Blishen scores were then divided into six class intervals as suggested by the authors with lower indices representing the higher socioeconomic strata. If two parents were working, the one with the more prestigious rating was included for analysis.

Subject's age at the time of interview was coded in years and months. Subjects were also classified into two age groups: late adolescence (17- to 21-years) and young adulthood (22- to 29-years).

Subject's status at the time of interview was classified as "student" (taking daytime courses), "employed" (fulltime job), or "unemployed" (not attending school and looking for a job) or "other" (e.g., housewife, taking a year off to travel).

The educational attainment of the control and LD subjects was coded both qualitatively and quantitatively. In both cases the code was based on the highest level attained by the subject at the time of interview and did not necessarily reflect the final educational attainment, which may have been achieved several years after the interview.

Number of years of education completed, a quantitative measure, was computed by assigning one point for every year of elementary, secondary, and post secondary school successfully completed (e.g., a score of 12 was assigned to subjects completing high school, and not continuing their education).

Educational level was classified into one of eight qualitative categories: "high school dropout;" "completed high school program" (did not continue education); "post high school vocational training;" "junior college in progress" (subject was in the first 2 years of a post secondary academic program); "junior college dropout" (subject left the program because of poor academic standing); "university in progress" (subject was in university having completed the first 2 years of the junior college program); "university dropout" (subject left university due to disinterest and not due to failure or dissatisfaction with the system); "university completed" (successful completion of undergraduate program).

The Occupational level of each subject employed at the time of interview was rated according to the Blishen Scale (Blishen & McRoberts, 1976). The Blishen scores were then divided into six intervals with lower indices representing the higher socioeconomic strata.

The basic skill levels of the LD and peer control subjects were measured by their performance on the reading, spelling, and math tests administered after the interview.

Asocial and deviant behaviors, which occured from the beginning of high school (early adolescence), were coded for the LD and peer controls. The data were based on parents' and subjects' interview responses. Two measures were used.

1. The first reflects the occurences of delinquent acts which were classified as "acts for which subject was sent to jail," "acts with police involvement," "acts with no police involvement." Coded delinquent acts included aggravated assault, larceny, auto theft, drunkenness and disorderly conduct, driving without a license, and possession of drugs.
2. The second measure of asocial and socially deviant behaviors reflected the frequency of intake of nonmedical drugs and alcohol. Problems were coded when the subject reported heavy use.

Social and psychological adjustments were coded for all LD and peer control subjects. The data were based on the subjects' and parents' reports throughout the interview and as such are based on their perceptions of adjustment rather than on a clinical judgement of adjustment. Adjustment in each of four major areas was coded by a psychiatric social worker, family therapist and clinical psychologist using similar guidelines to those summarized for the coding of childhood problems. Overall, there was interjudge agreement for 91% of the cases.

Family relationships at follow-up were judged in terms of the subject's ability to function within the primary nuclear family, the degree of conflict and antagonism with each parent, and the degree to which the subject's interactions with these family members affected the quality of the family life. Problems were coded that were not related to specific personality styles of the parent (which may have affected interactions with all family members) but which were specific to subject–parent interactions. Family relationships were judged as "adequate" if all interviewees agreed that they got along, and did not mention any areas of unusual difficulty or conflict. Family relationships were judged as "poor" when subjects reported severe difficulties interacting with both parents (or in the case of a single-parent family, with that one parent) and when these perceptions were confirmed by the parent(s). In all cases these subjects did not fit into the family and caused particular difficulties in terms of the total family relationships. For those subjects not living at home who were coded as "poor," it was often the case that they did not live at home because they were not welcome. In many cases when the subject was living at home either the parent or child expressed the notion that they would like to leave home. "Moderate" difficulties were coded when subjects had particular difficulties with only one parent, but related well to the other parent. In these cases problems were due to particular personality clashes and were not age specific as they had persisted over a period of time. Again there was agreement among the interviewees on the presence of the conflict. Finally some subjects and parents indicated the presence of "mild" difficulties which, although disturbing, were not as disruptive or as troublesome as the "moderate" or "severe" problems but which could be clearly differentiated from those subjects showing no problems. For the purposes of some analyses, mild, moderate and severe problems were collapsed into one category "family problem."

Peer relationships with the same sex were coded as "moderate" problems when family members agreed that the subject had few friends, was lonely, and had trouble making friends. "Mild" problems were coded if the subject was shy, had difficulty making social contacts, but had a few friends and was secure in these relationships. For the purpose of some analyses "moderate" and "mild" problems were collapsed into one category.

Peer interactions with the opposite sex (dating) were coded as "poor" for subjects who had infrequent interactions with the opposite sex because of shyness, lack of social skills, or disinterest. These subjects had never or rarely dated since adolescence.

Psychological adjustment reflected an overall judgment of each subject's personal or emotional well-being. Data about anxiety, depressions, emotional lability, temper tantrums, extreme sensitivity, and so on, were extracted from the interview along with information on whether any of the interviewees felt the subject needed counselling or therapy for emotional problems. Problems that directly reflected poor family or peer relationships were not coded in this section (e.g., extreme lack of self-confidence in social situations), nor were problems specifically related to jobs (dissatisfaction with present job), or to school (anxiety around exam times), unless these problems affected the subject's total psychological adjustment and interactions in all spheres of life.

Each subject's overall psychological adjustment was coded in terms of the presence of certain behavioral reactions that most typified their common responses. Subjects were classified as "withdrawn" if they were either depressed, highly sensitive, somewhat withdrawn, or constant worriers. Subjects classified as "acting-out" were best described by their immature and volatile reactions to stress or conflict. They would lose self-control and become easily angered; they seemed very vulnerable to criticism. Subjects with "conduct disorders" were repeatedly aggressive in an antisocial manner and around the time of interview, they had committed a number of serious delinquent acts. Subjects with "situational disorders" expressed general dissatisfaction with their present life because of unrealistic perceptions of, or inability to deal with, specific problem areas. For example, one subject described her physical attractiveness as the cause of her inability to sustain employment because employers would initially take unfair advantage of her and then fire her. She attributed her poor occupational and general status to these "unfair" firings. The justification for unemployment seemed unwarranted to the interviewers and her parents who attributed her unemployment to poor job skills. Subjects were coded as "well adjusted" when they and their parents indicated throughout the interview, that the subject was well adjusted, happy and coping adequately for an individual of that age.

For the purposes of many analyses the qualitative categories were dichotomized into "problems" and "no problems" in psychological adjustment.

RESULTS

Descriptive Data

Characteristics of the LD and control subjects at follow-up are summarized in Table 3.1. The ratio of males to females in the LD sample is similar to those reported for other clinic samples (Coleman & Sandhu, 1967). The subjects were predominantly from middle class backgrounds (6% of the LD subjects were from lower working class backgrounds; 6% of the peer control subjects from similar backgrounds).

TABLE 3.1. Characteristics of Learning Disabled and Control Subjects

	Group		
Characteristics	Learning Disabled (*n* = 101)	Peer Control (*n* = 50)	Sibling Control (*n* = 51)
Age			
Years (M)	21.10	20.71	21.20
Late adolescents (%)	55	54	53
Young adults (%)	45	46	47
Sex			
Females (%)	21	24	22
Males (%)	79	76	78
Family SES			
Blishen Scale (M)	2.74	2.14	2.67
Parentage			
Adopted (%)	11	0	8
Biological (%)	89	100	92
Civil Status			
Single (%)	92	96	80
Married (%)	7	2	16
Divorced (%)	1	2	6
Subjects with children (%)	3	0	not available
Living Arrangements			
At home with parents (%)	61	72	42
On own (%)	39	28	58

In addition to the information presented above, the following data, extracted from the clinic files, school records and interviews, present a general description of the LD subjects' cognitive profiles, academic experiences and learning disabilities during childhood and early adolescence. The average age of the first clinic contact and assessment occurred at 8-years-old (Grade 2). At entry, the subjects' IQ scores were in the average range ($M = 103$, $SD = 11.22$). All subjects were assessed as having primary problems with written language (reading and spelling). In addition, 75% were experiencing difficulties in the area of mathematics. Examinations of their childhood educational and psychological assessments indicate that the specific learning difficulties were associated with poor visual processing and/or spatial skills for 45% of the cases, with poor auditory processing and/or language skills for 6% of the cases, and with both poor visual/spatial and poor auditory language skills in 48% of the cases. A breakdown of the severity of learning disability ratings indicates that 43% of the subjects were in the severe range, 31% were in the moderate range, and 27% were in the mildly disabled range. The subjects' difficulties in elementary and secondary school are indicated by the number of grades repeated (59% repeated in elementary, 27% repeated in high school) and by the special help they received for their school problems; in elementary school, in addition to clinic remediation received by 50% of the subjects, 45% had specialized help in school, 59% received private tutoring; in high school 25% received specialized help in school, 55% received private tutoring. On the average each subject received 4.47 years of special assistance for their learning problems. In the total sample there were only 4 of the 101 subjects who never received any special remedial teaching or coaching for their school difficulties.[3]

In summary, these descriptive data in conjunction with the criteria for subject selection indicate that follow-up subjects had *primary learning disabilities,* which were diagnosed during childhood. These subjects encountered sufficient difficulty in acquiring basic school skills as to cause parents and teachers to refer the child to a professional who made a diagnosis of specific learning disabilities. In addition, although the severity of disability varies within the group, in all but 4 cases, subjects received some special assistance for their problems.

Persistence of Learning Disabilities

In order to determine whether the LD subjects continued to have persisting difficulties in basic skills, their performance on the reading, spelling, and math tests was compared to that of the peer control group (see Table 3.2). On all measures there were significant differences between the two groups. The peer group always performed better than the LD group.

Although the data indicate that learning disabilities persist, four additional analyses of the test score data indicated that, under certain conditions, basic skills continued to improve after adolescence for LD subjects. The results of the first analysis indicated that the LD subjects who were working at the time of the follow-up study generally did not perform as well on the tests as LD subjects who were fulltime students, despite the fact that the two groups were comparable in terms of family socioeconomic status, educational attainment (total years of schooling), severity of childhood learning disability and childhood full scale IQ[6] (see Table 3.3). These data suggest that the LD ''students' '' higher levels of skill acquisition at follow-up was related to their recent experiences with practicing and using these skills in demanding literacy environments, and that while the ''working'' LD subjects had attained the same educational levels as the LD students, their poorer test performance may be associated with lack of continued

---

[6]Similar analyses were not carried out for the peer control group for two reasons. First, they did not match the LD subgroups in terms of chronological age and educational attainment. Second, there was a ceiling effect on the control subjects' test scores.

TABLE 3.2.   Learning Disabled and Peer Control Subjects' Basic Skill Levels

Test	Learning Disabled	Peer Control	t
Gray Oral			
Total score (M)	65.50	95.78	48.06**
Grade level	9.0	12.0	
SDRT Comprehension			
Standard score (M)	661.73	794.70	77.76**
Grade level	10.2	12.0	
SDRT Rate			
Standard score (M)	630.94	728.38	68.88**
Grade level	9.1	12.0	
WRAT Reading			
Raw score (M)	84.48	94.46	22.23**
Grade level	9.7	13.7	
WRAT Spelling			
Raw score (M)	52.50	60.46	20.61**
Grade level	8.7	13.0	
WRAT Math			
Raw score (M)	42.18	50.54	20.71**
Grade level	6.5	10.0	

**df = 149, $p < .001$

exposure and practice of basic skills in highly demanding literacy environments. The results of the second analysis indicated that in addition to recency of participation in highly demanding literacy environments, the cumulative amount of participation was related to the basic skill levels of the LD subjects.[6] LD subjects who had completed an undergraduate university program generally performed better on the literacy tests than the LD subjects who were completing the last 2 years of the university program (see Table 3.3). Because the two groups were similar in terms of family SES, severity of learning disability, and childhood IQ, the between-group differences seem best associated with differences in years of schooling and amount of direct practicing of reading and writing skills.

In order to explore in greater detail the relative contributions of years of education and age at follow-up to test scores, a third analysis computed simple and partial correlations between the years of education and test scores removing the effects of age, and between age and test scores removing the effects of years of education for the LD group and control group respectively (see Table 3.4). For the control group, neither sets of partial correlations reached significance ($p < .05$) (although in some cases education and age at follow-up were significantly related to test scores). For the LD group the relationships between years of education and test scores, removing the effects of age, were highly significant

TABLE 3.3. Basic Skill Levels and Background Characteristics of Subgroups of LD Subjects

	Status at Follow-up			Educational Level at Follow-up		
	Student (n = 38)	Employed (n = 51)	$F(df = 1,87)$	University in Progress (n = 9)	University Completed (n = 11)	$F(df = 1,18)$
Test Scores						
Gray	75.08	63.31	6.97**	74.78	79.36	.59
SDRT Comprehension	698.11	652.39	3.62**	712.78	790.18	6.36**
SDRT Rate	650.58	634.08	.66	661.87	714.27	6.02*
WRAT Reading	88.16	83.80	3.79*	87.00	94.18	5.47*
WRAT Spelling	55.87	51.41	7.78***	55.22	59.91	4.47
WRAT Math	42.82	42.47	.07	45.00	47.82	.94
Background data						
Family SES	2.44	2.82	2.34	2.44	2.09	.52
Age at interview	19.64	22.59	22.98***	21.05	24.80	23.59**
Years of education	14.42	13.67	2.26	15.56	18.55	19.45**
Severity of disability	3.04	3.35	1.24	2.94	2.45	1.09
Full Scale IQ	103.68	103.45	.01	107.11	110.00	.46

*p < .05
**p < .01
***p < .06

although age was not significantly related to test scores after removing the effects of education. These results suggest that skills developed as a function of educational experience and not automatically as a function of maturation. Finally, to determine whether severity of childhood learning disability or intelligence confounded the relationship between education and literacy skills for the LD subjects (i.e., perhaps the subjects who had the better test scores were those who were initially brighter and less disabled and therefore could become better educated), partial correlations were carried out on the LD data in which number of years of education was correlated with test scores removing the effects of age at follow-up, childhood intelligence and severity of disability (see Table 3.4). These partial correlations were highly significant. These data suggest that after adolescence, continued exposure to literacy tasks in demanding situations are associated with the continuation of literacy skill development in learning disabled individuals.

In order to gain a broader understanding of the persistence of learning disabilities and of the nature of the difficulties experienced by the LD subjects at follow-up, the interview data were examined. Subjects and their parents were asked to evaluate the subjects' basic skills in terms of daily activities and to indicate, when relevant, how childhood disabilities interfered with daily functioning. For example, they were asked whether they enjoyed reading, whether they had problems understanding certain written materials (e.g., questionnaires,

TABLE 3.4. Correlations and Partial Correlations Between Test Scores and Years of Education, Age at Follow-up, Childhood IQ and Severity of Learning Disability

Tests	Education	Age	Education (removing age)	Age (removing education)	Education (removing age, IQ, severity)
Learning disabled					
Gray	.45**	.26**	.37**	.03	.27**
Comprehension	.64**	.49**	.52**	.23*	.43**
Rate	.51**	.36**	.40**	.12	.34**
WRAT-Read	.53**	.43**	.39**	.21*	.30**
WRAT-Spell	.54**	.31**	.47**	.02	.43**
WRAT-Math	.55**	.37**	.45**	.10	.35**
Controls					
Gray	.25	.32*	.05	.21	
Comprehension	.29*	.25	.17	.06	
Rate	.14	.23	−.03	.19	
WRAT-Read	.35**	.39**	.12	.22	
WRAT-Spell	.44**	.40**	.25	.14	
WRAT-Math	.10	−.03	.17	−.14	

*$p < .05$
**$p < .01$

instructions, menus), whether they required help with writing letters, or job applications, or with balancing a checkbook. These data are summarized in Table 3.5 for both the LD and peer control groups.

The data indicate that the most commonly reported difficulties related to spelling and written expression. For example, the majority of LD subjects described frequent problems writing reports, letters, and filling out applications. Parents, siblings, or friends were commonly asked to proofread their written materials. Although half of the subjects reported problems in the area of spelling, surprisingly few (28%) of this subgroup used a dictionary as an aid. By contrast, few control subjects described similar problems.

In terms of reading skills, the most important finding concerns the relatively high number of LD subjects who rarely read for pleasure (this included books, magazines, and newspapers). Interestingly, these reports were not accompanied by remarks such as "I don't read because it's too hard," or "I can't understand what I read, so I don't read." When asked about their knowledge of and interest in current events, most of the infrequent readers felt they were well informed and

TABLE 3.5.   LD and Peer Control Subjects' Perceptions of Disabilities

Difficulties	LD (%)	Control (%)
Writing Skills		
Spelling/Writing problem	75	10
Frequent spelling errors	54	8
Poor sentence structure or organization	46	2
Needs help with applica- tions/questionnaires	23	0
Reading Skills		
Does not read for pleasure	43	12
Reads too slowly	18	0
Rereads to get main point of text	9	0
Difficulty understanding written instruc- tions	36	0
Math Skills		
Has problems with math	42	4
Problems with measurement, or money	27	0
Motor and Spatial Skills		
Poor handwriting	41	6
Poor Motor coordination (can't ride a bike, clumsy, poor in sports)	8	0
Does not drive or have a license	24	22
General		
Still has learning disabilities	49	0

that they obtained the necessary information from radio, television, friends, or parents.

Math was also mentioned as a common problem. However, it is not clear whether these problems were academically related (i.e., these subjects did poorly in math courses) or whether these remarks about poor math skills reflected basic problems with daily activities. When specifically probed about math difficulties, fewer, but a significant proportion of LD subjects reported problems such as balancing checkbooks, counting change in a store, estimating or taking measurements.

It is important to note that, in general while most LD subjects and their families described difficulties associated with reading, writing and math skills, it was rare that these problems were regarded as a handicap or as a hindrance to the subjects' daily functioning and adjustment. Most subjects did not consider themselves as "learning-disabled" and in most cases they and their families remarked that they had either overcome or learned to compensate for the originally diagnosed childhood learning disability.

While the interview data and the test score data indicate that most LD subjects had sufficient skills to function in a variety of situations, that most subjects considered any cited difficulties to be minimally significant, and that on the average subjects reading and writing skills were at the Grade-9 level (see Table 3.2) because these data are based on group averages, they do not indicate the number of LD subjects who had failed to acquire minimal levels of basic skills. Therefore, in order to estimate the proportion of semi or illiterate subjects in the LD sample, the number of LD subjects scoring below the Grade-6 level on each of the tests was calculated. Because these rates varied among tests (see Table 3.6), a number of criteria were set to classfiy subjects as low functioning: The most stringent was that subjects had to perform below Grade-6 level on all 6 tests; the least stringent was that they had to perform poorly on 3 of the 6 tests. Because these rates reflect difficulties with reading, writing or math, another set of estimates was constructed to reflect low skill levels with respect to reading and writing skills only. Therefore the number of subjects performing below the Grade-6 level on all 5 reading and writing tests, on 4 of the 5 tests, and on 3 of the 5 tests was calculated. Referring to Table 3.6, it appears that between 3% to 16% of the subjects were low on all skills, and that between 3% to 10% were low on reading and writing skills.

The profiles of the low functioning subjects (using the least stringent criterion, $n = 16$) indicate that all were males, that all but one had been rated as having severe childhood disabilities, and that their IQ scores were below that of the LD sample ($M = 93.62$). However, these data do not indicate that severe childhood problems and lower IQ signify a poor prognosis in terms of basic skills. While 43 subjects had severe childhood disability ratings, 27 (Mean IQ = 95.42) had acquired facility (i.e., above Grade-6 level) in basic skills. Thus while severity

TABLE 3.6.   Estimates of Percentage of LD Subjects with
Low Basic Skill Levels at Follow-up

	% Below Grade 6
Individual Tests	
Gray Oral	24
SDRT-Comprehension	8
SDRT-Rate	5
WRAT-Reading	11
WRAT-Spelling	21
WRAT-Math	32
Estimates of Poor Functioning: Reading, Spelling, Math	
6/6 tests	3
5/6 tests	5
4/6 tests	9
3/6 tests	16
Estimates of Poor Functioning: Reading and Spelling	
5/5 tests	3
4/5 tests	6
3/5 tests	10

of initial childhood learning disability may be a necessary condition for predicting adult basic skills, it is not a sufficient condition.

To summarize, in confirming results of previous studies (e.g., Hardy, 1968; Howden, 1967; Muehl & Forrell, 1973–1974) these data indicate that learning disabilities are a syndrome that is not specific to the childhood years, it has a long lasting history. However, although individuals with learning disabilities were not "cured," the interpretation or the psychological significance of these findings does not present a negative outcome when tempered by three qualifications. First, even though the subjects had difficulty in certain skills areas, most had sufficient skills in reading, writing, and math to function in a wide variety of activities. As will be detailed in the next section, many of the subjects were able to meet the literacy demands of higher education and skilled professional environments. When questioned, only a negligible number of subjects felt that they were limited by their lower level of skills, and most did not consider these shortcomings as a burden or handicap. In fact, the general impression is that they had learned to deal with their disabilities and that they did not feel stigmatized or embarrassed by them. Second, breakdowns of the reading test scores by grade level indicate that there were only a few semiliterate or illiterate subjects. The majority were all coping well on the tests, although not as well as the peer controls. Thus the LD subjects who, as children, had great difficulty acquiring literacy skills and who, upon initial assessment, were extremely retarded in terms of reading and writing skills, did acquire sufficient proficiency in terms of reading and writing skills to cope in today's society. Third, literacy skills continued to develop after adolescence, especially in LD individuals who continued to be exposed to literacy skills in demanding contexts. That is, those LD subjects who continued their education after high school, continued to acquire facility in literacy skills as a function of the number of years in which they continued their schooling.

The Long Term Consequences of Learning Disabilities

Even though childhood learning disabilities persist into adulthood, this does not necessarily lead to the conclusions that learning disabilities will cause or will be associated with educational failure, poor employment, social deviance, or social and psychological maladjustment. In this section, some of these common hypotheses concerning the long-term consequences of learning disabilities are addressed.

Educational Achievement

Comparisons between the LD and peer control subjects' number of years of education indicated that the LD group had not received as many years of schooling as the peer controls, $t(200) = 4.95$, $p < .001$. A comparison of the LD and peer control group in terms of the qualitative breakdown of educational attainment was also highly significant: $\chi^2(7) = 29.34$, $p < .01$ (see Table 3.7).

Comparisons of the peer control group's level of education with data issued by Statistics Canada (1976), local school boards, junior colleges, and universities suggest that these subjects were highly educated and that their educational attainments were not representative of those of the normal population. For exam-

TABLE 3.7. Comparison of LD and Control Subjects' Educational Attainment

Variable	LD	Peer Control	Sibling Control
Years of education (M)	13.76	15.10	14.08
Qualitative categories (%)			
High School dropouts	10	2	12
High School completed only	20	2	14
Vocational training	12	2	0
Junior College in progress	22	46	26
Junior College dropouts	6	0	4
University in progress	9	20	18
University dropouts	11	8	14
University completed	11	20	12

ple, local high school dropout rates ranged from 6% to 12% (vs. 2%) of the peer controls, $n = 1$. Estimates of students who entered junior colleges between the years of 1975 and 1979 ranged from 50% to 68% (vs. 96% of the controls). The dropout rates in community colleges were approximately 10% (none of the peer controls had dropped out). The failure to obtain a more representative sample of the nonlearning-disabled population can be explained by several project-specific factors. First, many of the learning-disabled subjects who nominated peers to serve as controls seemed biased toward naming their smartest friends. This was indicated by frequent comments such as "I've got a really good one—he's always been great at school." Second, when subjects nominated a peer who was not so successful, the peer often had been in remedial classes with the subject, or had repeated a grade, or had received some tutoring. Since these events might signal the possibility of a learning disability, these peers were ineligible for the study. Finally there appeared to be a self-selection factor within the nominated sample pool of peers. That is, some potential peer controls refused to participate because there was no personal gain or they felt no commitment. The typical peer control, then, was either a college student (see Table 3.8) with time to participate or an educated individual who appreciated the importance of the project in particular and of research in general.

TABLE 3.8.   Percentage of LD, Peer Control, Sibling Control Subjects who were Students, Employed, and Unemployed at Follow-up

Age by Status	LD	Peer Control	Sibling Control
Late adolescents[a]			
Student	51	92	73
Employed	33	4	15
Unemployed	16	4	12
Young adults[b]			
Student	22	52	25
Employed	74	48	67
Unemployed	4	0	8
Total[c]			
Student	38	74	50
Employed	52	24	40
Unemployed	11	2	10

[a]LD vs. Peer Control $\chi^2 (2) = 13.83, p < .001$
    LD vs. Sibling Control $\chi^2 (2) = 3.72, p < .10$
[b]LD vs. Peer Control $\chi^2 (2) = 26.5 , p < .001$
    LD vs. Sibling Control $\chi^2 (2) = .62, p < .80$
[c]LD vs. Peer Control $\chi^2 (2) = 20.77, p < .001$
    LD vs. Sibling Control $\chi^2 (2) = 2.17, p < .30$

Because of the biased nature of the peer control group, it would be misleading to compare their educational levels to that of the LD group who, by comparison, would appear relatively uneducated. Thus, in order to obtain a more realistic estimate of the educational attainments of a nonlearning-disabled group (within the time limitations of the study), the educational attainments of the LD subjects' normal siblings, as reported in the interview, were examined and compared to that of the LD subjects.

The sibling controls received the same number of years of education as the LD subjects, t (150) < 1, (Table 3.7). Chi-square analyses of the qualitative educational measures indicated that, while more LD subjects (12% versus 0%) entered a vocational training school after completing high school, the same proportion of LD and sibling control subjects dropped out of high school (these rates were comparable to those reported by the local school boards), completed the formal requirements of their specific high school program, and continued their schooling after high school. Of those who entered an academic stream after completing high school, similar numbers of LD subjects and peer controls had completed the program, dropped out of the program, or were in the program at the time of interview.

In that many of the subjects were still in school at the time of the interviews, many of the statistics do not reflect the final educational achievements of the groups. We predict that were they to be interviewed at a future date, the numbers of subjects completing university programs would be greater than those reported in the present chapter. Also, even though it is not reflected in the coding categories, it should be noted that of the 11 LD subjects who had completed their undergraduate courses, 8 had continued their education. For example, 2 were in Ph.D. programs, 4 were in graduate business programs, 1 was in a graduate psychology program, and 1 had received an M.A. in communications.

The interview descriptions given by the LD subjects and their families of their college and university experiences suggest that, while they were functioning well in the academic program (their grades were in the average range, and there were few instances of course failures), by no means did they find their schooling easy. For example, most LD subjects indicated that they felt school was harder for them than for their classmates, that in order to cover the same material they had to work harder, and that they had to reread texts several times before they could understand the basic ideas. Most subjects said that writing term papers or reports presented the most difficulty. Often they asked members of the family to edit, proofread, and to type these assignments. Many subjects in postsecondary academic streams had taken reduced academic loads (31%) and thus required an additional year to complete their college or university program. It appears that many of the LD college and university students would have had a less difficult time if the staff of these institutions had been more aware of and sensitive to the problems of the LD individual. It seems that certain modifications could have been made for them (e.g., extending time on exams; tutoring programs) just as they are made for students with more visible handicaps (e.g., the blind or the deaf).

Examination of the characteristics of the subjects who attained various academic levels reveals two interesting findings. First, the 6 subjects from lower class backgrounds, either dropped out of high school ($n = 2$), or only completed high school ($n = 4$). In other words, 6% of the sample accounted for 20% of the dropout rate and for 20% of the "completes high school" rate. These data highlight the importance of controlling for, or examining the effects of, social class on follow-up measures. One suspects that follow-up studies, which reported poor outcomes for LD individuals, included a larger proportion of non-middle class subjects than were included in other studies, which reported more positive outcomes. The results of the former studies may thus reflect the effects of social class on follow-up status rather than of a learning disability as such. A second point of interest concerns the relationship between severity of childhood learning disability and educational attainment. The results indicate that children with the most severe disabilities were most at risk for dropping out of high school (of the 10 drop-outs, 6 were in the severely disabled group) and were least likely to continue their education after high school (44% of the most disabled group continued their education vs. 61% of the moderate group, and 77% of the mild group). However, many of these severely disabled subjects also continued their education after high school. Of the 43 subjects with severe childhood disabilities, 28% were in university at the time of interview (vs. 28% of subjects with moderate disabilities and 38% of subjects with mild disabilities). Furthermore, once the subjects had entered a postsecondary academic stream, dropping out of the program was not associated with severity of childhood learning disability. Thus, the severity of learning disability is associated with academic achievement to the extent that those with the most severe problems are least likely to complete high school or to continue their education after high school. However, individuals with severe childhood disabilities who do enter a postsecondary academic stream have an equal chance of success as those with less severe problems. These data indicate the importance of characterizing the severity of problems of the learning-disabled subjects in follow-up studies. If only the most disabled subjects had been examined, the results would not have been as positive as reported.

To summarize, the prognosis for the academic achievement of children with primary learning disabilities is positive. They are *not* at risk for dropping out of high school. Although they may require more time than nondisabled peers, they will complete high school, and many will successfully continue into higher academic streams. Because learning disabilities persist, these individuals will continue to encounter difficulties with academic skills, but these difficulties will not necessarily impede their academic careers. These findings are consistent with those reported in previous studies (Balow & Blomquist, 1965; Preston & Yarrington, 1967; Robinson & Smith, 1962).

Employment Rates and Occupational Levels

The employment rates and occupational levels of the LD subjects were first compared to the peer control subjects. As can be seen from Table 3.8, most of the peer controls were students and not in the job force at the time of interview. This was especially true in the case of the late-adolescent control group. While the unemployment rates of those who were not students were similar for the two groups (see Table 3.9), the significance of this result is difficult to interpret in that there was only one unemployed peer control subject. Comparisons of the employed LD and employed peer control subjects indicate that the peer controls held higher level jobs (see Table 3.10).

Examination of the employment data issued by Statistics Canada (1978) sug-

TABLE 3.9.   Unemployment Data for LD, Sibling Controls, and Peer Controls[a]

Age[b]	LD	Sibling Control	Peer Control	Statistics Canada
15–19-year-olds				
Unemployed (n)	7	3	1	
Eligible for employment (n)	19	5	2	
Unemployed (%)	37	60	50	21
20–24-year-olds				
Unemployed (n)	4	2	0	
Eligible for employment (n)	27	12	4	
Unemployed (%)	15	17	0	15
25-years and over				
Unemployed (n)	0	0	0	
Eligible for employment (n)	17	8	7	
Unemployed (%)	0	0	0	7
Total Group				
Unemployed (n)	11	5	1	
Eligible for employment (n)	63	25	13	
Unemployed (%)[c]	17	20	8	15

[a]Unemployment rates are calculated by dividing the number of unemployed subjects by the total number of subjects eligible for employment.

[b]Statistics Canada reports unemployment rates according to specific age categories. Our data were anlayzed to conform to these age classifications.

[c]χ^2 analyses comparing LD and sibling unemployment rates and LD and Peer Control unemployment rates were nonsignificant.

TABLE 3.10.   Occupational Levels of LD, Peer Control and Sibling Subject

Variable	LD (n = 49)	Peer Control (n = 12)	Sibling Control (n = 20)
Blishen rating[a] (M)	4.08	3.25	4.2
Educational level of employed subjects	13.67	15.83	13.90
Age of employed subjects	22.54	24.50	23.40

[a]LD vs. peer control, $t = 2.28$, $df = 59$, $p < .025$; LD vs. sibling control, $t < 1$, not significant.

gests that the peer control subjects were atypical of the general population in that, for their age level, few were in the job force and of those who were working, the occupational levels were extremely high. Because the peer control employment data were not representative of the normal population (see above for possible explanations), relevant data from the sibling control subjects and from Statistics Canada (1978) were used to evaluate the employment status of the LD subjects.

Relative to the sibling controls, similar numbers of LD subjects were in the labor force (Table 3.8). Overall, the unemployment rates were similar for the sibling controls and for the LD subjects; and these rates, except for the younger subjects,[7] were comparable to those issued by Statistics Canada (Table 3.9). In both groups, most of the unemployed subjects were late adolescents who had poor educational and employment histories. Thus, 45% of the LD unemployed, late adolescents were high school dropouts. All had been previously employed, but their job histories had been short due to being fired, laid off, or leaving an uninteresting job. This pattern was similar to that found for the late adolescent siblings controls—two of the three were high school dropouts. In contrast the two unemployed young adult LD subjects were in a transitional period; they had recently completed jobs and were interviewed while waiting to hear about future job possibilities. One had completed a B.A. and had recently moved home from a job in Europe; the other subject was trying to find work so she could have enough money to complete her hours for a pilot's license.

In terms of occupational levels, the sibling controls and LD subjects had similar Blishen ratings (Table 3.10). The occupations of the LD subjects were highly varied and included such professions as social workers, radio installers, mechanics, computer analysts, nurses, accountants, shippers, dispatchers. Occupational achievement was not associated with severity of learning disability.

---

[7]The high rate of unemployment among the late adolescent group may be purely an artifact of the statistics used. That is, the employment rate is expressed as the ratio of unemployed subjects to total number of subjects elegible for employment (i.e., not students). Since the number of subjects actually elegible for employment was small (especially among the sibling controls), the rates may reflect our sample sizes and are probably highly inflated.

Information concerning the levels of job satisfaction, salaries, and occupational responsibilities of the LD subjects were obtained from the interviews. Briefly, these data indicated that, on the whole, the LD subjects were satisfied with their jobs; most stated that they would like to eventually change jobs to more responsible or skilled placements. Most of the subjects felt that they had the requisite skills to function competently in their occupation. There were only a few instances where the subjects did not behave appropriately (they were late, they did not go to work, they argued with fellow employees). Very few subjects felt they were "underemployed." Except for a few younger subjects who were new to the job market and who were being trained, most of the LD subjects held skilled jobs and were functioning efficiently in these situations.

To summarize, when compared to the sibling controls, the LD subjects had similar employment rates and held similar types of jobs. The data do not indicate that a learning disability as such is a precursor of unemployment or underemployment.

Deviant and Asocial Behaviors

The frequency of various delinquent and asocial acts committed by the peer control and LD subjects are presented in Table 3.11. On all measures the groups were comparable. There was no association between measures of delinquency, drug/alcohol abuse, severity of disability, or social class variables.

These data indicate that LD children are not at risk for becoming juvenile delinquents, drug addicts, or alcoholics, and in general are law abiding citizens.

A review of the clinical and research literature suggests a common belief that learning disabilities are a precursor to antisocial behaviors (cf. Mauser, 1974). In many cases this belief is based on the results of correlational studies indicating

TABLE 3.11. Percentage of LD and Peer Control Subjects with Histories of Deviant Asocial Behaviors

Behavior	LD	Peer Control	Significance
Delinquent acts			
Jail	3	2	$\chi^2 = 5.47$, $df = 3$, n.s.
Police involvement (no jail)	15	12	
Delinquent acts with no police involvement	9	0	
No delinquent acts	73	86	
Drug and alcohol use			
Heavy Drug Use	12	8	$\chi^2 = .53$, $df = 1$, n.s.
Heavy Alcohol Use	5	6	$\chi^2 = .07$, $df = 1$, n.s.

that incarcerated or delinquent individuals frequently have histories of poor school performance and do poorly on academic achievement tests (cf. Mauser, 1974, for a review). These data have led to the conclusion that these subjects were learning-disabled. There are two major problems with such conclusions. First, because the subjects in such studies had not been diagnosed in childhood as learning-disabled, their poor performance could be due to antecedent emotional, physical, intellectual, or cultural factors rather than to a learning disability. Second, the data are retrospective; they do not indicate whether identified LD children are more at risk for becoming delinquent than a nondisabled group. In the present study, a group of subjects with identified, childhood learning problems were followed into late adolescence and early adulthood. While there were occurrences of deviant acts, these typified a minority of the sample and were of similar frequency and quality to those reported by subjects who had not experienced academic problems. These results are consistent with recent interpretations of the literature and with recent data indicating that there is no clear link between learning disabilities and juvenile delinquency (Keilitz, Zaremba, & Broder, 1979; Lane, 1980; Murray, 1976; Spreen, 1981).

Social and Psychological Adjustments

The social and psychological adjustments of the LD group at the time of interview were compared to those of the peer control group. The analyses involved comparing the proportion of subjects in each sample with significant problems in family relationships, peer relationships, and overall psychological adjustment. The effects of age at interview and of sex on social and psychological adjustments were also examined. The rates of reported problems at follow-up were also compared to those reported in childhood for the LD group only (Table 3.12). In addition, for the LD group only, the association between severity of childhood learning disability and social–psychological adjustments was examined.

In terms of family relationships, similar numbers of LD and control subjects experienced difficulty in their interactions with their parents, χ^2 (1) = 1.95, p < .20. There were no age differences, but there were sex differences within the LD group. That is, relative to LD males, significantly more LD females experienced family problems, χ^2 (1) = 5.33, p < .05. There was no significant relationship between the severity of childhood learning disabilities and family relationships at follow-up. There were no between group differences in the qualitative distribution of family relationship problems (i.e., mild, moderate, severe). Finally, it is noted that there was little change in the overall rates of family problems from childhood to adulthood for the LD group. Closer inspection of these data indicate that 75% of the LD subjects with reported family problems at follow-up, also had problems in childhood. Thus the follow-up rates

TABLE 3.12. Frequency of LD and Peer Control Subject's Family, Peer and Psychological Adjustment Problems at Follow-up

	Family		Peer (same sex)		Peer (opposite sex)		Psychological Adjustment	
	LD	Control	LD	Control	LD	Control	LD	Control
Age Comparisons								
Late Adolescents	29(16)	19(5)	22(12)	14(4)	15(8)	11(3)	38(21)	15(4)
Young Adults	17(8)	9(2)	24(11)	9(2)	16(7)	4(1)	35(16)	26(6)
Sex Comparisons								
Male	19(15)	13(5)	21(17)	11(4)	15(12)	10(4)	35(28)	24(9)
Female	43(9)	17(2)	29(6)	17(2)	14(3)	0(0)	43(9)	8(1)
Quality of Problem								
Severe	58(14)	57(8)	57(13)	0(0)				
Moderate	24(6)	26(4)	43(10)	100(6)				
Mild	17(4)	14(2)						
Withdrawn							46(17)	50(5)
Acting-out							30(11)	0(0)
Conduct							14(5)	30(3)
Situational							11(4)	20(2)
Overall Rate at Follow-up	24(24)	14(7)	23(23)	12(6)	15(15)	8(4)	37(37)	20(10)
Overall Rate in childhood	31(31)	n/a	33(33)	n/a	. . .	. . .	85(85)	. . .

aThe data represent the percentage of subjects within the designated categories with problems. Percentages for Quality of Problems represent the distribution of specific problems within the group of subjects with reported problems. Raw subject frequencies are enclosed in parentheses.

for the LD group reflect long-standing family difficulties rather than adolescent or recently occurring difficulties.

Similar proportions of LD and control subjects had peer relationship problems with the same sex. There were no sex or age differences associated with this measure. Severity of childhood learning disability was not associated with peer relationship problems at follow-up. Although similar rates of problems were found for the control and LD subjects, the results of the qualitative analyses indicate that the types of problems reported at follow-up differentiated the two groups. All problems reported by the peer control were ''mild.'' These subjects were primarily shy, and thus had difficulty initiating social contacts, but they did have a small group of friends with whom they enjoyed good relationships. While ''mild'' problems were also experienced by some of the LD subjects, more than half of LD subjects with peer relationship problems (vs. none of the controls) had ''moderate'' problems. These subjects were socially isolated, lonely, and not competent in making or keeping friends. While the reported rates at follow-up were similar to those reported in childhood for the LD group (90% of subjects with problems at follow-up had problems as children), it should be noted that 39% of the subjects with childhood problems were enjoying good peer relationships at follow-up.

There were no differences in the proportions of LD and control subjects who had infrequent (dating) interactions with the opposite sex. These rates were equally distributed by age group. Inspection of Table 3.12 indicates that there was a trend for LD females to date less frequently than the female controls (no χ^2 test was run because of the small n). Severity of childhood disability was not related to this measure.

In the area of psychological adjustment, the LD subjects had significantly higher rates of problems than the peer controls, $\chi^2 (1) = 4.32$, $p < .04$. The greater incidence of problems, is associated with three factors. The first factor is age. LD adolescents had significantly more problems than the adolescent controls, $\chi^2 (1) = 4.67$, $p < .03$, while LD young adults and control young adults had similar rates. The second factor is sex. LD females had significantly more problems than control females, $\chi^2 (1) = 4.31$, $p < .05$, while LD males had similar rates to control males. The third factor is type of problem. The LD group exclusively demonstrated difficulties in terms of controlling temper and dealing with frustration (acting-out). Severity of childhood learning disability was not related to psychological adjustment at follow-up.

The finding that part of the greater incidence of psychological adjustment problems may be associated with age is difficult to interpret. The finding does not support the hypothesis that the poorer adjustments of the LD adolescents reflect a developmental lag which is not a permanent state. Closer inspection of the data indicate there are no changes in the problem rates for the LD subjects from late adolescence to young adulthood, but rather that the control young adults had higher (although not statistically significant) rates of problems than the control adolescents. Because of the small number of control subjects with adjustment problems (if one more control adolescent had been classified into the problem category, there would have been no significant between-group differences), clear-cut explanations for the differential rates are not possible. One working hypothesis is that the rate for the late-adolescent control group was depressed relative to the older control group because 95% of the adolescent control subjects (vs. 51% of the LD late adolescents, 22% of the LD young adults, and 52% of the control young adults) were in school at the time of interview and were not faced with the daily pressures and normal stresses of employment and self-support faced by the other subgroups.

While the data on psychological adjustment do indicate that the LD group was not as well adjusted as the controls and that there was no improvement in functioning for the LD group from late adolescence to young adulthood, it is important to note that many of the problems noted in childhood for the LD group disappeared with age: 53% of the LD subjects with childhood problems were considered to be well adjusted at follow-up.

Taking into account the very general nature of the data on social and psychological functioning a number of conclusions can be drawn from our results. First, there was an absence of extreme forms of deviance within the LD group. Only a small minority of LD subjects ($n = 5$) had recent histories of counselling or psychiatry. Most of the subjects and their parents concurred that any stated problems were not of clinical significance and did not require professional assistance. Thus in most cases the behaviors coded as problematic were probably representative of the common difficulties experienced by many young adults or late adolescents. Aware of the possibility that only the better adjusted LD subjects agreed to participate in the study, we attempted to determine whether there were any signs of gross psychopathology in those who had refused. This occurred in only three cases: one subject was psychotic; one was extremely aggressive and destructive; and one was too depressed to come in for the interview. These three cases represented 1.5% of the subjects in the located sample pool. This figure is low by any standards, and indicates that childhood learning disabilities are not a precursor of extreme forms of adult psychopathology.

Second, the data indicate LD females were particularly at risk for having social and emotional problems. Similar data on the poorer adjustments of the LD female child have been reported in the literature (Bryan, 1974; Scranton & Ryckman, 1979). While there are no existing empirical data to explain these patterns, a number of hypotheses can be advanced. LD females may have more adjustment problems because they deviate from the cultural sex-role stereotype that, relative to school-aged boys, girls will be academically successful (reviewed in Brophy & Good, 1974). Violation of this cultural expectation may make it more difficult for parents, teachers, and peers to accept or to understand the failure and disability of a female child and may lead many to label the LD female child as deviant or as undesirable. These reactions may cause emotional and social problems for the child, which may last into adulthood. Also, LD girls may not display more deviant social or emotional behaviors but rather, relative to boys, these behaviors may be less tolerated by teachers, parents, and peers whose reactions may lead to the suppression or aggravation of the unacceptable behavior and lead to more negative adjustments at a future date. Last, it is speculated that within the LD population girls do not have more social or emotional problems than boys, but that within the subsample of LD children referred for diagnosis, girls may have more adjustment problems than boys. This hypothesis is based upon recent evidence that, while boys outnumber girls in clinic samples of LD subjects by 5:1, in nonclinic samples similar numbers of boys and girls have been found to have positive diagnoses of learning disabilities (Lambert & Sandoval, 1980). These data suggest that within the LD population, proportionately more LD boys are referred to clinics than LD girls and therefore that the criteria for referral vary as a function of sex. It is possible that the criteria for referring girls may involve the presence of both a learning disability and adjustment problems, while for boys only a learning disability is necessary.

Third, while the LD subjects experienced more ''moderate'' peer relationship problems than the controls, this finding must be tempered by two considerations. The first concerns the sampling procedure of the control subjects. The peer controls participated in the study because they were friends of one of the LD subjects who nominated them. Thus each control subject *automatically* enjoyed a minimal level of peer interaction. The LD subjects were not sampled on this social nomination basis. (Not all LD subjects could suggest a peer control.) Second, even though 13% of the LD sample had moderate problems relating to peers of the same sex, and even though they compared unfavorably to the controls, this figure is not representative of the LD sample's functioning in the area of peer relationships. The majority (77%) of LD subjects enjoyed good peer relationships. Based on these two qualifications, it is suggested that the data do *not* warrant the conclusion that children with learning disabilities will, as adults, experience poor peer relationships. That they may be more at risk for having such problems than a nonlearning-disabled sample must be confirmed by further comparisons to a more unbiased control group than was sampled in the present study.

Last, while the data on psychological adjustment indicate that the LD group experienced more problems than the controls, it is not clear to what extent this poorer adjustment is associated with differences in the daily experiences of the two groups or to the pervasive long-term effects of childhood learning disabilities. Despite the ambiguities of the adjustment data, however, it is important to emphasize that many of the problems that were noted in childhood for the LD subjects did not persist into adulthood. These data are consistent with those of follow-up, and retrospective studies of other clinic or normal populations (cf. Robins, 1979).

SUMMARY

The academic, occupational, social, and emotional status of 101 late adolescents and young adults who had been diagnosed as learning-disabled during childhood was assessed and compared to a control group of tested, nonlearning-disabled peers, and to an untested group of age-matched, nonlearning-disabled siblings.

While the data indicate that the learning disabilities clearly persist into late adolescence and young adulthood, these findings must be qualified by two points. First, while the majority of LD subjects were considered nonreaders when assessed as children, at follow-up there were extremely few who were illiterate. Most had the necessary skills to function adequately in various situations. Second, while learning disabilities persist, the data suggest that continued exposure to literacy tasks in demanding situations can result in the continuation of skill development in the learning-disabled population. Because skills continued to develop as a function of exposure to literacy tasks, it is hypothesized that, if the LD subjects who were students had actually received special tutoring in reading, writing, or math (none had), their skill levels may have increased to an even greater degree. Clearly, judging from their test scores and interview reports, the LD students would have benefited from extra tutoring in reading, writing, and study skills. Although remedial reading or remedial math courses are offered in many post-secondary institutions, it is not clear whether this approach would be most beneficial to the LD student who, like LD children, may require programs that are specifically designed to meet their academic needs as well as their cognitive strengths. This is an area that deserves further research.

The data on academic and occupational achievements were most encouraging. In terms of unemployment, the LD sample had similar rates to sibling controls. The LD subjects were not underemployed. They represented a wide range of occupations, and only a few subjects held unskilled jobs. The children with learning disabilities were not at risk for becoming high school dropouts. Similar numbers of sibling control and LD subjects did go on to higher education where, despite their specific problems, the LD subjects became successful students. As was noted in this study and previous others (e.g., Balow & Blomquist, 1965; Preston & Yarrington, 1967), the LD individual can achieve academically, but it may take him or her longer than the nondisabled peer. In the present study, the added time dimension in postsecondary streams was accounted for by students deliberately deciding to take a reduced course load and, only in a few cases, reflected students failing courses and having to take extra time to make them up.

It should be emphasized, however, that all the LD students (even those who were in postgraduate programs) reported mild to moderate difficulties with their academic studies. Although these difficulties stem from the learning disabilities and are permanent, there are several suggestions that may alleviate some of the problems. One area in which the LD student requires assistance involves helping the student to take over the advocacy tasks that were previously assigned to their parents. Specifically in the present setting, one of the goals of the clinic assessment procedure was to explain to parents the kinds of difficulties that their child was encountering so that they could then talk to teachers to explain these difficulties and, when appropriate, to request teachers to make specific modifications for their children. By the time the students were in college it was no longer appropriate for parents to continue with this task, although many did do it right through high school. However, the same explanations and requests to professors were still necessary; unfortunately, none of the students had learned how to approach the task. These students could have benefited from learning, as their parents did, how to explain their problems to professors as well as how to request specific modifications (e.g., oral exams, outlines of lectures to assist with note taking). However, in order for the LD students to make successful requests, the teachers in postsecondary institutions must be knowledgeable or sympathetic concerning these students' problems. Current experience suggests that this is not the case. The common attitude among staff in these institutions is that college students should be literate and no allowances in workload or style of presentation should be made. With lower requirements for enrollment in many postsecondary institutions and recent high rates of unemployment, enrollment rates are rising for the first time—many different types of students are entering the stream. This would be an opportune time to sensitize faculty to the backgrounds not only of the nontraditional, nonmiddle class student, but also to the handicapped.

Comparisons with the peer control group on measures of social deviance indicated that there was no association between juvenile delinquency, problems of drug and alcohol abuse, and childhood learning disabilities.

The social and emotional data indicate that while the quality of family relationships of the LD subjects were similar to those of the peer controls, LD subjects may be at risk to show problems in the area of peer relationships and psychological adjustment. These results require confirmation with a more representative peer control group. However, the data also revealed an absence of extreme forms of deviance in the LD group. Only a small minority of subjects had recent histories of counselling or psychiatry. Most of the other subjects and their parents concurred that any stated problems were not of clinical significance and did not require professional assistance. The social and emotional status of the LD adult requires more careful examination and analysis. It is suggested that more clinically oriented interviews be employed by professionals to determine whether some of the differences, found in the present study and in previous studies, (e.g., Balow and Blomquist, 1965; Spreen, 1982) are true indicators of poor functioning and maladjustment.

The major value of the present study has been to present a comprehensive picture of the adjustment of the LD adult. The data indicate that while learning disabilities persist, LD individuals lead well adjusted and productive lives—a conception that is at odds with current beliefs of a poor prognosis for this clinical population. There are several explanations for why these findings are more optimistic than those generally reported in the literature. First, all the subjects were identified at a young age. For many early identification led to early intervention; thus, many were taught skills they could not normally acquire in the classroom. For all subjects, early identification was accompanied by counselling for parents and teachers who were explained the nature of the problems. In the interviews many years later, parents reported the benefits of these early debriefing sessions—they did not perceive their child's school problems as a sign of poor intelligence or emotional disturbances. In many cases the parents were primary advocates for their child; they went to school several times a year to explain to teachers the nature of the child's problems. The parents' and teachers' attitudes may have decreased many of the pressures on these children and led to a more positive attitude toward education and learning in general. A second factor, which contributed to the positive outcomes, was a methodological one. The sample was carefully defined. All potential subjects with childhood symptoms which, by themselves, may have been antecedents of poor adult outcomes were excluded from the study. The present study examined the outcomes of children with primary learning disabilities. A third factor concerns the variability of learning problems within the sample. Although all the subjects encountered problems with reading and writing skills, the severity of their problems varied. Many previous studies have focused on only the most disabled (a small proportion of the learning disabled population), and thus those results have limited applicability. In the present study, the results are more general because of the greater variability in terms of the LD sample examined.

REFERENCES

Achenbach, T. M., & Edelbrock, C. S. (1978). The classification of child psychopathology: A review and analysis of empirical efforts. *Psychological Bulletin, 85,* 1275–1301.

Balow, B. (1965). The long term effect of remedial reading instruction. *Reading Teacher, 18,* 581–586.

Balow, B. J., & Blomquist, M. (1965). Young adults 10–15 years after a severe reading disability. *Elementary School Journal, 66,* 44–48.

Belmont, L. (1980). Epidemiology of minimal brain dysfunction. In H. E. Rie & E. D. Rie (Eds.) *Handbook of minimal brain dysfunction.* New York: John Wiley.

Blishen, B., & McRoberts, H. (1976). A revised socioeconomic index for occupations in Canada. *Canadian Review of Sociology and Anthropology, 13,* 71–79.

Brophy, J., & Good, T. L. (1974). *Teacher-student relationships: Causes and consequences.* New York: Holt, Rinehart, & Winston.

Bruck, M. (1981, August). A follow-up of learning disabled children into late adolescence and young adulthood. Final report submitted to Health and Welfare Canada.

Bryan, T. (1974). Peer popularity of learning disabled children. *Journal of Learning Disabilities, 7,* 261–268.

Bryan, T., & Bryan, J. H. (1978). *Understanding learning disabilities.* (2nd. ed.) Sherman Oaks, CA: Alfred Publishing.

Carter, R. P. (1964). A descriptive analysis of the adult adjustment of persons once identified as disabled readers. Unpublished doctoral dissertation, Indiana University, IN.

Coleman, J. C., & Sandhu, M. A. (1967). A descriptive study of 364 children referred to a university clinic for learning disorders. *Psychological Reports, 20,* 1091–1105.

Dykman, R., Peters, J., & Ackerman, P. (1973). Experimental approaches to the study of minimal brain dysfunction: A follow-up study. In Cruz, Fox, & Roberts (Eds.) *Minimal Brain Dysfunction,* New York Academy of Sciences.

Farnham-Diggory, S. (1978). *Learning disabilities.* Cambridge, MA: Harvard University Press.

Gottesman, R., Belmont, I., & Kaminer, R. (1975). Admission and follow-up status of reading disabled children referred to a medical clinic. *Journal of Learning Disabilities, 10,* 642–649.

Hardy, M. I. (1968). Clinical follow-up of disabled readers. Unpublished doctoral dissertation, University of Toronto, Ontario. As cited in B. Herjanic & E. Penick, (1972). Adult outcomes of disabled child readers. *Journal of Special Education, 6,* 397–410.

Howden, M. E. (1967). A nineteen-year follow-up of good, average and poor readers in the fifth and sixth grade. Unpublished doctoral dissertation. University of Oregon, Eugene, OR. As cited in Herjanic, & E. Penick, (1972). Adult outcomes of disabled child readers. *Journal of Special Education, 6,* 397–410.

Keilitz, L., Zaremba, B. A., & Broder, P. K. (1979). The link between learning disabilities and juvenile delinquency: Some issues and answers. *Learning Disability Quarterly, 2,* 2–11.

Koppitz, E. M. (1971). *Children with Learning Disabilities: A five year follow-up study.* New York: Grune & Stratton.

Lambert, N. M., & Sandoval, J. (1980). The prevalence of learning disabilities in a sample of children considered hyperactive. *Journal of Abnormal Child Psychology, 8,* 33–50.

Lane, B. A. (1980). The relationship of learning disabilities to juvenile delinquency: Current status. *Journal of Learning Disabilities, 13,* 426–435.

Mauser, A. J. (1974). Learning disabilities and delinquent youth. *Academic Therapy, 9,* 389–402.

Muehl, S., & Forell, E. (1974). A follow-up study of disabled readers: variables related to high school reading performance. *Reading Research Quarterly, 9,* 110–123.

Murray, C. A. (1976). *The link between learning disabilities and juvenile delinquency: current theory and knowledge.* Washington, DC: U.S. Government Printing Office.

Pearl, R. A., Donahue, M. L., & Bryan, T. M. (1979). Children's responses to nonexplicit requests for clarification. Presented at Boston University Conference on Language Development, Boston, MA.

Preston, R. C., & Yarrington, D. J. (1967). Status of 50 retarded readers eight years after reading clinic diagnosis. *Journal of Reading, 11,* 122–129.

Quay, H. C. (1979). Classification. In H. C. Quay & J. S. Werry (Eds.) *Psychopathological disorders of childhood* (2nd ed.) New York: John Wiley.

Rawson, M. (1968). *Developmental Language Disability.* Baltimore, MD: Johns Hopkins Press.

Robins, L. N. (1979). Follow-up studies. In H. C. Quay & J. S. Werry (Eds.) *Psychopathological disorders of childhood* (2nd ed.). New York: John Wiley.

Robinson, H. M., & Smith, H. (1962). Reading Clinic Clients—ten years after. *Elementary School Journal, 63,* 22–27.

Schenck, B. J., Fitzsimmons, J., Bullard, P. C., Taylor, H. G., & Satz, P. (1980). A prevention model for children at risk for reading failure. In R. Knights & D. J. Bakker (Eds.) *Treatment of Hyperactive and Learning Disordered Children.* Baltimore, MD: University Park Press.

Scranton, T. R., & Ryckman, D. B. (1979). Sociometric status of learning disabled children in an integrative program. *Journal of Learning Disabilities, 12,* 402–407.

Silver, A. A., & Hagin, R. A. (1964). Specific reading disability: Follow-up studies. *American Journal of Orthopsychiatry, 34*, 95–102.

Spreen, O. (1981). The relationship between learning disability, neurological impairment and delinquency: Results of a follow-up study. *Journal of Nervous and Mental Diseases, 169*, 791–799.

Spreen, O. (1982). Adult outcome of reading disorders. In R. N. Malatesha & P. G. Aaron (Eds.), *Reading disorders: Varieties and treatments*. New York: Academic Press.

Statistics Canada. (1976). Demographic characteristics, school attendance and level of schooling. Census of Canada. Ottawa, Ontario.

Statistics Canada. (1978). Labor Force Information, Ottawa, Ontario.

Trites, R., & Fiedorowicz, C. (1976). Follow-up study of children with specific (or primary) reading disability. In R. Knights & D. J. Bakker (Eds.), *The neuropsychology of learning disorders: theoretical approaches*. Baltimore, MD: University Park Press.

Yarrow, M. R. (1963). Problems of methods in parent–child research. *Child Development, 34*, 215–226.

4

Continuity Between Home and Day Care: A Model for Defining Relevant Dimensions of Child Care

Florence Long, Donald L. Peters, and Laurie Garduque
The Pennsylvania State University

INTRODUCTION

In the past decade, increasing numbers of young children have entered day care. According to estimates based upon the National Child Care Consumer Study, as many as 15,551,000 children under the age of six may spend part of each week in the care of someone other than a member of their nuclear family (Rodes & Moore, 1975). Most current projections indicate the number is likely to increase rather than decrease over the next 10 years (Hofferth, 1979). Yet, there continues to be concern, both within the general public and among researchers, that day care experience may be harmful to children (Peters, 1980; Peters & Benn, 1980; Woolsey, 1977).

This concern with the "harmful" effects of day care experience has focused researchers' attention on such questions as:

1. Does day care *damage* the attachment between the infant and the mother?
2. Does day care *retard* cognitive development?
3. Does day care produce children that *lack* self-control, who are *overly* aggressive or *overly* passive?
4. Does day care lead to *too great* a reliance on peers?
5. Does day care *usurp* the mother's responsibility for the child? (Peters, 1980, p. 22)

The current state of our knowledge seems to suggest a qualified "No" answer to each of these questions (cf. Belsky, Steinberg, & Walker, 1982; Fein, 1977;

Kagan, 1977; Kilmer, 1979; Peters & Belsky, 1982; Radloff, 1977; Ricciutti, 1977). As a result, several researchers have indicated the time has come to move on to more sophisticated research questions (Belsky, Steinberg, & Walker, 1982; Garduque, Peters, & Long, in preparation). To do so requires an understanding of the assumptions underlying the prevailing concerns. We shall examine these assumptions in the context of the historical development of child care. It will be shown that these assumptions presume discontinuity between home and day care, with day care being, in some way, inferior to home care.

What evidence is there to support these assumptions? Remarkably little. Indeed, the whole issue of continuity versus discontinuity between home and day care hardly has been approached.

CONTINUITY OF CHILD CARE: WHAT DOES IT MEAN?

Webster's New Collegeiate Dictionary (1981) defines continuity as "an uninterrupted connection, persistence without essential change." Discontinuity, according to the same source, is defined as "lack of continuity or cohesion," that is, lacking unification of principles, relationships, or interests. The term *discontinuity of child care* has been used loosely in the day care literature to refer to several dimensions of real and/or potential differences between the experiences of children at home and in day care that reflect this concern for cohesiveness in the child's experience. For example, parents and caregivers may display different *behaviors* toward the child. Their behaviors may be predicated upon different *beliefs* or world views about how children develop or learn, or upon their experience-based *perceptions* of the child's abilities. These beliefs and perceptions may lead parents and caregivers to challenge the child in different ways. The physical and social *environments* of the home and day care center also may differ, giving the child different opportunities for exploration, stimulation, or exposure to risks, as well as different opportunities for social interaction with peers and adults. Intuitively, each of these dimensions may present points of "discontinuity" or "continuity" between the day care and home environments. Yet they have seldom been studied either singly or in combination. We recognize intuitively that differences between home care and group care exist, but these differences have not been documented. The assumption underlying the suspected differences between home and day care is that differences imply discontinuity and that discontinuity is disruptive to the development of young children. This assumption has led researchers to examine the effects of day care attendance as a unidimensional variable without considering variability across programs or across the experiences of individual children (Anderson, Nagle, Roberts, & Smith, 1981; Garduque, Peters, & Long, in preparation). Furthermore, forms other than center-based day care, like family day care, have received virtually no research attention. Perhaps the differences we recognize intuitively as existing between home and day care have no significant influence on child development. Or perhaps their influence is positive rather than negative. In either case, we will not be able to judge the importance of continuity and discontinuity between home and day care before we (a) adequately operationalize the dimensions of discontinuity, (b) embed these dimensions in a relatively comprehensive model of the process of day care, and (c) relate these dimensions to important child development outcomes.

Perhaps the concept of continuity has neither been adequately conceptualized nor operationalized because two contradictory views of continuity exist in the child care field. These two views stem from the convergent development of day care from welfare services for needy families and from services for families seeking alternatives to traditional child care arrangements. On the one hand, it is assumed that most families provide an ideal learning and development environment for children. For these children, continuity between day care and the home is valued to ensure that this "ideal" growth environment exists in day care as it is assumed to at home. On the other hand, some families—notably low-income families—may not provide this ideal environment. In this case *discontinuity* is stressed: Day care provides developmental experiences that children lack when reared at home. In addition, sometimes discontinuity is acceptable, as when peer contact in day care is viewed as necessary for an only child to "learn to get along with others."

Because discussions in the literature have focused on either the "welfare" base or the "child care alternative" base of day care, a clear conceptualization of the need for continuity (or discontinuity) has been difficult. Embedding the dimensions of continuity in a comprehensive model of the process of day care may help to focus attention on research questions that can support or refute some of the assumptions that create concern over discontinuity. To be truly useful this model must relate day care process to some important developmental outcomes for children.

This review will develop a framework for defining dimensions of continuity and discontinuity between home and day care by focusing on the experiences of children in family day care homes. Family day care has been selected for the setting of this review for methodological and practical reasons. Even though family day care constitutes the most common form of out-of-home care employed by families in the United States (Administration on Children, Youth, and Families [ACYF], 1981), little research has been conducted in this setting. In the past, center-based day care received most attention because of concerns over the negative effects of "institutional" care. However, as we have learned more about family day care, new issues have surfaced. The majority of family day care providers are untrained and unsupervised, raising concerns over the quality of care children receive in family day care. The need to document the care these children receive is great, but the practical difficulties faced by researchers attempting to conduct studies in family day care homes discourage many. Family day care homes are difficult to locate except by word of mouth. Turnover in caregivers and families is high. Caregivers are often reluctant to participate in research, especially when they are unlicensed (Wandersman, 1981).

Family day care as a setting for research has its advantages as well. Research on family day care offers some methodological controls that would not be available in a study of day care centers. In family day care, as in homes, there is likely to be a single caregiver and a small number of children. Differences in interaction between home and family day care are more likely to be attributable to the behaviors of a single caregiver than to the dynamics of a group containing many adults as well as strong peer group influence. The difficulties inherent in determining who is the child's primary caregiver in center day care are also avoided in family day care. Family day care takes place in a family-like setting. Environmental differences between the settings are related to the child-rearing environment the adults create rather than to the spatial and organizational differences imposed by a center. Thus, a study of family day care, by focusing attention on the central variable of adult–child interaction, allows us to examine the assumption that differences between parents and caregivers have an effect on the child (Siegel-Gorelick, Everson, & Ambron, 1980).

Before turning to the literature comparing parents' and caregivers' interactions with children, we briefly review the historical developments that contribute to our conflicting assumptions about child care.

HISTORICAL CONCEPTS: CONFLICTING ASSUMPTIONS OF A DUAL SYSTEM

The Welfare Tradition

Throughout its early history, dating back to the 1880s, day care was viewed as a child welfare service to provide care and protection for "children of destitute widows and those with sick husbands" (Fein & Clarke-Stewart, 1973, p. 26). It was conceived in the settlement house tradition and was intended to relieve women "bent under the double burden" of caring for their children and at the same time trying to earn the money to support their families.

This early beginning, in which day care was judged to be a legitimate form of child care only under conditions of dire necessity and family deviance, has its vestiges in present day legislation. In 1962, for example, amendments to the initial Social Security Act of 1935, under Title IVA, provided federal funds to state departments of public welfare for the development of day care facilities. By 1974, the program, which was targeted to the economically impoverished, provided child care for over 500,000 children (Kamerman & Kahn, 1976). Similarly, in 1962, Title II of the Manpower Training Act mandated the provision of child care for children of the hard-core unemployed who were provided jobs or vocational training. The 1967 Work Incentive Program (WIN) also required states to provide child care for children whose welfare-recipient parents were required to obtain work or undergo training.

Title XX of the Social Security Act, the largest source of federal monies for day care, had a slightly more liberal philosophy. Under this act, while social services, including day care, were still primarily targeted for the poor, eligibility was more universal—at least in theory. For families with incomes below 80% of the state median income, day care services were to be available free; graduated fees were mandated for the more affluent. In reality, Title XX services were usually not available to other than welfare recipients (Kamerman & Kahn, 1976). In 1981 Title XX was superceded by the Social Services Block Grant, which eliminated income-related eligibility requirements. The fact remains, however, that states will continue to provide child care funds (if at all) primarily to low-income families.

Similarly, the early intervention movement that was mandated by federal legislation creating Head Start reveals this response to family inadequacy veiled as family enhancement. Head Start was begun in part to give children experiences they did not receive at home—that is, to actively create discontinuity between home and day care. At the same time, parental involvement ensured that parents would take into the home skills learned in the Head Start center, thus reducing over time the discontinuity between home and day care as the home approximated an environment thought to be optimal for child development.

Briefly, then, the history of federal involvement in day care has been deeply rooted in a welfare tradition in America. And, as Ruderman (1968) argues (and Etaugh's 1980 review reiterates), because of its welfare tradition, day care is still regarded as a response to family inadequacy—a problem service for problem families.

The Second System

Since the end of World War II, there has been within American society considerable confusion between idealized concepts of the "traditional" American Family and the reality of the "typical" American family. Our demographics as a nation belie traditionally held beliefs. The number of women in the work force has doubled since World War II, and is projected to continue increasing. By 1990, it is expected that 3 out of every 4 mothers will work, leaving 10.5 million preschool-aged children in need of day care (Peters & Belsky, 1982; Urban Institute, 1980).

The number of single-parent families is also on the rise. Census Bureau data show a great increase in single-parent households over the past two decades, especially in households containing children under the age of 6. Census projections also suggest that the "baby-boom" generation will soon contribute to an expansion of the number of preschool-aged children in our population (Hofferth, 1979). Thus the trends suggest that the need for child care will continue to increase in the near future.

The reality of these demographic changes has not entirely escaped the federal legislature. For example, the 1962 amendments to the Social Security Act set forth two goals: (a) to provide necessary supportive services for adults seeking to escape the cycle of poverty (consistent with the welfare tradition), and (b) to meet social needs of children and families stemming from the increased number of working women.

From the perspective of this latter goal, day care is viewed as a major component of an emerging "personal social service system" (Kamerman & Kahn, 1976). This segment of the field has evolved into a middle-class, child-rearing alternative—a purchasable convenience for the single-parent or 2-worker family (Peters, 1975), and a rapidly growing industry (Lake, 1980).

CONFLICTING BELIEFS AND ASSUMPTIONS

The welfare-tradition image of day care is well embedded in the public consciousness. The concept of day care as a service for problem families seems to have widespread acceptance—although this is no doubt changing (Etaugh, 1980). Research indicates, for example, that while 29% of mothers have been found to reject the use of day care for other people's children under normal circumstances, 44% of these same women reject this option for their own children (Sibbison, 1973). Similarly, many women accept the notion that "working women miss the best years of their children's lives," and 1 in 5 believes that working women neglect their children (Rodes & Moore, 1975). That is, "traditional" family beliefs are held even though the "traditional" family and the "typical" family are quite different (Peters & Belsky, 1982).

Typical families (including single-parent families and dual-worker families), however, still try to fulfill traditional family roles (Blehar, 1979). Two decades ago family experts claimed that working mothers were becoming so common they could no longer be regarded as deviant (e.g., Bronfenbrenner, 1961). Twenty years later society still holds parents primarily responsible for bringing up children under the age of 3 (Etaugh, 1980). This causes many parents conflict between their desire to advance career goals or maintain an adequate standard of living and their desire to rear their children themselves. Indeed, Etaugh suggests that parental guilt stemming from these demands may cause more harm than the split roles parents fulfill. Because traditional values are still upheld by our society, these parents receive little reinforcement for trying to restructure their work and child-care roles. To be a good parent means to be at home caring for the child *and* to provide an adequate standard of living. For many parents, these demands create an insoluable dilemma.

Several critical assumptions about families and about day care underlie these beliefs about the family's role in child care. With respect to families, these assumptions include:

1. A principal function of the family is childrearing.
2. Most families are "traditional" in structure and include a father, non-working mother, and children.
3. This type of family is the one against which all other family forms should be judged—usually to be inferior or inadequate.
4. Most middle-class families provide the ideal learning and development environment for children; most poverty families do not.

The day care assumptions include:

1. Day care is closely akin to institutional child care; that is, it provides children with little more than a minimal custodial environment.
2. Day care represents a major separation of parent and child.

Acceptance of these assumptions suggests day care would be harmful to middle-class children, and they, therefore, should be raised at home while poverty children would be no worse off (or perhaps better off) for day care experience. In either case, the fundamental assumption is that there is a discontinuity between the day care and the home environment for all children. Day care substitutes for a principal family function, yet it fulfills this role inadequately precisely because it is not a family.

Although child development theory has not been applied to the issue of continuity between home and day care, predominant theoretical positions have indirectly upheld these assumptions by promoting the early-experience view of child development (Goldhaber, 1979; Hunt, 1981). From the early experience viewpoint, children are malleable creatures but, since development is cumulative, early experiences have implications for later competence (Goldhaber, 1979; Evans, 1975). The first experiences of young children are not only necessary to development but sufficient causes of later outcomes. Because parents have traditionally cared for very young children, parents bear the responsibility of providing these essential early experiences.

The emerging life-span view, on the other hand, stresses temporal continuity in experiences and the potency of the current environment (Goldhaber, 1979). This theoretical position is based on empirical findings regarding the lack of predictability between early trauma and later developmental delay (e.g., Scarr-Salapatek & Williams, 1973; Werner, Bierman, & French, 1971), and washouts of effects in longitudinal follow-ups of early intervention "graduates" when the family was not involved (e.g., Bronfenbrenner, 1974). Other recent evidence has suggested that early experiences are important but can be moderated or overruled by later-life events (Kagan & Klein, 1973; Sameroff, 1975). From this viewpoint continuity across settings facilitates and maintains developmental gains.

Discontinuity could arise between home and day care simply because parents, that is, mothers, are not present to care for their children. Additional discontinuities on other dimensions may arise: differences in the physical environment, social environment, educational opportunities for children, child-rearing beliefs held by adults, or strategies of socialization employed by adults. In addition, the dimensions of discontinuity possible vary with the type of child care employed: in-home care, family day care, or center-based care.

FAMILY DAY CARE AND CENTER-BASED CARE

Family day care—care provided in an occupied residence for not more than 6 children from more than one unrelated family—accounts for the largest proportion of children cared for outside their own homes in the United States (45% of all child care arrangements, according to the National Day Care Home Study [ACYF, 1981]). It is estimated that as many as 1.3 million family day care homes serve an estimated 2.4 million full-time children (over 30 hours per week). Another 19.5 million children attend family day care for some part of each week (Fosberg, 1980). Unfortunately the accuracy of these figures is in doubt because of the private and transient nature of many family day care arrangements. If anything, they underestimate the prevalence of family day care.

Family day care homes have been classified into three categories (Belsky, Steinberg & Walker, 1982). *Unregulated homes* are not licensed or recognized by any public agency. These homes probably represent the predominant form of child care in this country in spite of the fact that it is illegal to operate without a license or registration in many states. Many parents and caregivers regard this kind of home care as an informal arrangement, especially when payment is not involved. *Regulated* or *licensed homes* have met the criteria set by public day care agencies and usually contain between 3 and 6 children. Some providers form networks or operate under the auspices of a supportive or supervisory child care agency; these *sponsored* or *supervised homes* are often licensed or regulated as well.

Advantages and Disadvantages of Family Day Care

Several advantages to family day care, when compared to center-based care, appear frequently in the literature (cf., Auerbach, 1975; Peters & Belsky, 1982; Wandersman, 1981). They include: (a) daily close contact with a small number of mixed-aged peers in a home setting, (b) its relative integration into the neighborhood and community (when compared to day care centers), (c) its relatively lower cost and greater flexibility in hours, (d) its convenient location, (e) its opportunities for individual adult attention to children, (f) the parents' ability to select caregivers who conform to parents' values, and (g) its informal atmosphere.

On the other hand, family day care has some potential disadvantages. Those most frequently cited are: (a) relative instability—that is, family day care homes open and close with great rapidity because caregivers get sick, lose interest, or find higher paying jobs (Saunders & Keister, 1972; Steinberg & Green, 1979); (b) there is little assurance that the day care provider has any formal training in child care or child development—caregiver educational qualifications are seldom regulated (ACYF, 1981); (c) the majority of family day care providers see their roles as custodial—providing for the safety and nurturance of the child— rather than educational or developmental (Howes, 1981; Peters, 1972; Willner, 1969); and (d) within unlicensed day care homes especially, there is little or no formal outside agency supervision to help assure health and safety standards.

When analyzed, these advantages and disadvantages have an interesting quality about them. On the one hand, family day care is considered desirable because it approximates a home and family environment. That is, on the surface at least, it appears to promote greater continuity in the physical and social environment than would a center-based alternative. On the other hand, the qualifications of family day care providers, the supervision they have, and the experiences they provide seem less desirable than those found in center-based care (at least the good quality center care that has been the focus of research). Day care centers are "preferred" to family day care homes precisely because they are usually educationally or developmentally oriented, have trained staff, meet fixed standards set by regulations, provide children group socialization experiences, and offer a child-care arrangement with long-term stability (Rothschild, 1978; Steinberg & Green, 1979). These aspects of center-based care make it attractive to parents, even though they represent discontinuities from home-based care.

Clearly the evaluation of continuity depends upon the nature of the home environment that is used as the comparison. In the literature, the implicit standard used is that of the idealized, "traditional" middle-class family life and home environment—one that census statistics suggest is becoming increasingly uncommon. This traditional family environment has been associated with positive child-development outcomes. The ideal child-care arrangement then becomes one that approximates this standard, rather than one that provides consistency between the actual home environment and the actual day care environment. To operationalize "quality care" and "continuity," this idealized standard needs to be made explicit, if only so that we can address the issue of quality day care in its own right. Then homes and day care settings may be analyzed to see how closely they conform to the standard. Such an examination may reveal that day care, rather than inadequately "replacing" the traditional family, provides different types of experience for children that are equal in importance to the experiences they undergo at home (Lewis & Schaeffer, 1981; Peters & Benn, 1980).

To understand the meaning of continuity, the basic assumption that most families (and only families) provide an ideal learning and development environment for children needs to be examined. For example:

1. What developmentally important experiences do families provide for children?
2. Do other arrangements provide these experiences?

Specifically applied to day care, we can ask,

1. What elements of child-rearing does day care share with the home environment, and what elements does it lack?
2. Do the differences between home and day care have significant implications for the child's development?

Research on parent–child relationships has demonstrated that multiple child-rearing strategies can lead to the same outcomes; conversely, the same parental strategies sometimes lead to different outcomes because of individual differences in children's reactions to socialization. If we apply these lessons to comparisons between home care and day care, perhaps we can set aside the "deficit model" of day care research. The result, hopefully, will be a better understanding of the meaning of setting differences in the lives of children, and some guidelines for optimizing the day care experience.

To address these issues a descriptive model will be proposed that places parent–child interaction in the context of a dynamic relationship between home and day care. The model is designed to allow definition of key dimensions of continuity and discontinuity in terms relevant to child development outcomes. We begin with a look at the optimal characteristics of the caregivers.

DEVELOPMENTAL EXPERIENCES PROVIDED BY FAMILIES

The "Ideal" Child-rearing Environment

Families have traditionally been regarded as providing the ideal child-rearing environment for several reasons. First of all, they can meet the child's physical needs for food and shelter. They provide adults who socialize children to pro-social behavior. They provide a secure base from which the child can diversify interpersonal relationships and gradually become independent. Families provide models for adult behavior. They provide cognitive and verbal stimulation necessary for intellectual growth.

But why are families especially suited for these purposes? A good day care arrangement can meet children's physical needs. It also has adults who socialize prosocial behavior. Many day care programs today provide intellectually stimulating activities, and they certainly foster independence and peer relationships (Belsky & Steinberg, 1978).

The concern with removing children from their families focuses on the unique relationship a child develops with a single, adult caregiver or a small number of adults. On the basis of the strong emotional tie between primary caregiver and young child, children become socially and intellectually competent. Within the context of this relationship, parents are assumed to provide special experiences that make them optimal socializers of young children. What special experiences do parents provide? To answer this question, we will examine the types of behaviors adults exhibit in their interactions with children and the quality of their interactions.

Types of Behavior Exhibited by Parents and Caregivers

Parents might differ from other adults and each other in how frequently they provide affection, physical contact, verbal interaction, play, discipline, or structured learning experiences for their children. Table 4.1 summarizes studies that have compared parents to day care caregivers on some of these behaviors. In general, parents (mothers) appear to equal or exceed day care caregivers in

TABLE 4.1. Differences and Similarities Between Homes and Family Day Care

Dimension	Similarity/Difference	Reference
Quality of adult-child interaction		
Physical contact	HC = FDC > CDC[a] carrying	Cochran, 1977
	HC > FDC hold, hug	Howes & Rubenstein, 1980
	CDC > FDC physical contact	Golden, et al., 1978
	HC > FDC physical contact	Siegel-Gorelick, et al., 1980
	FDC > HC	Tyler & Dittman, 1980; Howes & Rubenstein, 1980
Positive affect		Siegel-Gorelick, et al., 1980
	HC > FDC	Peters, 1972
	FDC more frequently low on praise than high	
Negative affect	HC > FDC	Siegel-Gorelick, et al., 1980; Cochran, 1977; Howes & Rubenstein, 1980; Wandersman, 1978; Tyler & Dittman, 1980
Verbal interactions	HC = FD > CDC cognitive verbal	Cochran, 1977
	HC > FDC verbal initiations by adults	Howes & Rubenstein, 1980; Howes, 1981
Quantity of social interaction	FDC + HC > CDC	Tyler & Dittman, 1980[b]
	FDC = CDC	Golden, et al., 1978
	HC = FDC > CDC	Cochran, 1977
	HC > FDC social interaction, one-to-one interaction	Clarke-Stewart, 1981; Wandersman, 1978; Prescott, et al., 1973
	HC = FDC > CDC one-to-one interaction	Yarrow, Rubenstein, & Pedersen, 1977
	Mothers > in-home babysitters	

Initiations by adults	HC = FDC > CDC	Prescott, et al., 1973
Controls, gives orders, restricts	HC = FDC > CDC	Cochran, 1977
	HC > FDC	Wandersman, 1978; Howes & Rubenstein, 1980
Frustration, interference with child's activity	HC = FDC > CDC	Prescott, et al., 1973
Complies with child's requests	HC = FDC response to sharing	Howes & Rubenstein, 1980
	HC = FDC Compliance (rank order)	Siegel-Gorelick, et al., 1980
	HC > FDC compliance (frequency)	Siegel-Gorelick, et al., 1980
Ignore	HC = FDC (rank order)	Siegel-Gorelick, et al., 1980
	HC > FDC (frequency)	Siegel-Gorelick, et al., 1980
Hostility	HC > FDC	Wandersman, 1978
		Siegel-Gorelick, et al., 1980
Discourage	HC > FDC	Wandersman, 1978
Teaching	FDC = HC > CDC	Cochran, 1977
Physical setting		
Toys and materials	FDC > CDC complex equipment (allows simultaneous use by more than one child)	Prescott, et al., 1973
	Few special adaptations of home for children in FDC	Peters, 1972
	FDC > HC	Clarke-Stewart, 1982
Numbers of adults and children present		
Child-designed space	within FDC, child-designed space positively related to positive affect, negatively related to restrictions	Howes, 1981
Exposure to activities of daily living	FDC > CDC	Tyler & Dittman, 1980

[a]CDC = center day care; HC = home care; FDC = family day care.
[b]Combined home care and family day care in comparisons with center day care.

143

exhibiting positive behaviors toward their children. They show more positive physical contact, more cognitive–verbal interaction, and more individual social stimulation. However, they also express more negative affect and restrict the child's behavior more than do caregivers.

Observations of adult and child behavior in family day care homes would provide the most direct information about continuities in the social experiences of children in family day care. However, only a handful of observational studies have been conducted in family day care (FDC) settings. In most cases children and adults in FDC homes have been compared to a different group of home-reared children and/or children in full-time center care. Clarke-Stewart (1981) has looked at the experiences of the same child at home and in the day care placement, but she has not yet presented a full analysis of her data.

The National Day Care Home Study (ACYF, 1981) provides a basis for describing the experiences of children in family day care homes, unfortunately without a comparison to home conditions. This large-scale study, funded by the Administration for Children, Youth, and Families, represents the first attempt to describe family day care on a broad basis. A core sample of 793 black, white, and Hispanic caregivers was identified from three types of urban, family day care homes (sponsored, regulated, and unregulated) in Los Angeles, San Antonio, and Philadelphia. From this core sample smaller groups were selected for inter-views and observations. In all, 352 day care providers were interviewed, 414 children and 303 caregivers were observed, and 348 parents were interviewed. Observations of caregivers and children are the focus of this discussion. Observers completed separate focal samples on a child and the caregiver for about 2 hours on two mornings. When possible a child between 1 and 3 years and another between 3 and 5 years of age were observed in each family day care home.

The study found that across all ethnic groups and types of care that caregivers spent almost half their time (46.4%) directly involved with the children. For another 16.3% of the time they were supervising the children or preparing activities for them. Most of the direct interaction time was spent in teaching, playing with, or helping the 1–5-year-olds (30.6% of the caregivers' time). Only 3.7% of the caregivers' time was devoted to controlling the children's behavior; only 0.3% of the time did the caregivers express negative affect toward any child. Caregivers in sponsored homes were directly involved with the children for more of their time than caregivers in regulated homes, and regulated care-givers were involved more than unregulated caregivers. This difference is caused mainly by the greater amount of teaching and play engaged in by sponsored caregivers. Limited data are available to suggest that caregivers do not differ from parents in how they spend their "caregiving" time. In one study that compared center, FDC, and home-reared children, parents and FDC caregivers were equal in the amount of time they spent teaching and supervising children. Both groups engaged in more teaching and supervision of the children than did caregivers in day care centers (Cochran, 1977).

One of the few research efforts that compares the process of child care in homes, FDC homes, and day care centers has been conducted by Howes and Rubenstein (Howes, 1981; Howes & Rubenstein, 1980). Their research has involved samples of center children, home-reared children and toddlers in FDC. In one study, Howes and Rubenstein (1980) compared the experiences of 20 toddlers in regulated FDC to 23 home-reared children and 35 in centers. Their work is particularly relevant to this review because they defined good quality nonmaternal care in terms of maternal behaviors that research has associated with positive child development. They looked at types of social stimulation engaged in by adult and child, adult responsiveness to the toddler, and affect, assessed during behavioral observations.

The results that pertain to FDC are included in Table 4.1. Mothers initiated more verbalizations to toddlers than did caregivers, and held or hugged their toddlers more. Mothers restricted their toddlers more, and reprimanded them or expressed negative affect more often than did caregivers. They found no differences among settings in toddler-peer behaviors, but they did not address the issue of whether caregiver initiations to the focal child are reduced because the caregiver or the focal child spends more time interacting with other children.

In a study of three types of child-rearing in Sweden, Cochran (1977) obtained similar results. His sample included 26 children in family day care homes as well as center-reared and home-reared toddlers. Intellectual development and attachment indices were collected on the children at 12-, 15-, and 18-months. Behavioral observations of adults and children were also conducted at these three times. Few differences were noted among children or adults in the three settings. Adult–child interactions in FDC were not significantly different from those in home care in areas where the interactions in day care centers did differ, such as in the amount of cognitive–verbal interaction, physical contact, and teaching activities. However, children at home received more negative affect and more restrictions than did FDC children.

Siegel-Gorelick, Everson, and Ambron (1980) observed 38 home-reared children and 38 children who spent at least 20 hours per week in FDC. Children's bids for attention and the quality of caregivers' responses to them were recorded, along with physical and verbal contacts between adults and children. Children in FDC made bids for attention much less frequently than children at home. Consequently, the FDC caregivers' frequency of responses was lower than that of mothers, but in rank order, the types of responses mothers and caregivers used were similar. Meeting the child's need for attention or help was the most frequent response of both mothers and caregivers, and hostility was the least frequent in both groups.

Further analyses showed that the quantity of adult responses was not related to either the number of children present in FDC or at home, nor to the ages of these children. This finding was interesting in light of the authors' hypothesis that infants might require more attention. Although Siegel et al. found no correlation between the number of children present and the number of initiations by children or responses by adults, their data collection and analysis did not address directly the issue of whether children in FDC made fewer bids to adults because they interacted more with peers. Siegel-Gorelick and her colleagues did find that children and adults at home had more interactions in which positive and negative affect were expressed than did dyads in the FDC homes. They concluded that the stronger affective tone of the parent–child relationship leads children to make more frequent bids for parents' attention than they do to caregivers.

The findings of Siegel-Gorelick and her colleagues support the reports of Howes and Rubenstein, but the former study raises the question that perhaps the child's behavior is the cause of different adult behaviors in each setting. Without examining the same child in different settings it is difficult to conclude whether the differences in initiation rate between home-reared and FDC children are due to the setting or due to differences between the two groups of children. In our search of the literature we encountered only one study that observed the same children both in their day care placements and in their own homes (Clarke-Stewart, 1981). Clarke-Stewart presents a variety of preliminary but suggestive findings based on both experimental and naturalistic observational procedures. In terms of verbal interaction, she found that children reared at home experienced consistency in interactions with their parents across the different situations in which they were observed (day time and dinner time). However, children who spent time in day care experienced greater amounts of verbal interaction at home than they did in their day care arrangements. (Clarke-Stewart looked at the range of day care settings including inhome care by family or a nonfamily member, family day care and fulltime center care, conceived as steps along a continuum with inhome parental care at one endpoint. Discrepancies from interactions characterizing home care increased with increasing distance along this continuum.) Parents and children in the home-reared group engaged in the same amount of verbal interaction at dinner time as did parents and children who attended day care. Thus parental behavior appeared stable; the child's experience varied depending on where he or she was. Since Clarke-Stewart only analyzed behaviors directed to the child, it is unclear whether differences in child behavior across settings contributed to the differences she found.

Two studies (Hock, 1978; Sibbison, 1973) indicate that mothers who rear their children differ from mothers who use day care in their attitudes toward the maternal role and toward child care. Children in child care may have particular characteristics that led parents to place them in day care rather than to rear them at home (Hock, Christman, & Hock, 1980). We know little about the dynamics of parent–child relationships that may contribute to the parent's decision to use outside child care.

Wandersman's (1978) work does shed some light on the interaction differences between day care and home-reared children and adults. However, she compared one caregiver's responses to different children rather than a particular child's behavior with different adults. Wandersman compared the interactions of caregivers and children in FDC with the caregiver's interaction with her own child, also present with the FDC child. Her sample consisted of 19 preschool-aged children in FDC homes where the provider also had her own child of the same age and sex in the home. Child and adult behaviors were sampled in observations alternating in 10-minute blocks between the day care child and the caregiver's own child. "Own" children (the children of the day care providers) engaged in more negative behavior and more activities with the caregiver than did day care children. Day care children played by themselves and with peers more than own children. Own children received more hostility from the caregiver and peers, and more restriction and discouragement than did day care children. Own children displayed more verbal behavior, and observed more than day care children. Caregivers spent more time observing and restricting their own children than the day care children.

These findings may reflect behavioral differences in children in their own homes in response to the presence of a peer who competes for mother's attention. However, Wandersman's report is consistent with other studies comparing children at home to children in day care (see Table 4.1). Clarke-Stewart's (1981) findings as well as Wandersman's suggest that when children come home, they engage in different interactions than they do in day care. We need to ask whether the day care children would look like "own" children in interactions with their own mothers.

Table 4.1 shows that studies comparing center day care to FDC alone or to both FDC and home care found FDC and home care to be similar on many variables. Differences were found in favor of both home settings over center day care. However, comparisons between FDC and home care that have not included a center day care sample (Siegel-Gorelick, et al., 1980; Wandersman, 1978) found differences between home and FDC. Looking at affective variables, parents were more likely than caregivers to express both positive and negative affect, and to initiate verbal and physical contact with the child. As Siegel-Gorelick and her colleagues (1980) pointed out, this may be a function of the number of bids made by children to adults, as well as relating to differences in the quality of parent child relationships as opposed to caregiver–child relationships. Howes and Rubenstein (1980) did find that children initiated more verbal interactions at home than in FDC, and several studies observed higher rates of social interaction at home than in FDC. Since individual differences of this type found between *parents* have been related to child development outcomes (e.g., Ainsworth & Bell, 1969; Brody & Axelrad, 1978; White, Watts, Barnett, Kaban, Marmor, & Shapiro, 1973), differences between parents and caregivers on these dimensions of behavior may also have implications for the development of the children in their care.

The Quality of Adult Response

One approach to describing discontinuity is to tally and compare frequencies of different types of behavior. A different approach would be to consider the qualitative aspects of adult–child interaction. The literature on parent–child interaction indicates that children's positive development is associated with certain qualities of parental behavior toward the child. One important characteristic of parental behavior is contingency, the latency of responding. Contingent responses follow the child's action within a period of time that allows the child to form associations between his or her own behavior and that of the parent (Lamb, 1981; Watson, 1972). It may be the case that day care providers do not respond contingently to young children. They may have many other children demanding their attention, or they may be unable to recognize or interpret accurately the child's bids for attention.

The second aspect of parental response is consistency, the repeated pairing of contingent responses with particular child behaviors. Consistent adult responses may help children learn that their actions have a predictable effect on the environment (Lamb, 1981). When each caregiver's responses are consistent within themselves, children may be able to attend to differences between adults and learn to discriminate between the demands for their behavior in interacting with each adult. If each adult who cares for the child is inconsistent in his or her own behavior, the child may not learn clear rules for interacting with that adult. Consistency between parent and caregiver in discipline and rule enforcement is a major concern for some parents (Steinberg & Green, 1979). From a behavioral perspective, consistent rule enforcement brings about faster learning and better maintenance of behavior across settings (Gewirtz, 1972). For the learning of prosocial behavior at least, consistency between caregivers may be important (Wahler & Dumas, 1981). In other aspects of child development, consistency between adults may not be so important as consistency within the behaviors of each adult.

One can also examine whether the parent seems to respond to the child with behavior that is matched in kind to the child's initiation (Ainsworth, 1974; Hinde, 1976). For instance, if the child seeks affection, does the adult respond with affection, or a rebuff? If the child seeks task-related assistance, does the adult meet this need? Through the course of their interactions most parents and children learn to interpret each other's behaviors and to respond to them in a way that fulfills the goals of the interaction. Parents meet their children's needs for contact and social interaction; children meet demands for age-appropriate prosocial behavior. Without this history of experience, the interactions between day care caregivers and children may not be as mutually satisfying as with parents. Thus parent–child interaction can be characterized as *reciprocal* in the sense of exchanging similar positive behaviors, and *synchronous* in the sense that the behaviors of each individual facilitate rather than frustrate the behaviors of the other (Ray, 1982).

Table 4.1 also presents findings relevant to the quality of adult responses. Parents are as likely as caregivers to ignore children's bids for attention (an indication of noncontingency). However, they are also as likely to comply with the child's requests (indicating reciprocity or a match between child and parent behaviors). These qualities of adult response are seldom explored in the day care literature, in spite of the fact that research on parent–child relationships suggests these are crucial elements of parent–child interaction.

Summary

The literature reviewed indicates that some differences exist between the behaviors of parents and day care providers. Research describing children's experiences in day care has been limited primarily to the study of a treatment—day care versus home care—on developmental outcomes for young children (Belsky & Steinberg, 1978; Etaugh, 1980). Few studies have examined the quality of the interactions between children and their caregivers, and even fewer have compared experiences of the same child in the two different settings. The literature suggests generalizations about "what parents are like" and "what caregivers are like." However, without examining the behaviors of the same child at home and in day care, we cannot draw conclusions regarding observed differences between care conditions. The adult–child interactions of parents and caregivers may actually be different. But parents who rear their children at home and parents who place their children in day care may also differ, obfuscating the meaning of results from studies comparing day care and home-reared groups.

Differences between parents and caregivers are ultimately meaningful only if they have impact on the child's development. Even though there appear to be some general discrepancies between parents' and caregivers' behaviors, these discrepancies may be more or less accentuated for each child–parent–caregiver triad. The degree of discrepancy between a particular parent and caregiver may determine the impact of discontinuity on a particular child. Each child's response to discrepancy may also vary depending on a number of factors including the child's temperament, previous experience, age, sex, and the opportunities for positive interactions offered by each setting.

The research that has been conducted in family day care is limited both in number of studies and in the methodological quality of these studies. The samples employed have been small, the quantity of observation limited. Researchers have chosen to describe the experiences of children in home care or children in day care without comparing the experiences of a particular child across multiple settings. If children in day care have similar experiences in their own homes as the home-reared samples described here, then the day care children may experience more diverse relationships with adults than do home-reared children. This diversity may be due to differences in the caregiving styles of mother and caregiver, or diversity may indicate that FDC children elicit different caregiving behaviors from their caregivers than children do from their mothers. To assess these differences, we need to observe the same child with his or her caregiver and with his or her mother. In addition, we need to relate observed differences and similarities to developmental outcomes for children. Perhaps even if differences exist, the differences are neutral or beneficial in their influence on child development.

In order to describe potential continuities or discontinuities between the behavior of parents and caregivers, we need to characterize the different types of behaviors adults exhibit in interacting with children as well as the qualitative aspects of adult behavior (contingency, consistency, and reciprocity). However, adults and children do not interact in a vacuum. Characteristics of the physical and social environment also influence adult–child interaction. This dimension of continuity–discontinuity between home and day care will be discussed in the following section.

THE CONTEXT OF INTERACTION

The context of adult–child interaction must also be considered in examining continuities and discontinuities between home and day care. Characteristics of the physical and social environments influence the quality and quantity of adult–child interactions. For instance, varying amounts of space or toys available may influence the child's explorations. The arrangement of the house or center may affect the child's opportunities for privacy. The number of risks present may be positively related to how frequently the adult must restrict the child's explorations and how carefully the adult must monitor the child. These are aspects of the physical environment. The social environment consists of the number and diversity of potential social interactors.[1] At home there may be few or no siblings and few adults. In day care there may be several peers and several adults. There may be few or many opportunities to have contact with people with diverse roles, or of diverse ages.

Most studies of the environmental characteristics of homes have examined

---

[1]Some include in the social environment aspects of social interaction (e.g., Yarrow, Rubenstein, & Pedersen, 1975. In this review a distinction is made between potential interactors and the qualities of the interactions they have with the focal subject.

individual differences between homes contributing to individual differences between children. The work of Prescott and her colleagues has compared different types of day care environments including home care (Prescott, 1981; Prescott, Jones, & Kritchevsky, 1967; Prescott, Kirtchevsky, & Jones, 1972). They characterized day care environments along several dimensions including variety and complexity of materials, organization of space, and program format decisions that structure children's use of space and materials. Unfortunately, their findings regarding homes and day care homes have not been presented systematically, but must be culled from their reports on center day care. They do not differentiate between homes and family day care, as they emphasize the distinction between any home environment and a center environment. Their work is helpful in pinpointing several dimensions that may be important to consider: social density of the play space, types of equipment, physical organization, opportunities for privacy, tactile responsiveness, and access to materials.

Prescott's dimensions (Prescott, et al., 1972) are similar to some items on the HOME scale. The HOME scale developed by Caldwell (1979) characterizes the physical environments, social environments, and social interactions between parents and children. Scores on the HOME have been positively correlated with Stanford–Binet IQ scores. They have not been related to indices of social behavior. Since these dimensions have predicted individual differences between children on intellectual test performance, they may be useful as well in examining the effects of home–FDC differences on the development of children in FDC.

In terms of the desirability of continuity on the dimension of environmental characteristics, again the dual system and purposes of child care appear. For children from middle-class homes, day care has been evaluated in terms of how it differs from the home environment (e.g., Prescott, 1981). For low-income children, however, we look to day care (center-based care at least) to provide cognitive stimulation compensating for opportunities missing at home. Middle-class homes are physically very different from day care centers, but there are no data to suggest that this difference has a negative impact on child development. Belsky and Steinberg (1978), in their review of the effects of day care, suggest that different types of competence are fostered by different settings. The cognitively stimulating materials frequently found in centers enhance perceptual–motor and problem-solving skills, while at home children may be able to engage in risk-taking and explore novel uses of common household objects. Differences found between home and the day care arrangement provide healthy diversity as long as the child lives in a home that meets the loosely defined ideal standard. If the home does not match this standard, however, discontinuity is stressed to give the child "needed" experiences. Among the crucial elements of the child-rearing environment potentially missing from homes not matching the standard are

1. Adequate social, cognitive, and verbal stimulation provided by toys, objects, and people.

2. Low social density allowing adequate privacy and opportunities for one-to-one interaction.
3. A safe and healthful physical environment that promotes exploration.
4. Exposure to the world beyond the household through visitors to the home or activities outside it (shopping, trips, etc.).

These elements have been associated with positive cognitive development in young children (e.g., Bradley & Caldwell, 1976; White, et al., 1973). In many cases, these environmental qualities have been found to overcome developmental delays associated with birth trauma or early social deprivation. Unfortunately, absence of these elements is also associated with low socioeconomic status, although there is great within-class variability (Bloom, 1964; Bradley & Caldwell, 1976). Much of the concern over the quality of environmental stimulation stems from early studies of sterile institutional environments. Recognizing that few homes are as sterile as institutions, the work of Caldwell and her colleagues (e.g., Bradley & Caldwell, 1976) using the HOME scale still suggests that there may be relevant individual differences between homes that have impact on the child's development and behavior. If a child's time is divided equally between home and day care, does a "dose" of good quality environment in one setting compensate for inadequacies in the other? Do two positive environments have an additive or even multiplicative effect? Perhaps there are shades of difference between environments that measures such as the HOME scale cannot detect yet which add richness and diversity to children's daily experiences. These are issues that day care research has yet to address.

Center-based programs for low-income children have attempted to provide essential elements of environmental stimulation. Concern is frequently expressed that family day care is provided in low-income homes where the ideal child-rearing standards for the physical environment may not be met. The sample employed by the National Day Care Home Study included white, black, and Hispanic family day care providers in sponsored, regulated, and unregulated homes. Median income for subsamples grouped by ethnicity and status of the home revealed a range from $17,250 for white caregivers operating sponsored homes, to $4,750 earned by black providers in unregulated homes. In general, providers in unregulated homes had lower incomes than providers in regulated and sponsored homes, and white caregivers in all types of homes had higher incomes than the other two ethnic groups (ACYF, 1981). Howes (1981) found, in a small sample of regulated day care homes, that only a small proportion of the day care providers were low-income, single mothers (3 of 20). Few comparisons between the physical environments of homes and family day care homes have been made, but studies comparing center day care and family day care suggest family day care is much like an average home (Cochran, 1977; Golden, et al., 1978; Prescott, et al., 1973). There is probably much variability in this: In

Howes's sample of family day care homes, quality varied from small, dismal apartments to homes with specially designed, child-oriented space ("centers within a home"). Peters (1972), however, found family day care providers made few special adaptations of their homes for the children in their care.

Aspects of the physical environment are more easily operationalized than the nurturant qualities of the caregiver. Because of this, qualities of the physical environment have received major emphasis in day care licensing requirements. Since all centers are required to be licensed by state and/or federal law, they may be more uniform in quality on the dimension of physical environment than family day care homes. Unregulated, regulated, and supervised day care homes may show greater variability in quality on this dimension. Before conclusions can be drawn about the importance of continuity between physical and social settings, the physical settings of homes and day care, especially family day care, need to be described. Description may reveal gaps between the idealized standard and the typical home setting, but these gaps may not have strong negative implications for child development outcomes.

Characteristics of Adults that may Affect their Responses to Children

In Howes's (1980) small sample of family day care providers, two characteristics mediated the adult's positive contingent responses to children. Marital status of the provider influenced how she balanced household chores and child-care responsibilities. Single mothers spent more time engaged in housework while caring for the children. Howes suggested that because they did not have a spouse who could share housekeeping responsibilities, single mothers were required to devote more time to household tasks and as a result responded less contingently to the children in their care.

The other relevant characteristic that emerged from Howes's analysis was family income, which was related to the space and comfort of the provider's dwelling. Caregivers who were not dependent on their day care income alone for support had larger homes with a greater amount of specifically child-designed space. (Single mothers often depended on their day care income alone.) They could close off areas of their homes that they did not want children to enter. Because of this, they did not need to restrict the children's behavior as frequently as providers with limited space. Though Howes's sample is too small to draw generalizations, her findings suggest an area for further exploration.

Wandersman (1981) also looked at characteristics of providers. She found that caregivers with more education and experience in child care enrolled larger numbers of children and provided a more formal structured educational program. They provided more specifically child-designed space and spent less time on housekeeping. These providers probably defined their role as professional rather than custodial. Thus characteristics of the adult may interact with the physical environment to influence their interactions with children.

CHILD BEHAVIORS ASSOCIATED WITH THE IDEAL CHILDREARING ENVIRONMENT

The theoretical literature on child development suggests several dimensions of the child-rearing environment that optimize social and intellectual development in young children. One dimension is the quality of parental response: the contingency, consistency, and reciprocity of the parent's behaviors toward the child. Other dimensions include the physical and social environments in which the parent–child relationship develops. The optimal environment offers children safe opportunities for stimulation and exploration, and provides feedback to children about their actions.

Children who have experienced caregiving that is contingent, consistent, and directed to meeting their needs learn that their efforts to act on the environment will be successful (White, et al., 1973; Yarrow, et al., 1975). Because they are rewarded for their attempts to elicit responses from others, they continue to take initiative in fulfilling their needs for nurturance, social interaction, and goal-directed activity (Lamb, 1981).

The connection between contingent, consistent, reciprocally matched adult behavior, and these child behaviors has been documented in two bodies of literature. Attachment researchers (Ainsworth, 1979; Sroufe, 1979) have found that children who were securely attached (who by definition had received contingent, consistent parental responses directed at fulfilling their needs) took initiative, actively explored the environment during the preschool years, and demonstrated persistence on problem-solving tasks as well. From another perspective, research on the social or instrumental competence of young children identified parents who responded contingently and consistently to their children and facilitated the child's goal-directed activity by providing information, cognitive challenges, and support. These children became actively engaged in the environment, able to use others to fulfill their needs, and to take control of activities in order to meet those needs (Carew, 1980; White, Kaban, Shapiro, & Attanucci, 1977). On a more global level, Baumrind (1967) found that parents who used consistent disciplinary styles, taking into consideration the child's viewpoint, had children who were independent, who took initiative in new situations, and who were socially skilled. Using inductive reasoning as a disciplinary technique, as these parents did, could be interpreted as being more reciprocal in its relationship to the child's behavior than other, more arbitrary forms of discipline.

The child behaviors of initiative, exploration, independence, and engagement in activity reflect an underlying ability of the preschool-aged child to adapt to environmental demands. These children are able to maintain interest and motivation in the face of changing environmental circumstances (Sroufe, 1979). Thus the optimal child-rearing environment appears to facilitate the child's adaptability, initiative, and task motivation.

There is some evidence to suggest that the consistent, contingent, and reciprocal caregiving a child receives at home facilitates his or her adaptation to other child-rearing settings (e.g., Arend, Gove, & Sroufe, 1979; Waters, Wippman, & Sroufe, 1979). However, it is possible that the child's adaptation to different day care settings is also supported by the characteristics of the day care caregiver (Anderson, et al., 1981; Carew, 1980). A stable and positive day care arrangement may substitute for an instable parent–child relationship (Farran & Ramey, 1977), or it may facilitate the child's transition from the home to his or her expanding world (Anderson, et al., 1981).

Our understanding of the outcomes of parent–child relationships as yet offers little assistance in predicting the effects of discontinuity between home and day care. Two perspectives may be helpful in evaluating the effects of discontinuity. Hartup (1979) has suggested that we consider other social systems outside the homes of children as independent but interlocking systems, each contributing different but equally important experiences to children. Others (Garbarino, 1982; Rutter, 1979) have noted the importance of social systems outside the home as supplemental resources to children who encounter nonoptimal parenting. In light of these perspectives three questions can be posed when we examine continuity or discontinuity between day care and homes:

1. If discontinuity exists, especially along the dimension of adult–child interaction patterns, is the discontinuity in itself beneficial or detrimental to the child?
2. Does discontinuity in the child's experiences across settings foster greater flexibility in the face of new environmental challenges?
3. When home conditions are not optimal, does a day care arrangement showing characteristics of the optimal child-rearing environment offset negative outcomes?

In order to answer these questions, the experiences and characteristics of *individual* children need to be considered. For the most part, because of the unidimensional approach researchers have taken to day care, this has not been done. However, some researchers have found parallels to optimal parental behaviors in the behaviors of preschool and day care caregivers toward young children (Carew, 1980; Prescott, Kritchevsky, & Jones, 1973). When investigators speak of "adjustment to day care" they refer to the complex of behaviors that indicate positive affect, absence of anxiety, and the ability to adapt to the demands of the day care setting in a way that meets the child's needs while engaging in harmonious interactions with others. The ability to take initiative and actively engage the environment is one indicator of adjustment that has been employed in studies of children in day care (e.g., Anderson, et al., 1981; Prescott, et al., 1973; Rubenstein & Howes, 1979). Children new to the day care environment are often described as anxious and as demonstrating less active interest in their surroundings. For example, McGrew (1974) found that children new to a nursery school displayed less active social involvement during their first week in the nursery than they did 19 weeks later. However, day care programs differ, and different children within the same program do not adjust equally rapidly or well to the setting. Prescott and her colleagues (Prescott, et al., 1975) have identified some of the physical characteristics that differentiate day care settings. In addition, they suggest that individual differences among children may contribute to the child's adjustment to day care. Their studies (Prescott, Jones, Kritchevsky, Milich, & Haselhoef, 1975) describe children who "thrive" in day care and those who appear less successful. Thrivers, or "thrusters," as they called the successful children, initiated more interactions with the physical and social environment, offered input that expanded or sustained activities, and sought task-oriented assistance more than they sought affection or comfort. Of the four settings they examined (centers with closed and open structure, FDC, and half-day nursery school, and home), children in FDC displayed the highest levels of thrusting behaviors. However, thrusters and nonthrusters were found in all settings.

The work of Prescott's group provides a basis for exploring interactions between setting differences and individual differences in children's responses to different care settings. Recent work by Anderson, et al. (1981) suggests that setting differences are important to examine. By simply considering high and low center quality and high and low involvement by caregivers, they found significant differences in attachment behavior displayed by children to caregivers in a modification of the strange situation. Studies of the temperamental characteristics of children (e.g., Thomas & Chess, 1977) and the coping styles children employ in encountering new situations (Murphy & Moriarty, 1976) also suggest important individual differences between children that may predict their adaptation to discontinuity between home and day care.

MEDIATOR BETWEEN HOME AND DAY CARE: ADULTS' CHILDREARING BELIEFS

In discussions of continuity between home and day care, concern is often expressed that the parents' and caregivers' beliefs about child-rearing may be incongruent (e.g., Clarke-Stewart, 1977; Powell, 1980; Winetsky, 1978). Congruence between the beliefs of parents and caregivers is relevant to the continuity between home and child care to the extent that beliefs reflect behaviors. Monitoring beliefs also gives parents and caregivers a basis for judging similarity or dissimilarity—beliefs indicate to them the continuity or discontinuity between their two child-rearing environments. Parents report that they prefer family day care because it allows them to select a caregiver whose values match their own (Steinberg & Green, 1979; Wandersman, 1981). Some parents express concern that they will lose control of their children's proper socialization if the children are cared for by people who do not share the parents' values (Blehar, 1979).

To understand why child-rearing beliefs are an important dimension of continuity, the relationship between beliefs and behaviors must be examined. Some researchers have argued (Hess, Price, Dickson, & Conroy, 1981; Newson & Newson, 1976; Sigel, McGillicuddy-deLisi, & Johnson, 1980) that parental child-rearing beliefs provide a framework that directs the parent's behavior toward the child. The link between beliefs and behavior may be tenuous because no single behavior is necessarily predicated on a generalized belief. The patterning of adult behavior over a series of interactions may indicate a style of behavior representative of the parent's conception of how children develop.

The relationship between beliefs and behavior is a dynamic one. The feedback the adult receives through interactions with the child modifies his or her conception of the child and his or her beliefs in general about how children develop. Thus the specific information the adult has about the child interacts with the adult's general beliefs about child development. Adults may have multiple sources of information about the child. Contacts with other children offer comparative feedback. When the adult has opportunities to see other adults interacting with the child, the adult may gain a more complete or accurate understanding of the child's behavior (Sigel, et al., 1980). For instance, a parent of only one child, who never sees her child play with peers, may believe that young children are incapable of harmonious social play, or that her child in particular is incapable of it. When she sends her child to day care where the children generally get along but her child is aggressive, she may conclude that young children in general are capable of social play but her child is not. As her child learns to get along with others, she may modify her beliefs so that she thinks that peer exposure facilitates harmonious social play even among young children.

Research on the relationship between child-rearing beliefs and parenting behaviors is limited but suggestive. Sigel et al. (1980) correlated a wide range of generalized, child-rearing beliefs held by parents with their behaviors in two structured task situations with their 4-year-old children. Specific predictions parents made about how they would act toward a particular child were not demonstrated in their interactions. However, there was a complex relationship found between parents' general, child-rearing beliefs and their distancing behaviors (behaviors facilitating the child's use of cognitive representation). Fathers' child-rearing beliefs were more strongly related to their distancing behaviors than were mothers' beliefs. Fathers engaged in the same distancing behaviors across situations, but mothers did not. Fathers and mothers shared similar child-rearing beliefs. Sigel et al. concluded that these mothers, who were full-time caregivers to their children, had more specific information about the child than the fathers did. This information led the mothers to modify their distancing behaviors to elicit appropriate behaviors from their children in each situation. Fathers, without this specific knowledge of the child's skill level, interacted with the child in the same way across situations. Fathers' interactions were based on their general assumptions about child development.

Johnson (1975) found that parents who spent more time with their preschool-aged children held more positive child-rearing beliefs (those related theoretically to favorable child development outcomes) than parents who spent less time with their children. Unfortunately Johnson did not present the relationship between specific parental behaviors and positive child-rearing beliefs. Perhaps these parents spent more time with their children because they believed their involvement was important to child development. On the other hand, perhaps their positive child-rearing beliefs grew from experiences with the child in which they were rewarded for involvement by the child's positive development. In other words, the child's behavior is part of a feedback loop contributing to the evolution of the parent's beliefs and behaviors over time.

It is important to parents that their children's caregivers share the parents' values and beliefs about how to raise children (Auerbach, 1975; Steinberg & Green, 1979). If disagreements exist, the distance between parent and caregiver may be moderated over time as they have opportunities to share ideas about child-rearing. Opportunities to compare and modify beliefs may be a function of the amount of communication between parent and caregiver or the duration of their association. When parents and caregivers have many opportunities to communicate, there should be less distance between perceived and actual concensus between them on child-rearing issues. When they communicate infrequently, they may perceive concensus that does not exist, or think they disagree when they do not (Garduque & Long, 1982).

Parent–caregiver contact in the context of caring for the child also enters the feedback loop between beliefs and behavior. Parents observe caregivers with their children and receive information that may modify their beliefs about the child. Parents may also vicariously learn new child-rearing skills by watching others interact with the child, as has been demonstrated in several home-based early intervention programs (Goodman, 1975; Levenstein, 1970). In return, the caregiver may learn about the child by observing the child with the parent. These principles have been applied in parent-training programs and home-based intervention programs. The technique of modeling appropriate behaviors by a parent educator is commonly employed. Home visits are often justified on the basis that the home visitor can both model appropriate behaviors and learn about children by observing them with their parents (c.f., Honig, 1975; O'Keefe, 1979). However, these principles have not been explored in family day care, nor have they been applied to what the caregiver learns from observing the parent with the child.

Specific perceptions of the child allow the parent to make appropriate demands and to respond to the child's needs at a level appropriate to satisfy the child. Understanding the unique characteristics of the child allows the parent to fit her behaviors to those of the child. For instance, if a parent knows that her child needs a long time to make transitions to new activities, she may prepare the child for naptime by giving warnings 20 minutes in advance. Thus the parent's understanding of the child leads her to behave in a particular way toward the child that (hopefully) facilitates the child's ability to meet adult demands. When a child enters a child-rearing environment outside the home, he or she encounters adults who may behave differently because of different perceptions of the child or of children in general. To extend the example used previously, the day care provider who does not know that the child needs a long transition may have difficulty at naptime because she does not give the child time to adjust (a difficulty which will hopefully resolve itself as the caregiver learns more about the child). Not all differences in perceptions between parents and caregivers are bound to lead to difficulties for the child. However, children presumably need to discriminate between the demands and expectations made by different adults and learn to adapt their behaviors accordingly. The concern over continuity implies as well that in certain (undefined) areas of child-rearing beliefs, agreement between parent and caregiver is better because agreement facilitates the child's transitions between settings.

The few studies that compare parents' and caregivers' child-rearing beliefs unfortunately have not tied their comparisons to specific adult behaviors (e.g., Johnson, 1975), nor to outcomes for the children. Winetsky (1978) evaluated parents' and center caregivers' responses to situations offering child-directed or adult-directed solutions. Caregivers more often than parents preferred child-directed choices; however, middle-class parents expressed preferences more similar to those of the caregivers than did working-class parents.

In the area of adult child-rearing beliefs and perceptions of children more research has been conducted in preschools than in day care centers or day care homes. There may be a distinction between the role perceptions of preschool teachers and day care caregivers that parents as well as child care professionals accept. That is, preschools are viewed as educational institutions while day care centers and homes serve a custodial function. However, this distinction is becoming increasingly blurred as parents expect day care caregivers to provide cognitive stimulation and educational experiences as well as custodial care. We reviewed the literature comparing parents' and preschool teachers' beliefs, however, because it may suggest potential areas of discontinuity worthy of exploration in day care. In addition, these studies sometimes address the issues that parents and child care professionals themselves view as important considerations in assessing continuity between home and alternative care settings.

Elardo and Caldwell (1973) administered objective checklists to parents and preschool teachers and compared their ratings of the importance of the objectives. They found only five significant differences between parents' and teachers' ratings of 75 objectives. Horner (1977) replicated their work, comparing parents' *perceptions* of teachers' ratings to actual parent and teacher ratings. (Horner's sample included preschool, day care, and FDC parents and caregivers, but he did not differentiate between groups in his presentation.) While the parents and teachers rated the objectives equally, parents predicted that teachers would value different objectives for preschoolers. In spite of this perceived dissonance, parents reported satisfaction with the program. When questioned about this, parents said that they believed the values they attributed to teachers were equally important, and to have different values emphasized at home than in preschool is acceptable. Thus parents distinguish between the goals for children and adults at home and in preschool settings.

Hess, Price, Dickson, and Conroy (1981) directly addressed the issue of continuity between parents' and caregivers' beliefs and the link between beliefs and behaviors. They asked parents of 4-year-olds and their preschool teachers to rank the importance of 10 areas of development in three different ways: 1) which are most important for preschoolers to learn; 2) which are given emphasis in preschool; and 3) which should be given emphasis in preschool. The two groups agreed more closely on what is important for 4-year-olds to learn than they did on what role the preschool plays or should play in teaching the skills. Parents assigned specific responsibility for language development and school skills to the preschool.

Hess and his colleagues (1981) did examine the relationship between beliefs and behaviors. They found that mothers emphasized independence more and used more directive teaching and control techniques than did teachers. These behaviors reflected their beliefs about child development: Parents expected children to achieve various developmental tasks at an earlier age than did teachers. Parents believed it more appropriate to demand compliance from their children without offering reasons for their demands. Teachers preferred reasoning methods and showed greater flexibility. This study substantiates the link between beliefs and behaviors. However, it falls prey to the common failings of day care-home care comparisons: It does not examine continuity in terms of *each* child's experience, nor does it relate continuity to child development outcomes.

Horner (1977) and Hess et al. (1981) found that parents perceived different roles for the preschool teachers than for themselves and had different expectations for the teachers' behavior. This analysis needs to be expanded to center-based and family day care. Since many day care providers, especially in family day care, see their role as more custodial than educational (Auerbach, 1975), the role distinctions between home and preschool may not be maintained in day care.

Alternatively, perhaps the role expectations for someone who conducts care in her own home are different than for those working in more "institutional" settings (both center day care and preschools). Differences in the physical setting may dictate differences in expectations for both adult roles and child roles in each setting.

As with generalized beliefs, the amount of communication or contact between parent and caregiver can mediate the accuracy of the two adults' specific conceptions of the child, since increased information exchange adds to the knowledge base of each. As parent and caregiver exchange information about the child, their knowledge of the child becomes more similar. Since beliefs about the child are reflected in the adults' behaviors, parents and caregivers who share the same conception of the child may act more similarly toward the child than two adults who perceive the child differently. Frequency of communication and length of association can both be considered measures of the amount of contact and information exchange between parent and caregiver. Children who have been in care longer periods have also had more opportunities to interact with the caregiver and thus provide her with more information about the child. Thus, the length of time the child has been in the current day care arrangement may be correlated with similarity between parents' and caregivers' beliefs about the child, and their behaviors toward the child. Walsh and Dietchman (1980) investigated the effect of length of time in contact by comparing parents' and preschool teachers' ratings of children on a developmental rating scale at the beginning and end of the school year. Parents rated their children more positively than teachers both times, but teachers' ratings changed from the beginning of the year to the end to more closely match the ratings made by parents. Parents may have opportunities to observe a wider range of the child's behavior, which the teachers also gain over the school year.

Studies of parent–caregiver communication have rarely addressed the relationship between type of communication and the adults' conceptions of the child. Indirect evidence is available from several early-intervention programs in which parent involvement (presumably indicating high parent–caregiver communication) was related to parents' increased flexibility and developmentally appropriate expectations for child behavior (Goodson & Hess, 1978). Since trained preschool teachers supposedly hold developmentally appropriate expectations for child behavior, parent involvement thus brings parent conceptions into closer agreement with those of the teachers.

Powell (1981) measured parent–caregiver communication more directly. He interviewed parents and day care caregivers to ascertain how much they communicated and what topics they discussed. The majority of parent–caregiver exchanges in his study were child-related, focusing on the quality of the child's day care day. As communication increased, the diversity of topics also increased. When communication occurred frequently, then parents and caregivers talked about the child. These findings now need to be extended to consider how communication between parent and caregiver influences each adult's conception of the child over time.

Several studies have considered the relationship between parent–caregiver communication and parental satisfaction with the program (Phillip, 1980; Powell, 1981; Winkelstein, 1981). When parents are satisfied with their child-care arrangement, it may suggest that they perceive agreement between their beliefs about child-rearing and those of the program (Auerbach, 1975). Parental satisfaction with child care may also reduce parental stress or guilt over separation from the child, thereby facilitating a positive parent–child relationship. The implications of parental satisfaction with day care need further investigation.

Summary

Child-rearing beliefs of parents and caregivers are a relevant dimension of continuity–discontinuity between home and day care to the extent that they reflect the behaviors of each adult with the child. Parents do not have many opportunities to observe the caregiver interacting with their children, but they do have opportunities to learn the caregiver's beliefs when they communicate. Shared values or child-rearing beliefs are a consideration frequently mentioned by parents in the process of selecting day care (Auerbach, 1975; Steinberg & Green, 1979). However, formation of beliefs is a dynamic process in which, over time, information received from the child and others who interact with the child confirms or modifies the adult's beliefs.

Is continuity in child-rearing beliefs between home and day care desirable? The assumptions of the ideal child-rearing environment and the dual system of day care must again be examined to answer this question. For middle-class families, the answer appears to be a qualified "yes." These families presumably meet the ideal standard of child-rearing beliefs. (What these beliefs are will remain unspecified for now.) Within the realm of acceptable beliefs, however, certain discontinuities are allowed when they conform to perceived role differences between parents and day care providers (Hess, et al., 1981; Horner, 1977).

For low-income families, continuity of beliefs (in the direction from home to day care) appears less desirable. Research on cognitive style (Hess & Shipman, 1967), teaching strategies and child-rearing beliefs (McGillicuddy-deLisi, 1981; Sigel, et al., 1980), and educational beliefs (Shipman, 1976) has found social class differences in these areas, with low-income families displaying beliefs that are considered less optimal for child development (or at least the beliefs of middle-class parents are more congruent with the currently accepted theories of child development and learning; see McGillicuddy-deLisi, 1981). Thus the focus of many early intervention programs has been to expose children to discontinuity in these beliefs and their concommitant behaviors. At the same time, interventions attempt to modify the parents' beliefs to approximate the ideal or optimal standard. Whether it is appropriate to modify child-rearing beliefs to conform with those of the dominant culture is not an issue here. The point is that our implicit assumptions about optimal child-rearing conditions have led us to stress discontinuity between home and day care when the beliefs held at home are thought to conflict with those of the ideal child-rearing standard.

CONCLUSION: A MODEL OF DAY CARE PROCESS

This chapter has reviewed aspects of the child-rearing environment that may differ between home and day care. The interface between home and day care settings forms a model of the interrelationships among three aspects of this child-rearing environment: (a) adult characteristics and behaviors, (b) environmental characteristics, and (c) child behavior. Although this discussion has focused primarily on effects on children resulting from environmental characteristics and adult characteristics and behaviors, we do not mean to neglect the possibility that children also may be the cause of discontinuity between settings, by presenting different behaviors in each setting. Thus, in the model presented in Figure 4.1, children and adults influence each other bidirectionally, and child behaviors feed back into the adult's conception of the child. This model can be applied to analyze adult–child interactions within a single environment or to compare interactions across environments.

Within each child-rearing environment the model describes reciprocal influences between adult and child. The adult's behavior is also related to general knowledge of child development, specific information about the child, and such adult characteristics as family structure and income.

Concern over continuity or discontinuity between home and day care has implied that differences may exist along one or more of these dimensions of the child-rearing environment. Since qualities of parent behavior, parent beliefs, and the physical and social environment of the home have been directly or indirectly related to important child behaviors, divergence from these qualities in the child's day care experience may present significant discontinuities in the child's life.

Since the same child is present in both settings, but not the same adult, the child's behavior in one setting may reflect qualities of interactions the child has outside that setting. For instance, a child may learn self-help skills from the caregiver in day care that lead him or her to be more independent at home. A child who is rewarded for tantrums at home might try this strategy with the caregiver as well.

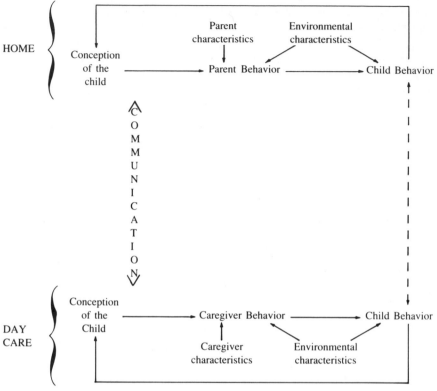

FIGURE 4.1.   A model of the child care process.

Parent and caregiver behaviors are more independent of each other because the adults have few opportunities to influence each other. However, their behaviors as well as their child-rearing beliefs may be mediated by the amount of contact or communication they have. As adults communicate about the child, the conception of the child held by each becomes more developed because they share additional information. Because beliefs interact with behaviors, we might expect greater conformity between the behaviors of parents and caregivers as a function of increasing communication. The length of time the child has been in the day care setting as well as frequency of communication between adults may provide us with measures of the amount of information exchanged.

This model raises several questions for empirical study. This review has suggested several dimensions of potential discontinuity between home and day care. Two further steps are needed now. First of all, the actual existence of continuity or discontinuity needs to be documented by examining the experience of day care children in their own homes and in their day care settings. The studies presented in this review offer limited evidence that some discontinuities exist. Since virtually no one has observed the same children across settings, we have little understanding of whether discontinuity actually exists in the lives of children attending day care. Second, the impact of discontinuity (or continuity) needs to be assessed in terms of child outcomes, that is, in terms of the child's behavior in each setting and parallels in his or her behavior across settings. These investigations would be more fruitful if based in a theoretical perspective that would allow predictions about why discontinuity is important. One potentially useful perspective might be to apply the concept of ''optimal discrepancy'' (Hunt, 1981; Wachs, 1977) to predict optimal or less positive child development outcomes based on the degree of discontinuity between settings. From this perspective moderate amounts of discontinuity may actually facilitate positive child outcomes while extreme discontinuity may be disruptive.

In the past, day care has been regarded as a unidimensional treatment (Belsky, Steinberg, & Walker, 1982; Garduque, Peters, & Long, in preparation). In some studies, in-home care by nonparents and family day care have been combined with the home-reared sample in comparisons with center-reared children (e.g., Gunnarrson, 1978). ''Day care'' does not reveal the diversity and richness of relationships children have outside their homes. The mounting evidence indicates many dimensions within the day care environment that merit investigation. For instance, we can examine the degree of discontinuity experienced by children as we proceed through increasingly more ''institutional'' settings, such as in-home care by a nonrelative, family day care, group home care, and day care centers. Clarke-Stewart (1981) has begun to do this. We can also use family day care, a setting that is similar to home care, to provide control over some dimensions of discontinuity while investigating the impact of other dimensions. This is the approach we have taken in studies in progress at The Pennsylvania State University. In either case it is important to consider the impact of day care experience as it relates to the individual child. A day care experience that is discontinuous for one child may be continuous for another.

As several reviewers have recently pointed out (Belsky, et al., 1982; Caldwell & Freyer, 1982; Garduque, Peters, & Long, in preparation) we know relatively little about the process of day care. Since day care is an increasingly common experience for most preschoolers, it is time to look more closely at how day care integrates with the home lives of young children. This can be accomplished by setting aside group comparisons in favor of examining the experiences of children across settings.

REFERENCES

Administration on Children, Youth, and Families. (1981). *National day care home study: Family day care in the United States. Summary of findings.* Washington, DC: DHHS Publ. No. (ODHS) 80-30287.

Ainsworth, M. (1979). Infant–mother attachment. *American Psychologist, 34* (10), 932–937.

Ainsworth, M., & Bell, S. (1969). Some contemporary patterns of mother–infant interaction in the feeding situation. In A. Ambrose (Ed.), *Stimulation in early infancy.* London, England: Academic Press.

Ainsworth, M., Bell, S., & Stayton, D. (1974) Infant–mother attachment and social adjustment: 'Socialisation' as a product of reciprocal responsiveness to signals. In M. P. M. Richards (Ed.), *The integration of a child into a social world.* London, England: Cambridge University Press.

Anderson, C., Nagle, R., Roberts, W., & Smith, J. (1981). Attachment to substitute caregivers as a function of center quality and caregiver involvement. *Child Development, 52,* 53–61.

Arend, R., Gove, F., & Sroufe, L. A. (1979). Continuity of individual adaptation from infancy to kindergarten: A predictive study of ego-resiliency and curiosity in preschoolers. *Child Development, 50,* 950–959.

Auerbach, S. (1975). What parents want from day care. In S. Auerbach & J. A. Rivaldo (Eds.), *Child care: A comparative guide. Vol. 1. Rationale for child care services: Programs vs. politics.* New York: Human Sciences Press, Inc.

Baumrind, D. (1967). Child care practices anteceding three patterns of preschool behavior. *Genetic Psychology Monographs, 75,* 43–88.

Belsky, J., & Steinberg, L. (1978). The effects of day care: A critical review. *Child Development, 49,* 929–949.

Belsky, J., Steinberg, L., & Walker, A. (1982). The ecology of day care. In M. Lamb (Ed.), *Childrearing in Nontraditional Families.* Hillsdale, NJ: Lawrence Erlbaum.

Blehar, M. (1979). Working couples as parents. In *Families today: A research sampler on families and children, Vol. I.* DHEW Publ. No. (ADM) 79–815.

Bloom, B. (1964). *Stability and change in human characteristics.* New York: Wiley.

Bradley, R., & Caldwell, B. (1976). Early home environment and changes in mental test performance from 6 to 36 months. *Developmental Psychology, 12,* 93–97.

Brody, S., & Axelrad, S. (1978). *Mothers, fathers, and children.* New York: International Universities Press.

Bronfenbrenner, U. (196i). The changing American child: A speculative analysis. *Merrill-Palmer Quarterly, 7,* 73–84.

Bronfenbrenner, U. (1974). Is early intervention effective? DHEW Publ. No. (OHD), 75–25.

Caldwell, B. (1979). *Home observation for measurement of the environment.* Little Rock, AK: Center for Child Development and Education, University of Arkansas.

Caldwell, B., & Freyer, M. (1982). Day care and early education. Unpublished manuscript.

Carew, J. (1980). Experience and the development of intelligence in young children at home and in day care. *Monographs of the Society for Reserach in Child Development, 45,* (6–7) Serial No. 187.

Clarke-Stewart, K- A. (1977). *Child Care in the Family.* New York: Academic Press.

Clarke-Stewart, K. A. (1981). Observation and experiment: complementary strategies for studying day care and social development. In S. Kilmer (Ed.), *Advances in early education and day care.* Vol. II. Greenwich, CT: JAI Press.

Cochran, M. (1977). A comparison of group day and family child-rearing patterns in Sweden. *Child Development, 48,* 702–707.

Elardo, R., & Caldwell, B. (1973). Value imposition in early education: Fact or fancy? *Child Care Quarterly, 2,* 6–13.

Etaugh, C. (1980). Effects of nommaternal care on children: Research evidence and popular views. *American Psychologist, 35* (4), 309–319.

Evans, E. (1975). *Contemporary influences in early childhood education.* New York: Holt, Rinehart, and Winston.

Farran, D., & Ramey, C. (1977). Infant day care and attachment behaviors toward mothers and teachers. *Child Development, 48,* 1112–1116.

Fein, G. (1977). Infant day care and the family. In *Policy issues in day care: Summaries of 21 papers*. Washington, DC: DHEW, Office of the Assistant Secretary for Planning and Evaluation.

Fein, G., & Clarke-Stewart, K. A. (1973). *Day care in context*. New York: Wiley.

Fosberg, S. (1980, April). Design of the National Day Care Home Study. Paper presented at the annual meeting of the American Educational Research Association, Boston, MA.

Garbarino, J. (1982). Sociocultural risk: Dangers to competence. In C. Kopp, & J. Krakow (Eds.), *The child: Development in a social context*. Reading, MA: Addison-Wesley.

Garduque, L., & Long, F. (1982, November). Continuity between day care and home seen from parent and caregiver perspectives. Paper presented at the annual meeting of the National Asociation for the Education of Young Children, Washington, DC.

Garduque, L., Peters, D. L., & Long, F. (in preparation). Day care research: Does it change anything? *Journal of Applied Developmental Psychology*.

Gewirtz, J. (1972). Attachment, dependence, and a distinction in terms of stimulus control. In J. Gewirtz (Ed.), *Attachment and Dependency*. New York: Wiley.

Golden, M., Rosenbluth, L., Grossi, M. T., Policare, J., Freenan, J., & Brownlee, M. (1978). *The New York City infant day care study: A comparative study of licensed group and family day care programs and the effects of these programs on children and their families*. New York: Medical and Health Research Association of New York City, Inc.

Goldhaber, D. (1979). Does the changing view of early experience imply a changing view of early development? In L. Katz, M. Glockner, C. Watkins, & M. Spencer (Eds.), *Current topics in early childhood education, Vol. II*. Norwood, NJ: Ablex Publishing Corp.

Goodman, E. (1975, January). Modeling: A method of parent education. *The Family Coordinator*, 7–11.

Goodson, B., & Hess, R. (1978). The effects of parent training programs on child performance and parent behavior. In B. Brown (Ed.), *Found: Long-term gains from early intervention*. Washington, DC: AAAS.

Gunnarrson, L. (1978, September). Children in day care and family care in Sweden: A follow-up. Research Bulletin No. 21, Gothenburg School of Education. (ERIC ED 180 665)

Hartup, W. (1979). Peer relations and the growth of social competence. In M. W. Kent & J. E. Rolf (Eds.), *Primary prevention of psychopathology, Vol. III. Social competence in children*. Hanover, NH: University Press of New England.

Hess, R., Price, G., Dickson, W. P., & Conroy, M. (1981). Different roles for mothers and teachers: Contrasting styles of child care. In S. Kilmer (Ed.), *Advances in early education and day care, Vol. II*. Greenwich, CT: JAI Press, Inc.

Hess, R., & Shipman, V. (1967). Cognitive elements in maternal behavior. In J. Hill (Ed.), *Minnesota symposium on child psychology, Vol. 1*. Minneapolis, MN: University of Minnesota Press.

Hinde, R. (1976). On describing relationships. *Journal of Child Psychology and Psychiatry, 17,* 1–19.

Hock, E. (1978). Working and nonworking mothers with infants: Perceptions of their careers, their infants' needs, and satisfaction with mothering. *Developmental Psychology, 14,* 37–43.

Hock, E., Christman, K., & Hock, M. (1980). Factors associated with decisions about return to work in mothers of infants. *Developmental Psychology, 16,* 535–536.

Hofferth, S. (1979). Day care in the next decade: 1980–1990. *Journal of Marriage and the Family,* 644–658.

Honig, A. (1975). *Parent involvement in early childhood education*. Washington, DC: NAEYC.

Horner, W. (1977). Value imposition in day care: Fact, fancy, or irrelevant? *Child Care Quarterly, 6* (10), 18–29.

Howes, C. (1981). Caregiver behavior and conditions of caregiving. Unpublished manuscript, University of California, Los Angeles.

Howes, C., & Rubenstein, J. (1980). Social experiences of toddlers at home and in two types of day care. Unpublished manuscript.

Howes, C., & Rubenstein, J. (1981). Toddler peer behavior in two types of day care. *Infant Behavior and Development, 4,* 387–393.

Hunt, J. McV. (1981). Toward a pedagogy for infancy and early childhood. In S. Kilmer (Ed.), *Advances in early education and day care, Vol. II.* Greenwich, CT: JAI Press, Inc.

Johnson, A. (1975). An assessment of Mexican-American parent child-rearing feelings and behaviors. Ph.D. Dissertation, Arizona State University.

Kagan, J. (1977). The effect of day care on the infant. In *Policy issues in day care: Summaries of 21 papers.* Washington, DC: DHEW, Office of the Assistant Secretary for Planning and Evaluation.

Kagan, J., & Klein, R. (1973). Cross-cultural perspectives on early development. *American Psychologist, 28,* 947–962.

Kamerman, S., & Kahn, A. (1976). *Social services in the United States: Policies and programs.* Philadelphia, PA: Temple University Press.

Kilmer, S. (1979). Infant-toddler group day care: A review of research. In L. G. Katz, M. Z. Glockner, C. Watkins, & M. J. Spencer (Eds.), *Current topics in early childhood education. Vol. III.* Norwood, NJ: Ablex Publishing Corp.

Lake, A. (1980, September). The day care business. *Working Mother,* 31–37.

Lamb, M. (1981). The development of social expectations in the first year of life. In M. Lamb & L. Sherrod (Eds.), *Infant social cognition: Empirical and theoretical considerations.* Hillsdale, NJ: Lawrence Erlbaum.

Levenstein, P. (1970). Cognitive growth in preschoolers through verbal interaction with their mothers. *American Journal of Orthopsychiatry, 40,* 426–432.

Lewis, M., & Schaeffer, S. (1981). Peer behavior and mother–infant interaction in maltreated children. In M. Lewis & L. Rosendum (Eds.), *The uncommon child: The genesis of behavior, Vol. III.* New York: Plenum Publishing Corp.

McGillicuddy-deLisi, A. (1981, May). The relationship between parents' beliefs about development and family constellation, socioeconomic status and parents' teaching strategies. Princeton, NJ: ETS Research Report No. 81-10.

McGrew, W. (1974). Aspects of social development in nursery school children, with emphasis on introduction to the group. In N. Blurton Jones (Ed.), *Ethological studies of child behaviour.* London, England: Cambridge University Press.

Murphy, L. B., & Moriarty, A. (1976). *Vulnerability, coping and growth from infancy to adolescence.* New Haven, CT: Yale University Press.

Newson, J., & Newson, E. (1976). *Seven years old in the home environment.* New York: Wiley.

O'Keefe, R. (1979). What Head Start means to families. In L. G. Katz, M. Z. Glockner, C. Watkins, & M. J. Spencer (Eds.), *Current topics in early childhood education, Vol. II.* Norwood, NJ: Ablex Publishing Corp.

Peters, D. L. (1972, December). Day care homes: A Pennsylvania profile. University Park, PA: The Pennsylvania State University, Institute for the Study of Human Development, CHSD Report No. 18.

Peters, D. L. (1975). Editorial, In D. L. Peters & J. Beker (Eds.), *Day care: Problems, process, prospects.* New York: Human Sciences Press.

Peters, D. L. (1980). Social service, social policy and the care of young children: Head Start and after. *Journal of Applied Developmental Psychology, 1,* 7–27.

Peters, D. L., & Belsky, J. (1982). The day care movement: Past, present, and future. In M. Kostelnik, A. Rabin, L. Phenice, & A. Soderman (Eds.), *Child nurturance: Patterns of supplementary parenting, Vol. 2.* New York: Plenum Publishing Corp.

Peters, D. L., & Benn, J. (1980, October). Day care: Support for the family. *Dimensions,* 78–82.

Phillip, C. (1980). Preschool programs for developmentally disabled children and their families: Are they meeting mothers' expectations? *Child Care Quarterly, 9* (3), 175–184.

Powell, D. R. (1980). Toward a socio-ecological perspective of relations between parents and childcare programs. In S. Kilmer (Ed.), *Advances in early education and day care, Vol. I.* Greenwich, CT: JAI Press, Inc.

Prescott, E. (1981). Relations between physical setting and adult/child behavior in day care. In S. Kilmer (Ed.), *Advances in early education and day care, Vol. II.* Greenwich, CT: JAI Press, Inc.

Prescott, E., Jones, E., & Kritchevsky, S. (1967). *Group day care as a child-rearing environment* (Final report to the Children's Bureau). Pasadena, CA: Pacific Oaks College.

Prescott, E., Jones, E., Kritchevsky, S., Milich, C., & Haselhoef, E. (1975). *Assessment of child-rearing environments. Part I: Who thrives in day care?; Part II: An environmental inventory.* Pasadena, CA: Pacific Oaks College.

Prescott, E., Kritchevsky, S., & Jones, E. (1972, October). The day care environmental inventory. Assessment of child-rearing environments: An ecological approach. Part I of the final report. Pasadena, CA: Pacific Oaks College. (ERIC ED 076 228)

Prescott, E., Kritchevsky, S., & Jones, E. (1973, March). Who thrives in group day care? Assessment of child-rearing environments: An ecological approach. Pasadena, CA: Pacific Oaks College. (ERIC ED 076 228)

Radloff, B. (1977). Average day care: Harmful or beneficial? *Carnegie Quarterly, 26* (3), 5–6.

Ray, M. (1982). Parenting in the single parent family. Unpublished manuscript, The Pennsylvania State University.

Ricciutti, H. (1977). Effects of infant day care experience on behavior and development: Research and implications for social policy. In *Policy issues and day care: Summaries of 21 papers.* Washington, DC: DHEW: Office of the Assistant Secretary for Planning and Evaluation.

Rodes, T., & Moore, J. (1975). *National child care consumer study: American consumer attitudes and opinions on child care.* Arlington, VA: Kappa Systems, Inc.

Rothschild, M. S. (1978). Public school center vs. family home day care: Single parents' reasons for selection. Master's Thesis, San Diego State University. (ERIC ED 162 759)

Rubenstein, J., & Howes, C. (1979). Caregiving and infant behavior in day care and in homes. *Developmental Psychology, 15,* 1–4.

Rubenstein, J., Pedersen, F., & Yarrow, L. (1977). What happens when mother is away: A comparison of mothers and substitute caregivers. *Developmental Psychology, 13,* 529–530.

Ruderman, F. (1968). *Child care and working mothers.* New York: Child Welfare League.

Rutter, M. (1979). Maternal deprivation, 1972–1979: New findings, new concepts, new approaches. *Child Development, 50,* 283–305.

Sameroff, A. (1975). Early influences on development: Fact or fancy? *Merrill-Palmer Quarterly, 21,* 267–295.

Saunders, M., & Keister, M. (1972). Family day care: Some observations. University of North Carolina, Greensboro.

Scarr-Salapatek, S., & Williams, M. (1973). The effects of early stimulation on low-birth-weight infants. *Child Development, 44,* 94–101.

Shipman, V. (1976). Notable early characteristics of high and low achieving black low-SES children. Project Report 76-21. Princeton, NJ: ETS.

Sibbison, V. (1973, June). The influence of maternal role perception on attitudes toward and utilization of early child care services. In D. L. Peters (Ed.) A summary of the Pennsylvania day care study. University Park, PA: The Pennsylvania State University, Institute for the Study of Human Development, CHSD Report No. 27.

Siegel-Gorelick, B., Everson, M., & Ambron, S. (1980, April). Qualitative vs. quantitative differences in caregivers in family day care and at home. Paper presented at the International Conference on Infant Studies, New Haven, CT.

Sigel, I., McGillicuddy-deLisi, A., & Johnson, J. (1980). Parental distancing beliefs and children's representational competence within the family context. Research Report No. 80-21. Princeton, NJ: ETS.

Sroufe, L. A. (1979). The coherence of individual development: Early care, attachment, and subsequent developmental issues. *American Psychologist, 34* (10), 834–841.

Steinberg, L., & Green, C. (1979, March). How parents may mediate the effect of day care. Paper presented at the biennial meeting of the Society for Research on Child Development, San Francisco, CA.

Thomas, A., & Chess, S. (1977). *Temperament and development.* New York: Brunner/Mazel.

Tyler, B., & Dittman, L. (1980). Meeting the toddler more than half way: The behavior of toddlers and their caregivers. *Young Children, 35,* 39–46.

Urban Institute. (1980). The subtle revolution: Women at work. Washington, DC: Department of Housing and Urban Development.

Wachs, T. (1977). The optimal stimulation hypothesis and early development: Anybody got a match? In I. Uzguriz & F. Weizmann, *The structuring of experience.* New York: Plenum.

Wahler, R. G., & Dumas, J. E. (1981). Changing the observational coding styles of insular and non-insular mothers: A step toward maintenance of parent training effects. Unpublished manuscript, The Child Behavior Institute, University of Tennessee.

Walsh, K., & Dietchman, R. (1980). Evaluation of early childhood programs: The role of parents. *Child Care Quarterly, 9* (4), 289–298.

Wandersman, L. P. (1978). An ecological study of the interaction of caregivers' own and day care children in family day care homes. *Cornell Journal of Social Relations, 13,* 75–90.

Wandersman, L. P. (1981). Ecological relationships in family day care. *Child Care Quarterly, 10* (2), 89–102.

Waters, E., Wippman, J., & Sroufe, L. A. (1979). Attachment, positive affect, and competence in the peer group: Two studies in construct validation. *Child Development, 50,* 821–829.

Watson, S. (1972). Smiling, cooing, and "The Game." *Merrill-Palmer Quarterly, 18,* 323–339.

Werner, E., Bierman, J., & French, F. (1971). *The children of Kauai.* Honolulu, HI: University of Hawaii Press.

White, B., Kaban, B., Shapiro, B., and Attanucci, J. (1977). Competence and experience. In I. Uzgiriz & F. Weizmann (Eds.), *The structuring of experience.* NY: Plenum.

White, B., Watts, J., Barnett, I., Kaban, B., Marmor, J., & Shapiro, B. (1973). *Environment and experience: Major influences on the development of the young child.* Englewood Cliffs, NJ: Prentice-Hall.

Willner, M. (1969). Unsupervised family day care in New York City. *Child Welfare, 48,* 342–347.

Winetsky, C. (1978). Comparisons of the expectations of parents and teachers for the behavior of preschool children. *Child Development, 49,* 1146–1154.

Winkelstein, E. (1981). Day care/family interaction and parental satisfaction. *Child Care Quarterly, 10* (4), 334–340.

Woolsey, S. (1977). Pied Piper politics and the child-care debate. *Daedalus,* Spring, 127–145.

Yarrow, L., Rubenstein, J., & Pederson, F. (1975). *Infant and environment: Early cognitive and motivational development.* New York: Halsted Press.

5
A Reanalysis of the Evidence for the Genetic Nature of Early Motor Development*

Micha Razel
Weizmann Institute of Science, Rehovot, Israel

INTRODUCTION

It is an accepted opinion in the field of developmental psychology and education that the early development of the locomotor skills is dominated by genetic factors. For example, Mussen, Conger, and Kagan (1979) stated in an influential textbook of developmental psychology that "sitting and standing will develop without any special teaching by adults" (p. 123). Hilgard, Atkinson, and Atkinson (1967) claimed too, in a widely used introductory textbook of psychology, that "motor development appears to be primarily a maturational process" (p. 70), where "maturation" is defined as "an innately governed sequence of physical changes that does not depend on particular environmental events" (p. 68). This view, stated in similar ways, can be found in most textbooks.

What is the evidence on which Mussen, his coworkers, Hilgard et al., and other psychologists and educators base this opinion? It seems to consist of four studies: the "early training" study by Arnold Gesell and Helen Thompson (1929), testing the effect of early training on the development of various motor skills; the "swaddling study" by Wayne and Marsena G. Dennis (1940), investigating Hopi Indian infants who were kept tied to their cradles during the first months of life; the "deprivation study" by the same researchers (e.g., Dennis, 1936), investigating the effect on two infants of a year-long experiment in deprivation of adult teaching; and the "study of Johnny and Jimmy" by Myrtle B. McGraw (1935), in which one of a pair of twins was given intensive motor training and the other—deprived of any teaching during the first 2 years of life. It is practically impossible to find today an introductory textbook on psychology or

*The author wishes to express his gratitude to Dina Feitelson, Carol Razel, Ozer Schild, and Philip R. Zelazo for reading various drafts of this paper and making useful suggestions. During the preparation of the final draft, the author was a Visiting Scholar at the Graduate School of Education, New York University.

human development in which a selection of these four studies is not cited (e.g., Dworetzky, 1981; Good & Brophy, 1980; Stone & Church, 1979).

In the following sections, it will be shown that the uncritical acceptance of the conclusion offered in these four studies, that early motor development is determined almost exclusively by genetic factors, is unjustified. The main aim of this chapter is to demonstrate that when these studies are analyzed properly, they usually provide strong evidence for the opposite point of view, namely, that motor development depends on learning opportunities and is even extremely sensitive to them. Moreover, when correctly presented, some of these studies demonstrate that the effects of motor training and deprivation are cumulative and that early motor training may have far reaching and permanent consequences for later motor behavior, intelligence, and personality characteristics such as fearlessness and independence. There are other studies, too, that provide evidence for this learning point of view. Some of these are reviewed at the end of this paper.

The student who is introduced to developmental psychology is usually told that "there are many problems of profound interest for which the experimental method is simply not appropriate or feasible" (Mussen, Conger, & Kagan, 1979, p. 37), such as the relationship between early deprivation and later outcomes. Perhaps the only two studies in which long-term, early deprivation of human subjects was administered experimentally and later outcomes observed are the Dennises' deprivation study and McGraw's study of Johnny and Jimmy. It is therefore of special importance to ascertain that the results of these studies are represented correctly as showing that when the infant is deprived of adult teaching no "maturation" takes place. This chapter contains an attempt to do so.

THE TRAINING STUDY

Arnold Gesell and Helen Thompson (1929, 1941, 1943) used a pair of identical twins, born July 3, 1927, who had been living in a child-caring institution since the death of their mother shortly after birth, in an experiment designed to test the effects of early motor training on development. They designated the twins "T" (for Treatment) and "C" (for Control). T received 20 minutes of daily training 6 days a week for 6 weeks starting with the 47th week of life. During 10 minutes each day, instruction was given in climbing a five-tread staircase, in crawling, in pulling up to standing, and in walking while holding on to furniture or an adult's hand. During the remaining 10 minutes, T was provided with training of finer motor coordination. Ten 1-in. cubes were placed on a table in front of her, and both spontaneous and directed play were encouraged. C received only 2 weeks of training, 1 week after T had ended hers. C's training included only practicing of stair climbing. The daily time for training of this skill was roughly the same for the two twins.

Data that Also Fit a Learning Theory: Faster Learning at an Older Age

Gesell and Thompson considered the fact that C, at an older age, learned faster than T, at a younger age, as most important. For example, C at age 56-weeks, after 2 weeks of training, climbed the stairs in a shorter time—14 s—than T at age 48-weeks, after 2 weeks of training—40 s—and even faster than T at 52-weeks, after 6 weeks of training—26 s. Or, C climbed the stairs without help on the first day of training while T was able to do so only after 15 days. Gesell and Thompson also attached much importance to the fact that some motor advantage of T seemed to disappear after some time. For example, T was able to climb the stairs 5 weeks before C. But this difference disappeared once C received her training.

According to the genetic theory, the more mature the organism, the less learning is needed to establish a particular behavior. And when it is perfectly mature, learning becomes absolutely superfluous. C's faster rate of learning was thus explained by her greater maturity at the time of training. Gesell and Thompson concluded that "these findings . . . point consistently to the preponderant importance of maturational factors in the determination of infant behavior" (1929, p. 114).

But C's faster learning can also be explained by any learning theory that assumes that an individual that has accumulated more knowledge and experience will be able to make faster progress when given directed instruction (cf. Carroll, 1963; Razel, 1977, 1984). Several investigators, such as Fowler (1983), Hunt (1961), J. R. Hilgard (1932), and Tyler (1964) have noted that since C was not kept in "cold storage" during her sister's training, it could be assumed that she received learning opportunities that helped her make faster progress during her subsequent training.

Evidence that C received stimulation outside the experimental training sessions from the staff of the institute in which the twins were raised, we find in the following quotation: "The nurses tended to play somewhat more with T because she was slightly the more responsive. She also received additional exercise in walking through the assistance of the nurses for the same reason. There can, therefore, be no doubt that the locomotor training advantages enjoyed by T were definitely greater in amount than those enjoyed by C, whether we have regard for the training periods themselves or the prevailing environments of the two children" (Gesell & Thompson, 1929, p. 54). Thus, C, too, received locomotor training outside the experimental framework. In addition, C was allowed to climb the stairs on at least 3 separate days before the beginning of her training, in the 46th, 48th, and 52nd weeks. These occasions were devised to compare the respective climbing abilities of T and C (Gesell & Thompson, 1929, Table 10, p. 65; Table 11, p. 70). Moreover, the day that C climbed the stairs without help for the first time, she climbed at least twice with help before she was able to do it by herself (Gesell & Thompson, 1929, p. 61). Therefore, Gesell and Thompson's claim that C's unaided climbing of the stairs at 53-weeks was achieved "without previous specific training and without any environmental opportunity to exercise the function of climbing" (1929, p. 60) was incorrect. C's faster learning can, thus, be explained equally well by a learning theory as by a genetic one.

The learning explanation of C's faster learning at an older age is further supported by the findings of Dennis (1938) and McGraw (1935), in studies to be reviewed in the following, that older children who were not given any environmental opportunity to exercise motor skills did not, at an older age, learn these skills faster than normal children at a younger age.

Data that Do Not Fit a Genetic Theory

According to the genetic theory, early motor training should not have any effect as early motor development is determined genetically. Any learning theory predicts, however, that the result of training in stair climbing, walking, standing, or crawling must be a more advanced motor development. This is exactly what was found. In Table 10 of the original report (1929, p. 65–67) Gesell and Thompson provided a summary of the locomotor effects of training up to the age of 1½-years. In the table it is noted that there was "no apparent difference between T and C in locomotor ability" (1929, p. 65) at the beginning of the experiment. But following the training, many differences could be observed. T climbed the stairs 5 weeks before C was able to do so. Even when C learned to climb the stairs, T's climbing time remained faster for a long time. For example, at the ages 53-, 56-, 70-, and 79-weeks, T's and C's fastest climbing times in seconds were 17 versus 45, 11 versus 14, 6 versus 10, and 7 versus 8, respectively. When the gap in stair-climbing time seemed to get smaller (evidently because of a ceiling effect), a new difference between the twins could be observed. T was able to climb in and out of her high chair, whereas C was less skilled at climbing in the chair and unable to climb out. At the end of the period covered by this report it was observed that C was climbing "hesitatingly" while T did so "with more alacrity and agility" (1929, p. 67).

T stood alone at 56-weeks, C, only 6 weeks later. But even when both twins were able to stand, finer measures taken at a later age could still reveal a difference in standing ability. For example, at the age of 1½-years, 5 months after the experiment, it was noted that C's standing stance was wider. T took one step alone at 56-weeks while C walked alone 4½ weeks later. But even when both twins walked alone, T's walking remained superior. For example, at 62-weeks T walked "all over" while C only took one or two steps. At 63- and 69-weeks C's walking was still less steady and slower. When the difference in balance seemed to decrease, new differences in walking ability could be observed. For instance, T was "more mobile than C" (Gesell & Thompson, 1929, p. 67) and she traversed "more ground in play" (p. 67). Beyond the specific skills, new differences in general motor disposition could be observed as time went by. For example, at 63-weeks C was characterized as "less supple than T" (p. 67), while at 79-weeks T was described as "more agile in her body movements" (p. 72).

The data provided in Table 10 (Gesell & Thompson, 1929) lend themselves to a statistical analysis. The table contains 37 comparisons. Of these, T surpassed C in 27, C exceeded T in 1, and there was parity in 9 comparisons. This advantage of T is statistically significant ($z=4.72$, $p<.05$, by a sign test, Hays, 1963, p. 625; following Guttman, 1977, the level of p was set in advance at .05 for all significance tests performed throughout this paper). The data clearly support the learning hypothesis and refute the genetic one. Faced with these data, Gesell and Thompson admitted that they "show a consistent locomotor superiority in T" (1929, p. 68). But in the summary of the report and in a later version of the paper (1943) Gesell and Thompson ignored the data and their own earlier recognition of T's superiority. They concluded that "there is no conclusive evidence that practice and exercise even hasten the actual appearance of types of reaction like climbing" (1929, p. 114). We have seen that the data showed how training hastened the appearance of climbing, standing, and walking.

Gesell and Thompson concluded from their study that early training was useless since "it had no marked effects upon ultimate skills" (1929, p. 72). The data just reviewed seem to contradict this claim too. The effect of training did not disappear when C learned to climb, stand, and walk; and the motor gap between the twins in motor skills did not seem to decrease during the whole period covered by Gesell and Thompson's first report (1929), that is, until the twins were 1½-years-old.

Locomotor Effects of Early Training in Later Years

In 1941, when the twins were almost 14-years-old, Gesell and Thompson (1941) published a paper summarizing the twins' development from infancy to adolescence. At age 2-years and 2-months they were returned from the child-care institution, where they had been living, to the home of their father and stepmother. The data published in this report reveal that T's motor superiority did not disappear with time.

At 3½-years, the twins were given a battery of motor tests twice. The tests included tasks such as stepping on blocks, and stepping into 8-in. (20 cm) rope hoops with alternating feet. On both occasions T was more skillful than C in both tasks (Gesell & Thompson, 1941, p. 43). Tests of walking on boards 2.72 yds (2.5 m) long, raised 39.37 in. (10 cm) from the floor, and of various widths, were made in 11 ages from 4½- to 12-years. In the majority of the tests T was quicker and kept her balance better (p. 43; see also Hilgard, 1933, p. 58). Gesell and Thompson also commented that "in natural stride, T tends to take the lead" (1941, p. 44). The picture is not completely black and white, as demonstrated by the fact that C rode the bicycle better than T at the age of 11-years. But such an advantage of C is only an exception. An analysis of two films showing the twins tap-dancing at 10- and 12-years indicated that "T moves more vig-orously . . . and completes her movements more perfectly. C . . . was rela-tively more lackadaisical and indecisive" (p. 35). For one of the films, a count indicated that out of 35 times in which there was a difference between the twins in the completeness of the movement, T executed the movement more fully 27 times, a statistically significant difference ($z=3.04$, $p<.05$). Gesell and Thompson also measured the time it took the girls to complete particular dance movements. Of the 51 instances in which there was a difference between the twins, T was faster in 35 ($z=2.52$, $p<.05$). T and C's play was observed from age 3½- to 10-years. It was concluded that "T's play was likely to be more active than C's" (p. 60). At 13-years, T won first prize in a track meet while C failed to make the team.

These data support the hypothesis that early motor training results in a life-long, general motor superiority. Gesell and Thompson argued that this study showed that "training does not transcend maturation" (1943, p. 216). But the data seem to contradict this claim.

Gesell and Thompson also concluded that the study demonstrated the "palpa-ble difference in favor of the efficacy of deferred training" (1929, p. 60). When the data are presented correctly, it is unclear how this study can be used to support this claim.

Cube Behavior and Fine Motor Coordination

Gesell and Thompson concluded that "it was found that the cube behavior was strikingly similar, both at the end of T's preferential training period and 11 weeks thereafter, and then again at 15 months and 18 months" (1929, p. 94). This conclusion was in line with the genetic theory of development according to which it is "impossible to deflect and distort the patterns of cube behavior even with the protracted period of training, because these patterns are basically deter-mined by the intrinsic mechanics of development" (p. 96). Gesell and Thompson's conclusion in 1929 was based on their focusing on the similar aspects and ignoring the differences in the twins' behavior. However, to give the experimental hypothesis a fair chance, scientific methodology requires that the focus be on the differentiating aspects. Luckily, these data were finally provided 12 years after the experiment had taken place (1941). In Tables 24, 25, 26, and 27 (1941, pp. 51–56), Gesell and Thompson provided information on both similarities and differences among the twins in tasks involving cube manipulation and building of towers, bridges, and gates. Faced with this presentation of the data they had to admit that "T's manner of manipulation tends to be superior to that of C" (p. 56). The tables include 25 comparisons of T and C in which the twins' performance was not identical, and which were recorded at various ages from 15- and 18-months to 7½-years. Of these, T displayed superior performance in 22 ($z=3.60$, $p<.05$). In a different section of the paper entitled "Fine Motor Coordination" (1941, p. 45) Gesell and Thompson provided the times in seconds required by T and C to complete four test situations: pulling a string to secure a lure; opening a puzzle box; building a bridge, gate, or tower with cubes; and putting pellets into a bottle. The tests spanned the age period from 18-months to 13-years. Thirteen of the comparisons given in Tables 17, 18, 19, and 20 (1941, pp. 45–46) represent data not included in Tables 24–27 discussed above, and indicate a difference in time to complete the task. Of these comparisons, T was faster than C in 10, a statistically significant result ($z=1.66$, $p<.05$). Even for the ages 15- and 18-months alone, these tables contain 9 differences out of which T was superior in 8, a statistically significant advantage ($z=2.00$, $p<.05$). Gesell and Thompson had earlier (1929) claimed to have found no differences for these ages.

Starting with age 8-years and until 13-years, the twins were given a more sophisticated, free construction task intended to measure also imagination and planfulness. The task involved blocks with holes, rods, wires, and wooden plaques that could be fitted together. Table 23 (1941, p. 50) included 13 comparisons of T and C in which a difference was observed. Of these, 10 indicated a superior performance for T, a statistically significant advantage ($z=1.66$, $p<.05$).

We may conclude that, contrary to Gesell and Thompson's claim in 1929, T superseded C in both quality and in speed of cube behavior and fine motor coordination, and hence in imagination and planfulness, at least as expressed in tasks requiring fine motor control. These data are congruent with the hypothesis that 6 weeks of playing with cubes at the age of 1-year give the trained child an edge that will generalize to different fine motor tasks and that will not fade over the years.

Intelligence and Scholastic Ability

From a learning point of view, mastery of motor skills opens up new opportunities for learning. Accordingly, after T received her training, she was better equipped than C to investigate her world and manipulate it to provide her with further learning opportunities, as was illustrated by the previously mentioned fact that the nurses played more with T because she was more responsive. It would, therefore, be predicted that early motor training has favorable effects on general cognitive development.

In the section dealing with the intelligence of the twins, Gesell and Thompson claimed that "twenty-two developmental examinations and intelligence tests were made between the ages 24-weeks and 13-years" (1941, p. 47). But Table 1 (1941, p. 9) indicates that 11 additional developmental examinations had in fact been performed, some of which, if not all, included intelligence measurements. For example, five such ratings, at age 4½, were reported in Hilgard (1933). Gesell and Thompson themselves, in a different section, provided information concerning scores on subsets of the Stanford–Binet test recorded at ages 8½ and 9½ (1941, Table 32, p. 76), ages not included in the 22 ages discussed in the section on intelligence. Combining the data from the three sources, we obtain 12 measurements in which there was a difference between T and C. Of these, T scored higher than C in 10 cases. This difference is statistically significant ($z = 2.02$, $p<.05$). A different way to evaluate the reliability of the intellectual difference between the twins is based on the information reported by Gesell and Thompson, that the 22 tests were based on 612 ratings of the twins' development. Of the 99 ratings that indicated a difference between the twins, 82 revealed a difference in favor of T. This result too is statistically significant ($z = 6.43$, $p<.05$). Gesell and Thompson's own conclusion is somewhat hesistant: "If there is a genuine difference in intellectual ability it is slightly in favor of T" (1941, p. 48). But the statistical analyses performed here show that there was such a difference. The difference amounted to 4 IQ points on the average between 6- and 13-years-of-age. The mean IQ of the twins was 86. This can be broken down into the following means: 78 for the period in which they were living in the institute, 90 for the ages 3–5, and 95 for the ages 6–13, indicating that the home environment progressively reversed the effects of the rearing conditions in the institute.

While these data are, in general, congruent with the notion that intelligence scores are affected by environment, they also indicate that among the many environmental factors that affect intelligence, early motor training is an important one. The difference of 4 IQ points may not be large, but the difference between T and C in duration of motor training was small, too, compared to differences in amount of motor training that parents can give to their children. The finding that early motor training has positive effects on later intelligence is replicated in other studies to be discussed in the following.

School achievement test scores are in line with the trend in intelligence scores: Out of the 39 tests in which there was a difference in performance between T and C (Gesell & Thompson, 1941, p. 71), T superseded C in 23 tests (a statistically nonsignificant result by itself). Gesell and Thompson concluded that T was "in general slightly better than C in scholastic achievement" (1941, p. 72).

Summary

In all of the 121 pages of Gesell and Thompson's later paper (1941), containing a wealth of data concerning the later differences between T and C, the possibility that any of these differences was caused by the experiment was mentioned only in one paragraph (p. 118) and summarily discounted. Instead, the authors stated that the identical twins were, after all, only "nearly identical" (1929, p. 113) and that "T was endowed (through the gene effects) with slightly superior potentiality" (1941, p. 110). It is of course impossible to reject this hypothesis, but Gesell and Thompson's conclusion seems rather unfair to the logic of scientific inquiry, as this logic requires that two alternative hypotheses be considered. Normally, one would conclude that a superiority of T supports the learning hypothesis. But the way Gesell and Thompson interpret their data, there exists no experimental outcome that could, in principle, support the learning hypothesis. Gesell and Thompson's conclusion is unfair in particular to the logic of the "co-twin control" method developed by these authors themselves. This method was presented as "an experimental method for analyzing the relations of growth and learning" (1929, p. 6), in which we are able "to compare the individual with himself as he would have been if not trained" (1943, p. 211). Instead of using the method as proposed, once differences between the twins were observed, the method of co-twin control was ignored and possible effects of learning not even considered.

Gesell and Thompson's theorizing about the underlying genetic and constitutional differences between T and C have an additional disadvantage. While such assumptions could explain the long-range differences between T and C, they could not explain the short-range effects of motor training, that is, that the training resulted in a sudden increase in performance.

Whereas some of the studies described in this chapter (Dennis, 1938; McGraw, 1935) show the effects of early motor training and deprivation in their extreme, Gesell and Thompson's bears evidence for the utmost sensitivity of human motor and general development to the availability of motor learning opportunities. It is remarkable that a relatively small difference in the amount of motor training provided at the end of the first year had effects on motor and general cognitive abilities lasting for 13 years and probably throughout T and C's lives. These findings contradict the low-threshold assumption of the genetic theory of motor development, according to which "environmental factors only enter the picture if they are extremely deviant, and then serve more to disrupt . . . than to generate distinctive developmental progression" (Ausubel, 1959, p. 248).

In sum, Gesell and Thompson's study yielded several findings. The one that seemed most important to Gesell and Thompson, C's faster learning at an older age, can be accounted for both by the genetic and the learning theory of development. The two findings that were ignored by Gesell and Thompson, that most motor skills were achieved earlier in the trained twin and that a superiority in motor and general cognitive ability remained after the experiment, support a learning point of view and not the genetic one. It is to be regretted that the citations of this study in scientific papers and introductory textbooks are typically incorrect. A. R. Hilgard and Atkinson (1967) wrote, for example, that "it did not matter at the end that one twin had three times the specific training of the other" (p. 66). Kohlberg (1968), in a very influential paper wrote that "an untrained twin became as adept at . . . stair climbing after a week of practice as was the trained twin who had been given practice in stair climbing over many weeks" (p. 1030). Likewise, conclusions such as Tyler's about the "ineffectiveness of 'early' practice" (1964, p. 217) that were usually assumed to derive from Gesell and Thompson's study, are based more on the interpretation that these authors gave their data than on the data themselves.

THE SWADDLING STUDY

Dennis and Dennis (1940) studied the custom of the American Hopi Indians to tie their babies to a 29.53 × 11.81 in. (75 × 30 cm), flat wooden board, and the effect of this swaddling on the age at which the infant first walked alone. The Hopi infant, lying on his back, his arms extended at his sides, was wrapped tightly in a blanket and was then tied to the board with strips of cloth so that he could not move his arms or legs. Only his head was relatively free to move. For the first 3 months the infant spent nearly all of his time bound to the board. Although he was taken off the board one or more times daily either for bathing or for replacing soiled clothes, these operations did not take many minutes—combined they did "not occupy more than an hour daily" (Dennis, 1943, p. 623)— and he was returned to the board when they were completed. The infant nursed while tied to the board. The Hopi swaddling is often incorrectly described (Whiting, 1972) as consisting of a way by which mothers carried the infants vertically on their backs. Pictures of back carriers are sometimes supplied portraying infants whose hands are completely free (Ruch, 1971, p. 122). But Dennis reported that the board, with the infant upon it, lay upon the floor or upon a bed. It was "never placed vertically, and . . . [was] seldom carried about" (Dennis & Dennis, 1940, p. 78). The purpose of this binding was "to insure that the infant will be straight and of good carriage" (Dennis, 1943, p. 623).

When the infant grew older, he was allowed to spend an increasing amount of time off the board. The average age at which the board was discarded was 9-months, with a range of between half a year and a year. Dennis and Dennis compared 63 infants that had been swaddled with 42 that had not. The latter had been reared in two Hopi villages where the inhabitants were influenced by

American culture "to the extent of giving up the use of the cradle [the board]" (Dennis & Dennis, 1940, p. 77).

The main finding of this study was that the mean age of first walking alone was 14.98-months in the group of swaddled babies and 15.05-months in the control group. The difference between these means was small and statistically insignificant. This finding did not seem to support the predictions of a learning theory. The Dennises' conclusion was, therefore, that restrictions on movement and on access to motor learning opportunities do not affect the age of walking alone. The theory that was employed to explain this conclusion was the genetic theory of development that views environment as a threshold variable: "Additional training or practice above a certain minimum has very little effect upon infant behavior" (1940, p. 82). The extent to which the genetic theory of development slights the importance of learning factors is remarkable: Even when the infant cannot move at all he receives a measure of training and practice that, according to this theory, is above the minimum that is required for normal development.

The difficulty with Dennis and Dennis's conclusion is that the obtained Hopi mean ages of walking are late in comparison with existing norms. For example, the median age of 14.4-months for walking alone obtained in the Hopi groups is 2.7 months behind the median age of 11.7-months for walking found by Bayley (1969) in a large and representative sample of American infants. Dennis and Dennis themselves tried to estimate the extent of retardation by comparing the Hopi mean walking-age with the means reported in nine studies of other groups of infants. The Hopi mean age was 1.00 to 1.8 months older than the means reported in these other studies. From the data supplied by Dennis and Dennis (1940), it can be calculated that the means of walking in the Hopi swaddled and unswaddled groups were between 2.5 and 5 standard errors behind the means of the other groups. Since the Hopi means of walking are based on relatively large numbers of children, it may be assumed that the sampling distribution of these means is approximately normal. The retardation of the Hopi children, is therefore, statistically significant ($p<.05$). The Hopi mean was slower than that found in samples of Chinese, Filipino, Haole, Hawaiian, Japanese, Korean, Portuguese (Smith, Lecker, Dunlap & Cureton, 1930), Belgian, British, French, Swedish, Swiss (Hindley, Filliozat, Klackenberg, Nicolet-Meister, & Sand, 1966), and Kenyan (Super, 1976) to name just a few different groups. It is altogether possible that this retardation was determined by the particular genetic endowment of the Hopi Indians. But the explanation that would be provided by any learning theory is that these infants had relatively few opportunities for motor learning. Indeed, what Dennis and Dennis report, concerning the Hopi child-rearing practices in the swaddled group, supports this hypothesis.

Although Dennis and Dennis noticed the developmental retardation of the Hopi infants, the explanations sought seem farfetched. The altitude in which these Indians live (about 2000 m above sea level) and the kind of food they eat were mentioned as possible causes for the slow development. The final conclusion was, however, that "the cause of this retardation of the Hopi children was not ascertained" (Dennis & Dennis, 1940, p. 86). Dennis and Dennis, like Gesell and Thompson in their study, ignored the logic of the investigation, which was designed to choose between the genetic and the learning theories of motor development by testing whether swaddling affected motor development or not. When Dennis and Dennis encountered evidence—the equality of the experimental and control groups—that indicated that motor development was not affected, they espoused the genetic theory and rejected the learning one. When another aspect of their data—the Hopi motor retardation—supported the learning theory, these investigators did not even consider this theory as a possible explanation.

Though the above analysis well establishes the fact that the Hopi children were retarded in walking, there are two reasons to suspect that their actual age of walking was later than 15-months. First, the ages of walking as reported by Dennis and Dennis (1940) were not actually recorded by them but given to them by the mothers of the children who, at the time of report, were between 2- and 6-years-old. Since Dennis and Dennis limited their sample to all parents who had children aged 2 to 6 and who were able to report an age of walking for their children, they could not have obtained the age of walking of a child who was older than 2 and was not walking yet at the time they were interviewing the parents. Second, Pyles, Stolz, and Macfarlane (1935) and McGraw and Molloy (1941) found that mothers' reports of their children's ages of walking was biased so as to portray a more precocious picture of their children. The tendency to produce a biased report seemed to increase with a decreasing level of social class, education, and intelligence of the mother and with time passed after the child had walked alone. In Pyles, Stolz, and Macfarlane's study, a group of mothers with a relatively high socioeconomic status, who were interviewed about 7 months after their children had walked alone, claimed that their children had walked 0.4 of a month earlier on the average than was true. In McGraw and Molloy's (1941) study, with a group of mothers of lower socioeconomic status, who were interviewed somewhere between 1½ and 7½ years after their children had walked alone, the average reported age of walking alone was 3.2 months earlier than it really had been. Since the Hopi mothers had little education and since they were interviewed between 1 and 5 years after their child had walked, it is possible that they too reported an age of walking that was several months earlier than the actual age.

What remains to be explained is the fact that the onset of walking in the group of unswaddled Hopi infants was also retarded. This would be explained by a learning approach if it could be assumed that these infants also were deprived of motor learning opportunities. The only evidence we have that could support such an explanation is the Dennises' report that, except for not being swaddled, the nursing customs and the child rearing practices of the control infants remained "virtually unchanged" (1940, p. 77) relative to those of the swaddled infants. This may mean that, during the first months, they too were kept all the time on their backs, that they too were not held during feeding, not held in a vertical or a sitting position, and that they too were not played with.

But even if the unswaddled infants were kept on their backs as much as the swaddled ones, why were the swaddled infants not more retarded in walking than the control ones whose movements were not restricted? It is probably the case that those movements that can be made by an unswaddled baby that is lying on his back do not facilitate the development of skills involved in walking. Dennis and Dennis (1940) argued that "the importance of the 'random movements' which occur during this period [i.e., the first months] has been stressed by many writers" (p. 79). However, no reference to any of these writers was given and there are several empirical findings that support the assumption that the "random movements" made by the infant when he lies on his back do not contribute to the development of walking skills. For example, Dennis (1960) himself showed 20 years later that keeping infants lying on their backs all hours of the day, not just for 9 months but until the infant walked by himself, could delay the onset of walking not by 3 or 6 months but almost indefinitely. In one Iranian orphanage he found that out of 33 children who were in their 4th year and who were kept lying on their backs all their life, only 5 were able to walk alone. In a second institution, only 3 children out of the 40 who were in their third year were able to walk. Held's (1965) study of the kittens who were deprived of the feedback that would normally result from their movements, and whose motoric development was impaired, provides additional support for the notion that movements that an infant makes while lying on his back and which do not result in feedback to the infant, have no effect on the development of walking. If this notion is correct, we might have an explanation for the retarded onset of walking in Dennis and Dennis' control group.

To summarize our discussion of the swaddling study—while the swaddled group was not more retarded in motor development than the unswaddled control group, which, prima facie, favors a genetic theoretical point of view—the fact that the swaddled Hopi infants were retarded in their motor development is consistent with the learning point of view. The Dennises' report does not contain enough information about the way the unswaddled infants were raised to give conclusive support to a learning explanation of these infants' retardation. But the little that is reported does not preclude such an explanation.

The fact that the average walking age of the Hopi children was later than that found in a normal population was forgotten in many of the quotations of this study in later sources. Ziv (1975), for example, summed up: "nevertheless, the Hopi infants start to walk at the age of approximately one year—just as most other children" (p. 244). Others have given similar summaries (e.g., Garrison & Jones, 1969; Whiting, 1972). It seems to us that the Hopi retarded development and the ambiguity of the results should disqualify this study from being repeatedly quoted as giving strong support to the point of view that motor development is not affected by the availability of learning opportunities.

THE DEPRIVATION STUDY

Del and Rey, two fraternal twins, were born January 19, 1932, in the University of Virginia Hospital. On the 8th day of life they were taken to the home of relatives, and on the 36th day they were removed by Wayne and Marsena Dennis to an isolated room in the Dennises' home, "which was specially prepared for the experiment" (Dennis, 1935, p. 18), designed to test the effects of minimizing social stimulation and adult teaching on development. They remained in this room until they were 14-months-old (Dennis, 1932, 1935a, 1935b, 1935c, 1936, 1938, 1940, 1941; Dennis & Dennis, 1951). During this period, Del and Rey were left alone in their room lying on their backs in their cribs. They were taken out of their cribs only for feeding and cleaning. Feeding took place at a schedule of once every 4 hours. While these activities took place, Mr. and Mrs. Dennis did not smile at the babies, talk to them, play, or interact with them in any way. They did not punish or scold the infants, nor did they reward them, by patting or special attentiveness. During the feedings, the hands of the infants were tied under a bib or handkerchief to prevent them from reaching and holding the food. The twins were kept lying on their backs during the feedings as well. The infants had no toy to play with, no interesting objects or picture to look at, and an opaque screen was hung between the cribs of the two twins so that they would not see each other. Except for very rare visits, no person entered Del and Rey's room except Mr. and Mrs. Dennis.

In later publications the Dennises attempted to portray the experiment in a more favorable way, successfully misleading many (Fowler, 1983; Stone, 1954; Watson & Lindgren, 1973). For example, in his article of 1938 Dennis implied that the depriving conditions lasted only 7 months. But this is contradicted by what Dennis said in the first papers on the experiment that were published in 1935: "Mrs. Dennis and I reared two infants from the end of the first to the end of the fourteenth calendar months of life under conditions of full experimental control" (Dennis, 1935c, p. 17; the same was said in Dennis, 1935a, p. 215, and Dennis, 1935b, p. 242).

In a paper that appeared 20 years after the experiment (Dennis & Dennis, 1951), the Dennises claimed that, since they entered the twins' room to observe the infants as well as to take care of them, "one or both experimenters were in the room about two hours per day . . . . This means that the babies were not 'isolated' " (p. 111). But in a paper of 1935 (Dennis, 1935b) we read that, even when the experimenters were in the room for the purpose of observation and recording, they "sat at the foot of the cribs and about four feet from them, in a position which made . . . [them] invisible to the twins" (p. 246).

Dennis' Main Test of the Twins' Development

Dennis (1938) compared the development of the two infants to the developmental norms that Dennis and Dennis (1937) had prepared based on a collection of 40 biographies of normal children. The norms contained the median age and age-range of first appearance, as reported in the biographies, for 50 behavioral items. In line with the claim that the depriving conditions lasted only 7 months, Dennis made the following test: "with respect to the items whose upper limits appear within the first seven lunar months [4-week months] the twin subjects with few exceptions fall within the age range of children with normal environments" (Dennis, 1938, p. 153). Dennis concluded from this that the twins' record of development was indistinguishable from those of normal children.

This test of the twins' development was methodologically incorrect on two counts. First, Dennis checked whether the twins' data fell within a range. But to show that the experimental deprivation had not affected development, it had to be shown that the data did not fall regularly in the slower part of the range. That Dennis was aware of this appears from a section on "statistical concepts" underlying the deprivation experiment, published 3 years earlier, in 1935: "I have spoken above as if the normal limits of the age of appearance of a given response are quite definite. This is, of course, an over simplification. Rather it is that slowness of development becomes more rare as it becomes more pronounced, but extensive studies would show a few cases four and five sigmas above the mean age of development of the response . . . . if our subjects fall more than 2.78 sigmas above the mean age of appearance of any response the probability that we have produced an experimental effect is 997 in 1000" (1935c, p. 21). That is, even if the experimental results fell within the range obtained in a particular sample, they might have been far enough from the mean to indicate that the twins' development was retarded.

The second methodological flaw was that Dennis did not compare the twins to the range that lay between the slowest and the most precocious child. Instead, he compared the twins' record to an artificial range that lay between the collection of the worst and the best performances that were contributed by different individuals in the normative sample. A child in this sample who contributed the slowest age to one item may have reached other items in relative early ages. Thus, if the twins' data fell in the slower parts of the age ranges of most items, their development may in fact have been much worse than that of any individual in the normative sample.

A Correct Test of the Twins' Development

One possible test of the twins development is based on the following considera-tion: If the twins' development was an average one, it would be expected that the twins would pass about half the items at an age earlier than the normative median, and the other half later than the median. Following Dennis (1938), we will first look at the 28, earliest behavioral items out of the 45 pertinent items of the norms (the age of first appearance for the twins was not established for 5 of the 50 items). The 28th item is the last one whose upper limit appears within the first 7 months (28 weeks) of life. The analysis is based on the data as they were given in several locations (Dennis, 1938, Figure 1, p. 152, Table 1, p. 155; Dennis & Dennis, 1937, Table 1, p. 351; Dennis, 1941, Table 1, pp. 174–177). For Rey we find that 20 items were reached at a later age than the norm's medians and only 3 at an earlier age (5 items were passed at the median age). In Del's case, 19 items were attained later than the median age and only 5 at an earlier age (4 additional items were achieved at the median age). This prepon-derance of items passed later than the norm's medians is statistically significant ($z = 4.38, p < .05$). The conclusion to be drawn from this test is unambiguous and opposed to the one reached by Dennis: The infants were slower than the average normative development. The findings support the hypothesis that condi-tions of deprivation will cause retarded development even in the first months of life.

To obtain information about the size of the twins' retardation we computed on Dennis and Dennis's (1937) norms a mean and standard deviation of the age of first appearance for each behavioral item, and translated the ages of the items' first appearances for each child in the comparison group, and for each twin to standard scores. Next, the mean standard score of the first 28 items was com-puted for each individual, providing a single, developmental index that summa-rized the individual's relative standing in the first 7 months of the experiment. The analysis indicated that the twins' average index was 1.9 standard deviations behind the mean index in the comparison group (2.06 and 1.72 standard devia-tion behind for Rey and Del, respectively). This index can be made even more meaningful by noting its similarity in structure to infant intelligence scores in that it reflects the average relative development of the twins compared to a normative sample and is based on a wide variety of behaviors. We can therefore say that this index is roughly equivalent to an IQ (or Developmental Quotient) of 70 (67 and 72 for Rey and Del, respectively), assuming a standard deviation of 16. This is identical with the mean DQ of 70 found by Dennis and Najarian (1957) in a group of 2- to 7-month-old infants reared in a Lebanese institution in conditions much like those prevailing in the Dennises' experiment. While Dennis (1935c) noted in 1935 that ''the socio-economic status of the subjects, their ancestry and inheritance are certainly represented in normal studies of infant behavior . . . . [and that] their essential normality in health and constitution'' (p. 21) can be documented, the present analysis reveals how, within 7 months, the twins' average developmental level deteriorated to one that can be found in only about 3% of the population.

The Twins' Development Following the 28th Week

Dennis (1938) summarized the twins' development in the second half of the experiment as showing ''some records beyond the range of comparison cases'' (p. 154). But the finding was, in fact, that the developmental records of each twin were beyond the ranges of the comparison group on 12 of the last 17 items. The comparison of the twins' data with the normative medians shows that, excepting one tie in the data of Del, the twins passed all the items at a later age than the median. These results are statistically significant ($z = 5.57, p < .05$).

An indication of the degree of retardation in the period covered by the last 17 items is given by the above described analysis, which yielded mean developmental indeces. Rey and Del lagged an average of 4.0 standard deviations behind the average child in the comparison group (Rey and Del lagged 3.04 and 4.96 standard deviations, respectively). Using the previously discussed analogy to add meaning to this result, this index would correspond roughly to an intelligence score of 36. This score is again comparable to the mean DQ score of 46 obtained by Sayegh and Dennis (1965) in a group of 11 infants 7- to 14-months-old reared in the same Labanese institution mentioned above. In other words, 7 additional months of deprivation caused further deterioration of the twins' development to a level that can be found only in less than 0.01 of 1% of the population. Dennis concluded that the deprivation experiment ''shows that normal behavioral development can occur in some infants when most of the first year is spent under conditions of minimum social stimulation and of very restricted practice'' (1938, p. 156). The data contradict this conclusion.

Epilogue

Very litle information has been provided about the twins' development in the years following the experiment. Dennis (1938) did report that at 4½-years of age, Del's IQ was 70 and Rey's IQ was 107. In light of these intelligence scores Dennis claimed that ''Rey throughout her history has been essentially normal'' (1938, p. 156). But the above analysis clearly indicated that this had not been the case. As for Del, Dennis claimed that she ''was retarded in practically nothing prior to nine months of age . . . . the retardation which appeared following the first year was in all likelihood due not to the experiment'' (1938, p. 156).

Dennis' argument is based on two, invalid considerations. First, contrary to Dennis' claim in 1938, the experiment did continue past the 7th month. Thus, even if Del's retardation would have appeared only in the 9th month, it still would have appeared within the experimental period. Second, it had been shown that Del was retarded even prior to the 9th month. The premise of Dennis' argument is therefore false, and the conclusion does not hold.

Translating the twins' intelligence scores at 4½-years to standard deviations and averaging, we obtain that the twins were about 0.7 standard deviations behind the average level of development. This is 3.3 standard deviations better than their level during the second half of the experiment. The improvement in standard deviations over this period was about the same for Del and Rey, that is, 3.1 and 3.5, respectively, and needs to be explained for both, probably by the same explanation. Thus there is no reason not to average the two intelligence scores, which will reduce the error in the estimate of their true intelligence, and regard the score of 89 as most representative of the twins' development at 4½-years. The improvement in their general development relative to the first year of life can be explained easily by the twins' moving out of the depriving experimental environment into a more favorable one. On the nature of the postexperimental environment we only know what the Dennises wrote 20 years after the experiment, namely, that "since the experiment ended, they [the twins] have been at times under the care of relatives and at times in an institution for children" (Dennis, 1951, p. 105). The twins' mean score of 89 is less than the mean IQ of 96 obtained by Dennis (1973) for 28 children 4½-years-old, on the average, who had been raised in the Lebanese institution mentioned above (Dennis & Najarian, 1957; Sayegh & Dennis, 1965), and who had been adopted before 2-years of age. The twins' mean score is above the mean IQ of 55 characteristic of those 1-to 6-year-olds who remained in the Lebanese institution (1973). Our analysis of Gesell and Thompson's study (1941) similarly demonstrated the increase in IQ when children are taken out of depriving environments and placed in better ones, just as this study and others (e.g., Dennis & Najarian, 1957; Sayegh & Dennis, 1965) show that IQ or general developmental level deteriorates progressively during early infancy the longer a child remains in a depriving environment.

When the twins were 6½-years-old, Dennis reported that "it has become apparent during the past two years that Del has some disability of the left arm and leg. Her left arm is much more awkward than her right in all respects and is almost unused by her. Her left leg is very inferior to the right" (1938, p. 156). She was brought to the hospital where it was established that there was no impairement in her bones and muscles and where she was given a diagnosis of "mild left hemiplegia probably referable to cortical injury at birth" (p. 156). The post hoc nature of this etiology is shown by the fact that the same explanation was rejected by Dennis 3 years earlier, in 1935, when the twins were just three years old. Dennis wrote then: "that the infants were retarded by organic motor disability is contra-indicated by the fact that they learned readily to sit and to stand and to reach when training was begun'' (1935c, p. 29). While it is impossible to prove that Del's hemiplegia was not caused by an injury at birth, the fact that her motor disability grew progressively worse with the duration of the experiment, until, by the end of the experiment, she could perform only few of the motor behaviors normally achieved by children her age, supports the learning hypothesis that the later retardation was a continuation of the earlier one and a direct consequence of the experimental deprivation.

In 1938 Dennis claimed that the hemiplegia ''became apparent'' only in the later years and that it had not made itself ''manifest at an early age'' (p. 156). And in 1951 the same claim was supported by saying that ''extensive movie records taken in the third month reveal no disability on the left side'' (Dennis & Dennis, 1951, p. 121). But in a study devoted to the manual dexterity of the twins, published in 1935 (1935b), Dennis reported data that indicated a gradual deterioration in the developmental status of Del's left hand. No right-hand preference was detected in Del in the early months. But, during the 7th through 9th lunar months, Del used a single hand rather than both in 87% of the times any manual behavior was observed, and of these she used her right hand in 82% of the times. In special tests given during the 11th through 15th lunar months, these percentages increased to 99 and 100, respectively. In the 17th lunar month, when Dennis restrained Del's right arm in order to test her ability to use her left arm, Del, sitting in a high chair, was unable, within the three trials allotted for this observation, to grasp a nursing bottle and pull it towards her mouth with her left hand. Dennis characterized this as a ''striking deficiency of the unpracticed hand'' (1935b, p. 249).

The true iteology of Del's left hemiplegia thus may well have been a gradual atrophy through increasing lack of practice. Dennis concluded, in line with the genetic theory of development, that his study showed that ''the infant within the first year will 'grow up' of his own accord'' (1938, p. 157). It seems to us that the results are congruent with the hypothesis that if an infant is not taught motor skills in the first year, there is a real danger that he will not learn some of these skills by himself and that in later years he will develop the equivalent of a partial paralysis.

The Motor Training of the Twins

The first report of data resulting from the deprivation experiment, published when the twins were 3-years-old (1935c), was concerned with training of motor skills that was begun in the 8th month. Dennis's conclusion from the motor training was that ''each response was readily established when practice was offered'' (1935c, p. 30). This conclusion reflected the tenet of the genetic theory that when the organism is mature for some behavior, a minimum of instruction is sufficient to bring it about. It is our claim, however, that Dennis unduly emphasized responses that seemed to be established readily and deemphasized, or altogether excluded from the report, responses that were not acquired at a fast rate. It seems to us that if all the data are taken into account, they support the conclusion that the average motor response was not established any faster in the twins at 8-months than in normal children who start to learn motor skills at birth.

One response that was established faster than in normal children was grasping a dangling ring, which was achieved after an average of 15, daily presentations. The twins had, however, some experience in grasping their bed clothes, hands and feet. For Del's left hand, which had had almost no practice in grasping, the presentation of the ring for 40 days did not constitute enough stimulation to establish a grasping response. This hand never grasped the ring in these trials. The fact that, by the age of 6½-years, this hand was still "almost unused" and mildly paralytic raises doubts that this hand learned to grasp faster than hands of normal children.

A second response was sitting alone, which the twins achieved after an average training period of 1½ months, which is faster than normal children.

A third response, standing for 2 minutes while supported under the arms, was achieved by the twins in less than 4 days of training. This seems to be a fast rate of learning indeed. But it was deemphasized in the report that Del and Rey were able to stand while holding furniture only much later, at 15- and 12-months of age, respectively, and that they were able to stand alone only at 25- and 15-months, respectively. Thus, while Dennis (1935c) claimed that the twins "learned to stand", this was not what is usually meant by standing nor what Dennis (e.g., 1938) himself meant by this expression in other reports on the twins, but rather what is commonly referred to as the "standing reflex", that is, the infant's temporary straightening of the legs to carry his weight. In light of Zelazo's (1976) findings, it seems that Dennis succeeded in eliciting the twins' latent, neonate standing reflexes and was unable, in 4 days' time, to bring these under voluntary control. Since the response can be elicited from the neonate, it does not seem that it was elicited faster in the twins than in normal children.

A fourth response was creeping. In the later reports of 1938 and 1941, Dennis reported that on day 254, or in the same period during which other motor training was provided, Del and Rey were placed prone on the floor for 5 to 30 minutes each day. This stimulation was provided "to give the subjects an opportunity for types of exercise which could not be gained when they lay supine" (Dennis, 1941, p. 163). Mention of this stimulation and its results was not made in the 1935 report on the training of various motor skills. The results did not support the prediction of the genetic theory and indicated that Rey started to creep only 5 months after the initiation of the training and that Del was "never" (1938, p. 155) able to do so. While Rey's rate of learning to creep was somewhat faster than normal children—creeping is normally achieved in 7 months (Bayley, 1969)—it was not very fast and Del's rate was clearly slower than that of normal children.

Finally, the achievement of two responses, standing alone and walking, was deemphasized in Dennis' (1935c) report. Following the training in the 8th month, it took Del and Rey 17 and 7 additional months, respectively, to learn to stand alone. Walking was achieved by Del and Rey 17 and 9 months, respectively, after the training. Rey's rate of learning cannot be viewed as very fast, and Del's was slower than the 11–12 months needed by the average normal child to learn to stand and walk.

To conclude, most responses were not established with "relative promptness" (1935c, p. 28), as claimed by Dennis, when training was provided at the age of 8-months. Some responses took longer to be established than they require in the average child who receives a normal amoung of learning opportunities starting from birth. The finding that an older, isolated child did not learn faster than a younger, normal child was replicated in McGraw's (1935) study to be reviewed next. The study thus demonstrates that if infants are relatively well deprived of adult teaching, as they were in this experiment, not much "maturation" takes place, as opposed to the experiment by Gesell and Thompson (1929) in which no control was exerted over learning that occurred outside of the experimental sessions.

No later than when the twins were 14-months-old, additional knowledge must have been acquired which showed that the damage caused by a year-long intensive deprivation was not going to be repaired "promptly" even by a month-long, training effort. This additional knowledge was not reported until 1941 (Dennis, 1941), after the theory concerning Del's birth injury had been developed. Here, Dennis wrote about the decision to return the twins to their mother, and "to bring . . . [Del] up to the normal performance for her age" (1941, p. 170). Dennis reported how he and his wife tried to place Del in the creeping position to get her to creep and how "she always dropped immediately to the prone position" (p. 170). The Dennises often placed her on a pad on the floor and put a rattle, of which she was fond, in front of her outside her reach to encourage her to creep. But "she did not creep" (p. 170). The Dennises led her many times in an attempt at getting her to walk. "But she would not try" (p. 170). They often stood her up in the crib, but "she preferred to sit down" (p. 170). Dennis concluded: "our efforts at training were apparently without effect" (p. 170), which is a perfect contradiction of his 1935 evaluation of the twins' motor training. This time Dennis' conclusion corroborates ours: Hardly any "maturation" was apparent in Del. Roughly speaking, the Dennises were as successful in training Del as they would have been with a neonate.

Summary

It is to be regretted that the deprivation study is always misrepresented in the literature. White's (1971) quotation of the study is typical: "With few exceptions, the behavioral development of these infants [Del and Rey] was largely unaffected by what appeared to be a significant degree of long term deprivation'' (p. 27). In an introductory textbook of educational psychology, Biehler (1974) concluded: "However, in still other studies [and here he quoted Dennis] . . . little or no evidence of retardation due to restricted experience was found'' (p. 101).

We have shown that when this study is analyzed correctly it demonstrates that, depriving infants of motor and other learning opportunities in the form of active adult intervention, results in extreme motor and general retardation that increases with the duration of the deprivation. Moreover, the effects on motor development seem to be lasting. Though the general developmental level of the twins improved somewhat after the termination of the experiment, 5½ years after the experiment the motor retardation of one of the twins was still so severe that it had to be described as a mild paralysis. When Dennis's attempt at motor rehabilitation of the twins is represented correctly, it shows that the twins were not able, on the whole, to learn motor skills faster at a later age than normal infants at an earlier age. This contradicts the genetic point of view espoused by Gesell and Thompon (1929) and leads to the conclusion that when infants are greatly deprived of stimulaton, no "maturation" occurs.

THE STUDY OF JOHNNY AND JIMMY

The Experiment

Johnny and Jimmy Woods, born April 18, 1932 (McGraw, 1942, p. 22), were chosen to serve as subjects in McGraw's experiment (1933, 1934, 1935, 1939) when they were identified, at birth, as identical twins. The purpose of this cotwin controlled study was "to evaluate the influence of exercise or use of an activity upon its development" (1935, p. 22). Johnny and Jimmy were brought to a clinic 5 days a week for 7 hours a day. While Johnny was stimulated and received training in various skills, Jimmy was placed "on a routine schedule with as little handling and stimulation as possible" (1933, p. 681). He was left virtually undisturbed in his crib except for periodic tests at weekly (during the first year, see 1935, pp. 56, 71), then biweekly, and finally monthly intervals, to compare his performance with Johnny's. The experiment started when the twins were 20-days-old and lasted until the age of 22-months, at which point Jimmy received 2½ months of training in an attempt to restore the experimental damage.

Though the study of Johnny and Jimmy lasted longer than the Dennises' deprivation study, Jimmy's deprivation was less severe than that of Del and Rey, because he spent the remaining part of the day at home. It seems that Johnny and

Jimmy were picked up at home at 9 a.m. and were back by 5 p.m. McGraw estimated that the twins slept at home an average of 10 hours a day. This leaves approximately 58 waking hours a week at home compared with 35 hours a week at the clinic, which probably included some sleeping also. Johnny and Jimmy thus spent only about a third of their waking time in the experiment. The experimental effects might have been further mitigated by the attitude of the family toward the experiment. We are told that "it was difficult for them [the family] not to favor Jimmy and not to try to make up for some things he did not get" (McGraw, 1939, p. 13). In addition, when the twins were returned home, Jimmy was wide awake and ready to play while Johnny was tired and ready to go to sleep.

Development During the First Year

According to McGraw, Johnny apparently occupied a disadvantaged position in the uterus. At birth, "Johnny presented a picture of utmost flaccidity, being not only more flaccid than Jimmy but more flaccid than many infants" (1935, p. 38). Unlike Jimmy, he displayed, in a weak form, only few of the reflexes that can be elicited from a normal baby. The description of the twins at birth (1935, pp. 38–39) permits making 14 comparisons of Johnny and Jimmy. In 13 of these Johnny's development was inferior to that of Jimmy's. In one comparison the twins were equal. By a sign test, Johnny's inferiority was statistically significant ($z = 3.33$, $p < .05$) It was Johnny's weakness that determined that he be stimulated and Jimmy deprived in McGraw's experiment.

Most of the development in the first year was reported in Chapter 3 of McGraw's book (1935). Here McGraw described the training of 11 behaviors. Johnny's Moro reflex was stimulated every 2 hours by sudden blows on the mattress on which he was lying. His suspension grasp reflex was stimulated daily by letting him grasp a rod that was lifted so that he was suspended in the air until he got tired and fell. McGraw held Johnny suspended by his feet every day for 15 seconds. In addition, McGraw trained his rolling-over from side to side, creeping, sitting, walking, and his reaching and prehension behavior. Reaction to rotation was trained by holding Johnny under the arms and spinning around rapidly. Reaction to cutaneous irritation was practiced by pricking the infant with a blunted pin-point in the leg, forearm, chest, and cheek.

The information provided by McGraw (1935) in her third chapter concerning the development of substages and various achievements related to these 11 areas of training, contains 104 comparisons of the twins in which differences between their respective achievements were noted. In 59 of these instances, Johnny's development was superior as compared with 45 cases in which Jimmy surpassed Johnny. This difference is not statistically significant ($z = 1.27$, $p > .05$). The present statistical result indicates, however, a clear recovery from the complete inferiority at birth. When McGraw concluded that the behaviors discussed in Chapter 3 were "not materially influenced by exercise" (1935, p. 118), she clearly referred to the twins' overall, apparent equality of development. But she ignored the fact that this final equality represented different rates of development due to the different starting points of Johnny and Jimmy. The existence of such different rates of development during the first year would be congruent with a learning point of view according to which the behaviors discussed in Chapter 3 were indeed affected by the respective training and deprivation of Johnny and Jimmy. The data concerning the twins' subsequent development render plausibility to the learning point of view.

The Twins' Development During their Second Year

Chapter 4 (McGraw, 1935) contains the description of Johnny's training in another set of 11 tasks. The average age at which training started was 1-year. Within an average period of 4 months, Johnny learned to swim without support, dive spontaneously, ascend inclines of 61 deg. to the top of a stool 63¼ in. (1.61 m) high, descend a 40 deg. slide prone and head first, walk up an incline of 40 deg., get off the 63¼-in. stool by hanging from the top and letting go, skate in a mode of a proficient skater, jump with "a spring" from the 63¼-in. stool into an adult's arms, jump from a 14½-in. (37 cm) stool to the floor, obtain a lure suspended at a height of 3.02 yds (2.78 m) by arranging several stools under it and climbing the stools, and obtain a suspended lure by stacking 3 boxes and climbing them. Johnny derived superb delight from engaging in all these activities. Regarding the majority of the tasks, McGraw evaluated that no other child under 2-years-of-age known to her had ever succeeded in reaching Johnny's level of performance. Concerning several tasks, such as walking up inclines, she concluded that Johnny's performance "excelled that of . . . adults" (1935, p. 151).

In his periodic tests, Jimmy did not succeed in performing any of the above tasks or simpler ones involving, for example, stools or slides as low as 7½ in. (19 cm) and inclined as little as 11 deg. Jimmy's diving and skating were not tested, apparently, because it was hopeless. The emerging picture of Jimmy in the test of the remaining 9 skills was pathetic. Jimmy's most outstanding behavior in these tests was crying, which he did consistently in 5 of the 9 tests. His second most characteristic behavior was "reaching vainly", which was his typical response to another set of 5 of the 9 types of tests. The third typical response was excessive clinging, which he demonstrated in 2 of the 9 tests, but of course in most tests the experimenter was too far to allow for clinging. Certainly, at this point, Johnny's and Jimmy's development were already "beyond comparison'' (McGraw, 1935, p. 151). Thus far the data support a learning theoretical point of view of early development in general and of motor development in particular.

The Speed of Learning at a Later Age

When Jimmy was 22-months-old he received 2½ months of training in 9 areas: activities on slides, getting off stools, skating, jumping, manipulation of stools, manipulation of boxes, tricycling, recall, and language comprehension (McGraw, 1935, Chapter 6). McGraw compared the speed by which Jimmy learned these skills to Johnny's rate of learning them at an average age of 13½ months. For each of 8 out of 9 training areas, Johnny's rate of learning exceeded Jimmy's, and for each of these 8 areas McGraw concluded unequivocally that ''comparison of the time required in their respective accomplishments . . . reveal greater achievements of Johnny within a given period of practice time than was shown by Jimmy during an equal interval of time'' (1935, p. 246), and that ''Jimmy's advanced age gave him no advantage'' (p. 243). Only for tricycling were the results reversed. The overall result of 8 out of 9 comparisons in which Johnny was superior is statistically significant ($z = 2.00$, $p < .05$). The finding that at 13-months-of-age Johnny's rate of learning was faster than Jimmy's at 22-months-of-age supports a learning theory (Carroll, 1963; Razel, 1977, 1984) that assumes that the learning rate depends on previous experience, since at these respective ages Johnny had had 1 year of training in various motor skills and Jimmy none. The finding refutes, however, the genetic theory proposed by Gesell and Thompson (1929) according to which learning rate depends on maturation that is determined solely be age. McGraw's data replicate what was found for the two girls deprived by the Dennises, and strengthens the conclusion that if a child is not taught, no ''maturation'' takes place. The data support the view that twin C's greater rate of learning at an older age, attributed by Gesell and Thompson (1929) to ''maturation,'' was actually caused by C's greater amount of accumulated experience at the older age. This part of McGraw's study, however, was simply ignored by educators, psychologists, and people in the medical professions, except, of course, for the tricycling part (Pontius, 1973; Stone, 1954).

The fact that Johnny's rate of learning at the end of the first year was faster than Jimmy's at the end of the second is significant also because it furnishes independent evidence that refutes McGraw's claim that the twins' development was the same during the first year. If the twins' levels of development had been equal at the end of the first year, Jimmy, at the end of the second year, would have been expected to benefit from his training as much as Johnny did at the end of the first year. The fact that Jimmy did not supports our conclusion that, toward the end of the first year, Johnny's development was more advanced than Jimmy's.

The Permanence of Johnny's Motor Superiority

Jimmy's training unquestionably had a beneficial effect even at an older age. But 2½ months of training could redress only a small part of a depriving condition that lasted 9 times as long. The results indicate that not only did McGraw fail in bringing Jimmy and Johnny to the same level at the end of the experiment, but she was also unable to bring Jimmy at 24½-months to Johnny's level at 16-months, the average age at which Johnny had had 2½ months of training in the skills under consideration.

In the paper of 1939 McGraw provided information concerning the twins' relative performance in activities on slides, getting off stools, jumping, manipulation of graded stools, manipulation of graded boxes, and swimming at the age of 6-years. She also discussed tricycling and skating, but without giving details of relative achievements. In all of the first 6 mentioned skills, Johnny's performance superseded Jimmy's, resulting in statistical significance ($z = 2.04$, $p < .05$). There was also no closing of the gap in general motoric behavior. McGraw noted that Jimmy "has never . . . attained the agility which Johnny manifests in his performance" (McGraw, 1939, pp. 5–6). Neither did he show Johnny's coordination, nor his abandonment. Rather, an inhibiting muscular tension was characteristic of his behavior.

The last report of Johnny and Jimmy was written by McGraw in 1942 when the twins were 10 years old. The article contained relatively little information, but McGraw did report that the motor superiority of Johnny was still intact: "Johnny handles himself more smoothly in physical activities . . . he shows more ease and grace. In some activities he is more skillful and confident" (p. 37).

The long follow-up provided by McGraw thus seems to indicate that the effects of early motor training never disappeared. This finding replicates the one obtained by the Dennises' that some of the early motor outcomes, such as Del's inability to use her left hand, never disappeared, and Gesell and Thompson's that T retained her gross and fine motor superiority over C for as long as we have accounts of their development.

Intelligence

McGraw concluded that there was "no evidence, that the early training of the experimental baby [Johnny] was of great advantage to him later in the solution of distinctly new problems'' (1934, p. 749; see also 1935, p. 280). But McGraw based this conclusion on a month-long experiment that followed Jimmy's retraining. In this experiment, 2-year-old Johnny and Jimmy were presented with test problems, mostly taken from a study with chimpanzees, that were too easy— except for one verbal problem that was too difficult—for both twins. This resulted in ceiling and floor effects, respectively. But differences between the twins in situations that tested new problems could be detected, of course, only by tasks that were neither too easy nor too difficult for both twins. Intelligence tests with their graded series of problems offer a good opportunity to test McGraw's conclusion.

McGraw administered two different tests when the twins were 22-months-old and again at the age of 25-months (1935, p. 278). In all tests, Johnny scored higher than Jimmy. Averaging these scores, we obtain 107 and 101 as average IQs for Johnny and Jimmy, respectively. McGraw assigned no importance to these findings, saying that ''the reliability and validity of the tests at the younger age level is highly questionable'' (1935, p. 278). But the analysis of the twins' Rorschach tests when they were 6-years-old indicated that the difference in intelligence had not disappeared. This analysis concluded that Jimmy's reasoning ''was not above average'' (1939, p. 16), while Johnny was intellectually ''above average'' (1939, p. 16). Thus, Johnny was rated superior in 5 out of 5 comparisons of intellectual ability, a statistically significant advantage ($z = 1.79, p < .05$). This finding supports the hypothesis that early motor stimulation results in a higher intelligence. These data duplicate what was found for T, C, Del, and Rey in the studies reviewed.

Other Effects of Early Stimulation and Deprivation

There are several additional differences between Johnny and Jimmy that deserve to be mentioned in order to take full advantage of the information emanating from McGraw's unique experiment.

Fearfulness

In the first year Jimmy started to display ''extreme caution'' (McGraw, 1935, p. 72). In the second year Jimmy grew to be fearful in situations that posed even a minimal degree of physical danger, such as descending an 11 deg. slide from a stool 7½ in. (19 cm) high. McGraw indicated, that there was no doubt that Jimmy did not lack the motor skills to perform some of these tasks. This was indicated by the fact that he did perform 3 of them (ascending, descending, and walking low inclines) a single time at the average age of 11-months. But these successes apparently only proved to him how "dangerous" the tasks were since they were never repeated until he received his training a year later. In contrast, McGraw testified that she had "never observed an infant or young child who could be so completely relaxed" (1935, p. 296) as Johnny. McGraw was of the opinion that the lack of training was the cause of Jimmy's fearfulness, and she proposed that "many childhood 'fears' may be attributed not necessarily to some unpleasant experience and resultant associations but to a natural growth imbalance" (1935, p. 290). The early effect did not seem to vanish with age. When the twins were 6-years-old, it was reported that Johnny's mother felt that Johnny had "no fears and . . . that he would be better off if he were a little more cautious, especially in his attitude toward dangerous occupations, such as crossing streets" (1939, p. 14).

These findings are congruent with the notion that early motor training nurtures fearlessness and physical security and, conversely, that neglecting this kind of training will result in a fearful child. This hypothesis is supported also by Gesell and Thompson's report that, subsequent to the experiment, C "was more afraid of falling than T" (1929, p. 67), and that while "T showed greater motor fearlessness, C's motor deportment suggested . . . fearsomeness" (p. 108), and by Dennis' account of Del's and Rey's apprehensiveness of unfamiliar objects and sounds (1941, p. 159). These findings are also congruent with those pertaining to animals. For example, Harlow and Harlow (1966), Levine (1960), and Wilson, Warren, and Abbott (1965) found that isolated monkeys, rats, or cats that did not receive handling—a simple form of motor stimulation—grew up to be fearful even in situations that are generally regarded as neutral. Levine (1960) singled out the stress component in handling as responsible for its beneficial effects. This was evidenced by the fact that electric shocks administered daily in the life of rats seemed to have the same effect as early handling. There is no doubt that some of McGraw's early motor training tasks were unusually loaded with a stress component, such as unexpectedly hitting Johnny's mattress with a stick every 2 hours, letting him hold a stick until he fell from fatigue, and pricking him with a needle in four areas of his body.

Though not perfectly in line with what was reported above, which pointed to Johnny's emotional stability, the psychiatrist that interviewed the twins at age 6 reported that "Johnny gives evidence of some tension; he was always a nail-biter, and the mother states that he . . . cannot sit still in a chair and from time to time displays quite restless sleep. In addition, Johnny has always been enuretic nightly" (McGraw, 1939, p. 13), though the latter was reported to be a family failing also with Jimmy wetting his bed occasionally. It was also reported that "Johnny, among all the Woods children, is a thumb sucker, this began in early infancy and continues at bedtime even today" (p. 14). The psychiatric interview at age 6 is the only source that indicates that Johnny had any emotional problems. It remains an open question if and in what way these problems were caused by the experiment.

Crying

The difference between the twins in their use of crying as a response developed already in the first year. Of the 11 kinds of stimulation provided by McGraw during that period, the more stressful 5—training the Moro reflex, grasping reflex, inverted suspension, rotation, and pin pricks—seem particularly relevant to the development of crying. In these five training areas, Johnny's early response, crying, was extinguished at an average age of 4-months. Jimmy's crying, on the other hand, continued as a typical response to these situations when presented in the periodic tests till the end of the experiment. Often he "cried so much as to preclude the test situation" (McGraw, 1935, p. 115). We have noted that Jimmy's typical response to 5 out of 9 tasks presented in the second year— ascending and descending inclines, getting off stools, jumping off high stools into an adult's hands, and jumping off a low stool onto the floor—was excessive crying. Towards the end of the experiment, the crying reached the level of "severe temper outbursts" (McGraw, 1939, p. 13). The relationship between the experiment and Jimmy's tendency to cry was well recognized by McGraw, who stated that "Jimmy, because of his restriction, was getting more and more tense and cranky and developing temper tantrums" (McGraw, 1935, p. 22). What was reported about the twins when they were 6-years-old indicated that the early patterns did ntot disappear with time: "Jimmy cries easily when things do not go his way or if he is scolded. He indulges in mild temper tantrums consisting of stamping his feet when he cannot get what he wants" (McGraw, 1939, p. 13), while with Johnny "there are no temper outbursts and he rarely cries" (p. 14).

The findings are congruent with the hypothesis implied by McGraw, that early motor training extinguishes crying as a general response set, perhaps by teaching alternative responses that, at an early age, are usually motoric in nature. The hypothesis fits Gesell and Thompson's finding that C, who received less motor training than T, developed a "greater susceptibility to crying and emotional disturbance" (1929, p. 70), as well as Dennis' (1941) report of Rey's and especially Del's tendency to cry in response to stimuli that would not elicit crying in normal infants, such as the sound of crumpling paper.

Dependence and Independence

The data of McGraw's experiment support the hypothesis that early motor training and its witholding cause the development of independent and dependent personalities, respectively. Jimmy's dependence in the second year was shown, for example, by his excessive clinging. Animal studies such as Harlow and Harlow's (1966) have also demonstrated that monkeys raised in isolation later show exaggerated tendencies toward partner clinging. Jimmy's dependence was also indicated in his reaching out helplessly in difficult situations. For instance, instead of manipulating the stools and climbing them to obtain a lure, "he would stand beneath . . . [the lure] reaching up vainly" (McGraw, 1935, p. 182). This situation illustrates how motor inability conditioned dependence. Johnny's independence, on the other hand, was founded on some skills reinforced through their repeated usefulness in solving motor problems. Thus, McGraw noted his exceptional "persistence and his manner of pausing at intervals to look the situation over before acting" (McGraw, 1935, pp. 182–183). An analysis of the twins' Rorschach tests at age 6 (McGraw, 1939, p. 16) described Jimmy as "more dependent, more appealing to adults" and as lacking "the capacity to preoccupy himself with imaginative and instructive games". It characterized Johnny as "more independent" and more "individual", whose "reactions to the environment are determined from within", and who is "on the whole . . . rather self confident". A psychiatric evaluation of Johnny and Jimmy concluded the same: "Johnny gives the impression of being able of weathering more serious environmental difficulties". These findings are similar to Gesell and Thompson's who observed 4 months after the experiment that C "had a greater amount of dependency" (1929, p. 111).

The lesson here seems to be that leaving a child alone in his crib does not nurture greater independence in the child, as is so often believed (Pikler, 1968). Positively put, it seems that greater engagement with the infant through motor stimulation results in his being more independent at a later age.

Language Development

The linguistic environment of Jimmy was very peculiar and its effects deserve to be documented. Since his crib had been standing behind an opaque screen in a busy nursery, he was able to hear all day long adults' conversation and children's chatter through the screen. In 1935 McGraw viewed this as "stimulation in language and comprehension" (p. 214), but it seems that the verbal stimuli must have sounded relatively meaningless behind the screen. The result of this unusual verbal stimulation was that "Jimmy could be heard daily behind his crib saying in fairly clear English, 'See der ball' or 'Dere der ball' innumerable times, though there was no ball in sight" (1935, p. 217). Jimmy's speech production was therefore consistently better than Johnny's, though he did not approach Johnny in understanding directions or in identifying objects by names. By the time Jimmy's deprivation had ended, the "sounds Jimmy emmitted during twenty-four hours would be many times the verbalizations of Johnny" (McGraw, 1935, p. 258). At that age he still "had a noticeable proclivity for repetition of the same phrase or sentence irrespective of the situation" (1935, p. 257). The specific linguistic effects of the early deprivation did not seem to disappear over the years. At age 6 it was observed that Jimmy was "all day as a rule chattering a blue streak about whatever comes into his mind" (McGraw, 1939, p. 13), but that he "was quite apt to grow almost incoherent in the rapidity with which he spouted out detail after detail and leaped from topic to topic'' (1939, p. 14). Jimmy "reacted to the questions immediately without taking thought as to how he answered'' (1939, p. 14). At age 10 he was "still a chatterbox'' (McGraw, 1942, p. 37) while Johnny was "the 'quieter' of the two . . . [and] more thoughtful'' (p. 37).

The unusual linguistic conditions that prevailed in McGraw's experiment thus furnish evidence for an unusual hypothesis: Early abundance of meaningless verbal stimulation results in a later tendency for abundant meaningless verbal productivity.

Straightness of Bones

McGraw indicated that Jimmy's recovery from the normal degree of infantile bowing of the legs occurred several months later than Johnny's and was "much slower . . . than that of other infants'' (1935, p. 297). McGraw provided the X-ray photographs of the twins' long leg bones at age 32-months and concluded that, at that time, the skeletal development of both was normal and that the experiment "had had no permanent effect upon their skeletal growth'' (1935, p. 298). A closer look at the bones indicates, however, that Jimmy's left and right tibiae were considerably more bowed than Johnny's, indicating perhaps that the effect was permanent nevertheless. These findings are congruent with the hypothesis that early motor training causes an earlier and greater straightening of the bones. This contradicts the Hopi belief that to achieve straightness of bones, it is desirable to keep the infant off his feet and swaddled to straight objects. The idea that bones will respond to stress involved in motor activities by straightening goes contrary to the genetic view of development that likens the infant to a plant that will bend as a result of pressure. McGraw who subscribed to the genetic view, looked for pressure that could have bent Jimmy's bones. Since Jimmy was sitting more than Johnny, she concluded that Jimmy's sitting put strain on the long bones of his legs and arms. It seems implausible that sitting puts more pressure on the arms and legs than do standing, walking, jumping, and carrying heavy boxes.

To recapitulate, it can of course not be proven that any of these developmental differences between the twins were caused by the experiment. But the data are congruent with such a hypothesis. Thus, contrary to what is commonly accepted, McGraw's study can be shown to indicate that early motor training can have enormous impact on the development of a less fearful, happier, more independent, more intelligent, better built, and motorically superior person.

McGraw's Presentation of the Main Findings

Like Dennis, McGraw chose to divide the experiment in 2 halves in the presentation of the results. Concerning the first half she then claimed that "there is no indication that such traits as the Moro, suspended grasping reflexes, sitting alone, erect locomotion, etc., can be modified appreciably by daily practice'' (1933, p. 681). As to the behaviors trained in the second half, she admitted that these skills ''can be greatly expanded through training'' (1933, p. 681). This is also the way the results are presented in the literature (Corbin, 1973). We have seen that the effects of the experiment, like the Dennises' deprivation study, were cumulative and progressive, in line with a learning theoretical view of development: The damage of deprivation and the benefit of training increased with the duration of the treatment. Of course, it was easier to single out the first half and claim that the experiment had no effect within that part. We have seen, however, that even such a claim could be made only by ignoring the initial developmental disadvantage of Johnny at birth.

Like Gesell and Thompson, McGraw (1935) employed the cotwin control method. In the first few months of life, the twins showed ''extraordinary correspondance'' (p. 34) and similarity. At birth, their being identical twins was established also by the existence of a single placenta. But ''the differences in personal appearance have become more noticeable as the children have grown older'' (p. 33). So much so that a ''study by the resemblance method cast doubt upon their single-ovum origin'' (p. 33). Dennis (1951), who reprinted and prefaced McGraw's 1939 paper, was quick to conclude that ''it became apparent . . . that the original diagnosis was in error'' (Dennis, 1951, p. 199). But the ''resemblance method'' is necessarily a ''subjective rating'' (McGraw, 1935, p. 31) that is based on standards and expectations deriving from twins who grew up in very similar environments unlike those of Johnny and Jimmy. Thus, like Gesell and Thompson, once differences between the twins were obtained, McGraw ignored the logic of the scientific design she was using. While in earlier reports (McGraw, 1933, 1934, 1935a) McGraw attributed the observed differences between the twins in ''attitude'' and ''emotional adjustment'' to the experiment, in the last report of the study it was emphasized that the ''personality differences may well be constitutional'' (McGraw, 1942, p. 27).

Like Dennis's reports of Del and Rey, the later the report, the more benign the description of the depriving conditions. In the earliest paper it was asserted that Jimmy had received ''as little handling and stimulation as possible'' (McGraw, 1933, p. 681). By the time 2 more years had passed McGraw claimed that Jimmy ''was by no means isolated'' (1935, p. 40), the reason being that his crib had been standing behind the opaque screen in the nursery and that he had been able to hear what went on in the nursery. McGraw claimed now that ''during the early part of the experiment Jimmy's activities were not restricted any more than would be customary for the average infant'' (1935, p. 40). In the report published when the twins were 10-years-old, McGraw asserted that ''during the first twenty-two months of the twins' lives, Jimmy played in his crib. He had plenty of company in the nursery, and was soon chattering a blue streak'' (1942, p. 22). Considering that he had nobody to play with and that ''objects were . . . witheld from Jimmy during the hours that he was in the clinic'' (1935, p. 103), claiming that Jimmy played in his crib was an inappropriate euphemism. The latter claim, that he had ''plenty of company'' was misleading too, since McGraw did not point out that all this ''company'' was kept behind an opaque screen and never had personal contact with Jimmy.

Concerning the twins' levels of intelligence, McGraw claimed in the last report that ''the boys always rated within the normal range on standardized intelligence tests'' (1942, p. 37). Like Dennis (1938) before, McGraw uses the concept of ''normal range'' to cover up differences, since we have seen that Johnny's intelligence was superior to Jimmy's. It is not clear whether McGraw refers here to new intelligence scores in addition to those obtained when the twins were 2-years-old. It is conspicuous, however, that this report, in contradistinction with Gesell and Thompson's (1941) later follow-up report, did not include easily accessible, quantitative information as school performance. Instead of providing differential information, McGraw emphasized that the twins were ''lively'', ''healthy'', and ''normal''.

The increasing tendency to withold information, ameliorate the description of the depriving conditions, and reject the earlier assumption of responsibility for the experimental results gives rise to the suspicion that, like in the Dennises' case, as time went by, the possible results of the experiment became ever more disturbing. For example, the photographs given of Jimmy in this last report (McGraw, 1942, p. 23) seem to show that as Jimmy grew older he became increasingly cross-eyed and suffered from a squint in his left eye. This defect was never mentioned by McGraw. It is entirely possible that this was caused by a mild left hemiplegia referable to a cortical injury at birth, or by any one of a great many other influences. But it is also possible that it was caused by a muscular weakness originating from a lack of visual and motor stimulation in early infancy.

In a single footnote, McGraw (1935, p. 34) indicated that the results of her experiment with Johnny and Jimmy were being checked with another pair of identical twin girls. John Dewey, too, in his introduction to McGraw's book made a footnote that mentioned these twins (1935, p. xiii). The present author was unable to locate any further references by McGraw to these twin girls. It would be of great interest to try to identify Del, Rey, Johnny and Jimmy and the two additional twin girls studied by McGraw and study their later development.

Summary

The study of Johnny and Jimmy shows that intensive levels of early motor training can produce outstanding, even prodigious, motor achievements, while deprivation results in slow development. The study indicates that the effect of training and deprivation is cumulative in line with a learning theory of development. The finding that a 2-year-old, isolated twin learned motor tasks slower than his trained brother at 1-year of age supports the learning theory and refutes the notion of a genetically controlled "maturation". The study raises the possibility that the effects of early motor training are not confined to the motor domain, but that it results in a higher intelligence as well as greater happiness, independence, fearlessness, and a better bone structure. A long follow-up indicates that the effects of early motor training and deprivation do not disappear with time.

DISCUSSION

In the foregoing sections, we have reanalyzed the empirical evidence most frequently cited as supporting the genetic theory of motor development according to which this development is not affected by the availability of learning opportunities. Our analysis indicated that motor development can indeed be accelerated by training and decelerated by conditions of deprivation. In addition to this evidence, there are many other studies showing the dependence of motor development on learning opportunities, and we will mention a few of these here. The extremely retarded motor development reported in Dennis's (1960) study of Iranian institutions for children was already mentioned. Comparing different institutions, Dennis also found that the extent of retardation was directly related to the degree of the child's neglect in the institution. Dennis (Dennis & Najarian, 1957; Sayegh & Dennis, 1965) similarly reported retarded motor development among children raised in a Lebanese institution in conditions of deprivation of learning opportunities. Kohen-Raz (1968) found retarded motor development among babies that were reared in five Israeli institutions.

Other evidence resulting from a "natural" experiment was cited by Super (1976). He found that the early motor precocity of Kenyan babies (compared with American ones) was related to active teaching of skills such as sitting, standing, and walking by their parents. Super (1976) recorded frequencies of educational activities and found, for example, that the Kenyan infant was sitting (e.g., on an adult's lap) 60% of his waking time during the first months of life compared with 40% for the American infants, much of whose sitting was in an infant seat, which requires little exercise of the trunk muscles. Super reported that 80% of the Kenyan mothers employed deliberate teaching methods such as holding the infant under the arms and bouncing him on her lap starting at 1-month of age, or sitting him down by himself with special support for his back at the fifth month. Super gathered some evidence that tends to rule out the genetic explanation of the African precocity. For example, he found that the Kenyan infants were slightly retarded in motor skills, such as crawling, lifting the head while in the prone position, and rolling over, in which they received less exercise than their American counterparts (e.g., they were lying down only 10% of their waking time compared to 30% in the American sample). Also, infants of Kenyan parents whose child rearing practices had been affected by western standards and who provided less training in upright locomotor skills than typical Kenyan parents but more than American ones, walked and sat at an age half way between the respective ages in the other two groups.

Pikler (1968) examined the motor development from birth to age 3 of 736 children raised in an institution in Budapest. Pikler reported that in 1946, based on her many years of experience as a pediatrician, she introduced a new educational regime in the institute. According to this method, "direct interference— i.e., 'teaching' by adults—is not a necessary condition for infants achieving gross motor skills" (p. 37). Moreover, requiring performances according to certain norms was viewed as "potentially harmful and disturbing to normal development" (p. 32). Thus, motor training, such as "keeping the child in a certain position, whether by adults or by equipment, or in any way causing him to make movements that . . . he is not yet able to execute by himself" (p. 31), was strictly avoided even if the child was rather slow in acquiring the normal motor abilities. The infant was thus not put in the prone, sitting, standing, or walking positions, was always carried and fed horizontally while lying supine. Toys were placed near the child on the bed but never in his hand nor hung within his hands' reach: "He must attain them himself" (p. 31). The rationale for this extreme form of "learning through discovery" strategy was the belief that these children would grow up to be "more independent, more sure in their movements, and, in general, more content and quiet in their behavior than . . . other children . . . reared in the customary way" (p. 33).

Pikler compared the mean ages at which turning from side to side, creeping, sitting, standing and two levels of walking were achieved by her children to the mean ages at which these were achieved by normal children as reported in six developmental scales. Pikler concluded that the ages of appearance of the motor skills in her children "agree surprisingly" with those of the norms (p. 35) and that her children "achieved stages of gross motor ability without appreciable delay" (p. 37). This conclusion was quoted in the literature as correct (see Whiting, 1972), but it is based on Pikler's subjective impression rather than on a statistical analysis of the data. It is possible to make 36 comparisons between Pikler's means and those of the norms. Of these, Pikler's infants lag behind the norms in 29 comparisons and are superior to them in 5 (there are 2 ties). The retardation of the children who were left to learn by themselves was thus statistically significant by a sign test ($z = 3.94$, $p < .05$). These data, too, are congruent with the assumption that denying children motor learning opportunities results in retarded motor development. Pikler did not report any data relevant to her hypotheses about her children's later independence, confidence in movements, happiness, or loudness of behavior. But had she known the correct results of the studies reviewed in this paper, the institute's children could have been spared, perhaps, Pikler's educational innovations.

Experimental evidence relevant to our discussion was provided by Hunt, Mohandessi, Ghodssi, and Akiyama (1976). The motor retardation found by Dennis (1960) challenged these investigators to test the effects of several educational interventions on improving various, mostly nonmotor, areas of development in infants reared in Iranian orphanages. It was found that reducing the infant/caretaker ratio from 10/1 to 10/3 (in a group designated "the third wave") advanced the mean age of standing with support from 16- to 9-months. Observation of the nurses led to the conclusion that their main educational activity consisted of holding the infants and carrying them about, which may, among other things, have stimulated the balancing mechanisms of the infants. The mean age of standing was improved to a slightly lesser degree—10- and 10.5-months—in two other experimental groups (the "fourth and fifth waves," respectively). The fourth wave consisted of audiovisual and tactile stimulation introduced by various objects, toys, and inanimate feedback systems. The fifth wave consisted of improving the infant/caretaker ratio to 3/1 or 2/1. The ratio in the fifth wave was superior to that in the third, but the nurses were directed this time to emphasize nonmotor and language stimulation while the nurses in the former group were allowed to interact with the infants in any way that was natural for them.

Other experimental evidence that appropriate motor training advances motor development had been provided by Zelazo and his coworkers (Zelazo, Zelazo, & Kolb, 1972; see also Zelazo, 1976) who trained a group of 1-week-old babies in standing and in walking by holding the babies under their arms for 3 minutes, four times a day. There were three control groups. In the "passive exercise group", the motor stimulation consisted of the infants having their mothers move their legs while they were lying or sitting down. A second control group received no training but was tested weekly for 8 weeks along with the experimental and passive exercise group. Each test lasted one minute in which the infant was held just like in the experimental group. A third control group was tested only once at 8-weeks of age. The results of 7 weeks of training were that the median age of walking alone in the practice group was 9.6-months, 2.4 months earlier than that of the control group. Moreover, the mean ages of walking of the four groups were nicely correlated with the amount of training they received. If these results are not chance (which must be determined in future research), they indicate that the age of walking is extremely sensitive even to small variations in amount of training. Zelazo et al. (1972) reported several other nonexperimental cases, including the Zelazos' own child, in which early training resulted in early walking. The experience of this writer, who trained the standing reflexes of his four children starting the first week of life, was similar. These children also received help and training in sitting, standing, and walking in the subsequent months and were given the opportunity to use the baby walker (a bicycle-type chair on wheels) and jumper (a seat hanging on a spring). The mean age of walking of these children was 9.8-months.

The possibility that early motor training has dangerous effects was raised by Gotts (1972) and Pontius (1973). But Zelazo et al. (Zelazo, Zelazo, & Kolb, 1972; Zelazo, Konner, Kolb, & Zelazo, 1974) pointed out that these authors merely expressed apprehensions for which no empirical support was provided. While the evidence of dangers in early motor training is apparently nonexistent, there is much evidence, part of which was reviewed in this chapter, indicating the concrete educational and developmental dangers that are involved in the prevention of motor training.

The significance of early motor training is not limited to early motor behavior. That early motor development affects later development has been demonstrated in studies that were analyzed in this chapter. Conceptually, it is easy to see how motor skills, such as sitting, standing, and walking would supply the infant with powerful means by which he could make better use of the learning opportunities available in his environment and investigate his world more efficiently. The view that walking on two feet accelerates the child's cognitive development is congruent with the opinion of anthropologists such as Napier (1967) who stated that man's way of locomotion "may be the most significant ability that sets him apart from his ancestors" (p. 56). If our analysis of the studies discussed in here is valid, the question seems not if early motor training affects later development but if there is any field of human education where teaching has greater and farther reaching consequences than early motor training. A theoretical framework for the notion that motor development is an instrument that accelerates development in other areas was given elsewhere (Razel, 1977, 1984). Empirical evidence that is in line with this idea can be found in the positive correlations between test scores of motor and mental development during infancy. The median correlation between the motor and mental subtests of the Bayley Scales within the age-range of 2- and 30-months is .46 (Bayley, 1969). This view is not shared by all psychologists. For example, Mussen et. al. (1979) claimed that "among normal children, there is no predictive relation between the age of walking or rate of physical development during the first two years and conceptual intelligence during the early school years" (p. 124). To be sure, the data contradict this claim. In a longitudinal study by Broman, Nichols, and Kennedy (1975), which was based on more than 26,000 subjects, it was found that, out of 169 prenatal, neonatal, infancy, and childhood variables, such as mother's education, socioeconomic status, and mother's intelligence, motor development at 8-months, measured by the Bayley Motor Scale (1969), was the fourth best (for white American children), or best (for blacks) predictor of intelligence at age 4. The correlations were .22 and .24, respectively, and quite reliable due to the large number of subjects. Such correlations are usually viewed as insignificant because they are low. But large correlations would mean that later intelligence depended almost exclusively on early motor development, certainly a rather unreasonable assumption. The low correlations are consistent with the view that intelligence at a later age can be raised or lowered by a number of factors, early motor development being one of them. Broman et al. (1975) also found that the average difference in mean IQ at age 4 between those scoring one standard deviation above and those scoring two standard deviations below the mean motor score at 8-months was 20 points.

The significance of our reanalysis of the four studies thought to provide the strongest evidence for the genetic view of motor development is two-fold. First, it has practical implications for motor education in infancy. The parent or the child's caretaker in day-care centers, hospitals, and other institutions for raising young children, who is interested in, or responsible for, the optimal motor and cognitive development of the child, must teach the child to sit, stand, and walk.

Second, our analysis has implications for education in the years beyond infancy as well. The educators that have stressed the role of heredity in development and have minimized the importance of learning factors, have derived much support for their point of view from the classical studies that purported to show that motor development is not affected by learning conditions. The existence of a human behavior that seemingly was not affected by environmental conditions was used to give credibility to claims that other behaviors as well are not affected by learning. For example, Kohlberg (1968), who gave an interpretation of Piaget's theory of cognitive development that shared "with maturationism a pessimism about the effect of specific teaching on cognitive-structural development" (p. 1029), repeatedly relied on the assumption that early motor development is "primarily maturational" (p. 1034). Moore, Moon, and Moore (1972), who presented a pronounced genetic point of view of human development and who recommended to delay any type of formal learning to adolescence, based their recommendations, among other things, on Gesell's conclusion that tasks such as reading, writing, and arithmetic "depend upon motor skills which are subject to the same laws of growth which govern creeping, walking, grasping" (p. 617). Even when learning theorists have attempted to point out some dangerous educational outcomes that result from the application of the genetic view of development to educational practice, their offensive was often curbed by the existence of motor development that, as it were, could not be construed by learning principles. Thus, Ausubel (1959) argued that "lack of maturation can . . . become a convenient scapegoat whenever children manifest insufficient readiness to learn, and the school . . . consequently fails to subject its instructional practices to . . . self-critical scrutiny" (p. 248). However Ausubel felt the need to concede that his criticisms did not apply to "such traits as walking and grasping" (p. 249). Gagné (1965) similarly stated that "a pupil is ready to learn something new after . . . he had acquired the necessary skills through prior learning" (p. 27) since the maturational view "is valid for only the very earliest years of life" (p. 27). We have pointed out that the genetic point of view is incorrect even for early motor development and for the first years of life, and our discussion thus provides support for those educators who stress the importance of learning and instruction in human development. If even early motor development, hailed by most psychologists and educators as the archetype of behavior which is "primarily maturational" (Darley, Glucksberg, Kamin, & Kinchla, 1984, p. 359) and unaffected by environmental factors, turns out to be so highly sensitive to instruction, then there probably is no human behavior whose development is not extremely dependent on educational efforts.

REFERENCES

Ausubel, D. P. (1959). Viewpoints from related disciplines: Human growth and development. *Teachers College Record, 60,* 245–254.

Bayley, N. (1969). *Bayley Scales of Infant Development.* New York: Psychological Corporation.

Biehler, R. F. (1974). *Psychology Applied to Teaching* (2nd ed.). Boston, MA: Houghton Mifflin.

Broman, S. H., Nichols, P. L., & Kennedy, W. A. (1975). *Preschool IQ: Prenatal and Early Developmental Correlates.* Hillsdale, NJ: Erlbaum.

Carroll, J. B. (1963). A model of school learning. *Teachers College Record, 64,* 723–733.

Corbin, C. B. (1973). *A Textbook of Motor Development.* Dubuque, IA: Brown.

Darley, J. M., Glucksberg, S., Kamin, L. J., & Kinchla, R. A. (1984). *Psychology* (2nd ed.). Englewood Cliffs, NJ: Prentice-Hall.

Dennis, W. (1932). Two new responses of infants. *Child Development, 3,* 362–363.

Dennis, W. (1935a). An experimental test of two theories of social smiling in infants. *Journal of Social Psychology, 6,* 214–223.

Dennis, W. (1935b). Laterality of function in early infancy under controlled developmental conditions. *Child Development, 6,* 242–252.

Dennis, W. (1935c). The effect of restricted practice upon the reaching, sitting, and standing of two infants. *Journal of Genetic Psychology, 47,* 17–32.

Dennis, W. (1936). Infant development under minimum social stimulation (Abstract). *Psychological Bulletin, 33,* 750.

Dennis, W. (1938). Infant development under conditions of restricted practice and of minimum social stimulation: A preliminary report. *Journal of Genetic Psychology, 53,* 149–158.

Dennis, W. (1940). *Infant reaction to restraint: An evaluation of Watson's theory. Transactions of the New York Academy of Sciences,* ser. II, *6.* 202–218.

Dennis, W. (1941). Infant development under conditions of restricted practice and of minimum social stimulation. *Genetic Psychology Monographs, 23,* 143–189.

Dennis, W. (1943). The Hopi child. In R. G. Barker, J. S. Kounin, & H. F. Wright (Eds.), *Child Behavior and Development.* New York: McGraw-Hill.

Dennis, W. (1951). (Ed.). *Readings in Child Psychology.* New York: Prentice-Hall.

Dennis, W. (1960). Causes of retardation among institutional children: Iran. *Journal of Genetic Psychology, 96,* 47–59.

Dennis, W. (1973). *Children of the Crèche.* New York: Appleton-Century-Crofts.

Dennis, W., & Dennis, M. G. (1937). Behavioral development in the first year as shown by forty biographies. *Psychological Record, 1,* 349–361.

Dennis, W., & Dennis, M. G. (1940). The effect of cradling practices upon the onset of walking in Hopi children. *Journal of Genetic Psychology, 56,* 77–86.

Dennis, W., & Dennis, M. G. (1951). Development under controlled environmental conditions. In W. Dennis (Ed.), *Readings in Child Psychology.* New York: Prentice-Hall.

Dennis, W., & Najarian, P. (1957). Infant development under environmental handicap. *Psychological Monographs, 71* (7, whole No. 436).

Dworetzky, J. P. (1981). *Introduction to Child Development.* St. Paul, MN: West Publishing.

Fowler, W. (1983). *Potentials of Childhood: Vol. 1. A Historical View of Early Experience.* Lexington, MA: Lexington Books.

Gagné, R. M. (1965). *The Conditions of Learning.* New York: Holt, Rinehart and Winston.

Garrison, K. C., & Jones, F. R. (1969). *The Psychology of Human Development.* Scranton, PA: International Textbook.

Gesell, A., & Thompson, H. (1929). Learning and growth in identical infant twins: An experimental study by the method of co-twin control. *Genetic Psychology Monographs, 6,* 1–124.

Gesell, A., & Thompson, H. (1941). Twins T and C from infancy to adolescence: A biogenetic study of individual differences by the method of co-twin control. *Genetic Psychology Monographs, 24,* 3–121.

Gesell, A., & Thompson, H. (1943). Learning and maturation in identical infant twins: An experimental analysis by the method of co-twin control. In R. G. Barker, J. S. Kounin, & H. F. Wright (Eds.), *Child Behavior and Development.* New York: McGraw-Hill.

Good, T. L., & Brophy, J. E. (1980). *Educational Psychology: A Realistic Approach* (2nd ed.). New York: Holt, Rinehart and Winston.

Gotts, E. E. (1972). Newborn walking. *Science, 177,* 1057–1058.

Guttman, L. (1977). What is not what in statistics. *Statistician,* 81–107.

Harlow, H. F., & Harlow, M. (1966). Learning to love. *American Scientist, 54,* 244–272.

Hays, W. L. (1963). *Statistics for Psychologists.* New York: Holt, Rinehart and Winston.

Held, R. (1965). Plasticity in sensory-motor systems. *Scientific American, 213,* 84–94.

Hilgard, E. R., & Atkinson, R. C. (1967). *Introduction to Psychology* (4th ed.). New York: Harcourt, Brace and World.

Hilgard, E. R., Atkinson, R. C., & Atkinson, R. L. (1975). *Introduction to Psychology* (6th ed.). New York: Harcourt Brace Jovanovich.

Hilgard, J. R. (1932). Learning and maturation in preschool children. *Journal of Genetic Psychology, 41,* 36–56.

Hilgard, J. R. (1933). The effect of early and delayed practice on memory and motor performances studied by the method of co-twin control. *Genetic Psychology Monographs, 14,* 493–567.

Hindley, C. B., Filliozat, A. M., Klackenberg, G., Nicolet-Meister, D., & Sand, E. A. (1966). Differences in age of walking in five European longitudinal samples. *Human Biology, 38,* 364–379.

Hunt, J. McV. (1961). *Intelligence and Experience.* New York: Ronald Press.

Hunt, J. McV., Mohandessi, K., Ghodssi, M., & Akiyama, M. (1976). The psychological development of orphanage-reared infants: Interventions with outcomes (Tehran). *Genetic Psychology Monographs, 94,* 177–226.

Kohen-Raz, R. (1968). Mental and motor development of Kibbutz, institution and city infants. *Megamot, 15,* 366–387. (In Hebrew).

Kohlberg, L. (1968). Early education: A cognitive-developmental view. *Child Development, 39,* 1013–1062.

Levine, S. (1960). Stimulation in infancy. *Scientific American, 202,* 81–87.

McGraw, M. B. (1933). The effect of practice during infancy upon the development of specific behavior traits (Abstract). *Psychological Bulletin, 30,* 681–682.

McGraw, M. B. (1934). The effect of specific training upon behavior development during first two years (Abstract). *Psychological Bulletin, 31,* 748–749.

McGraw, M. B. (1935). *Growth: A study of Johnny and Jimmy.* New York: Appleton-Century.

McGraw, M. B. (1939). Later development of children specially trained during infancy: Johnny and Jimmy at school age. *Child Development, 10,* 1–19.

McGraw, M. B. (1942, April 19). Johnny and Jimmy. *New York Times Magazine,* 22–23, 37.

McGraw, M. B., & Molloy, L. B. (1941). The pediatric anamnesis: Inaccuracies in eliciting developmental data. *Child Development, 12,* 255–265.

Moore, R. S., Moon, R. D., & Moore, D. R. (1972, June). The California Report: Early schooling for all? *Phi Delta Kappan,* 615–621, 677.

Mussen, P. H., Conger, J. J., & Kagan, J. (1979). *Child Development and Personality* (5th ed.). New York: Harper and Row.

Napier, J. (1967). The antiquity of human walking. *Scientific American, 216,* 56–66.

Pikler, E. (1968). Some contributions to the study of the gross motor development of children. *Journal of Genetic Psychology, 113,* 27–39.

Pontius, A. A. (1973). Neuro-ethics of "walking" in the newborn. *Perceptual and Motor Skills, 37,* 235–245.

Pyles, M. K., Stolz, H. R., & Macfarlane, J. W. (1935). The accuracy of mothers' reports on birth and developmental data. *Child Development, 6,* 165–176.

Razel, M. (1977). Educational Learning Theory and the timing of learning tasks. *Studies in Education, 17,* 101–126. (In Hebrew).

Razel, M. (1984). The intelligence test as a measure of knowledge. In preparation.

Ruch, F. L., & Zimbardo, P. G. (1971). *Psychology and Life* (8th ed.). Glenview, IL: Scott, Foresman.

Sayegh, Y., & Dennis, W. (1965). The effect of supplementary experiences upon the behavioral development of infants in institutions. *Child Development, 36,* 81–90.

Smith, M. E., Lecker, G., Dunlap, J. W., & Cureton, E. E. (1930). The effects of race, sex, and environment on the age at which children walk. *Journal of Genetic Psychology, 38,* 489–498.

Stone, L. J. (1954). A critique of studies of infant isolation. *Child Development, 25,* 9–20.

Stone, L. J., & Church, J. (1979). *Childhood and Adolescence: A Psychology of the Growing Person* (4th ed.). New York: Random House.

Super, C. M. (1976). Environmental effects on motor development: The case of 'African infant precocity'. *Developmental Medicine and Child Neurology, 18,* 561–567.

Tyler, F. T. (1964). Issues related to readiness to learn. In E. R. Hilgard (Ed.), *Theories of Learning and Instruction, 63rd Yearbook, Part 1, National Society for the Study of Education.* Chicago, IL: University of Chicago Press.

Watson, R. I., & Lindgren, H. C. (1973). *Psychology of the Child* (3rd ed.). New York: Wiley.

White, B. L. (1971). *Human Infants: Experience and Psychological Development.* Englewood Cliffs, NJ: Prentice-Hall.

Whiting, H. T. A. (1972). Learning motor skills. In J. E. Kane (Ed.), *Psychological Aspects of Physical Education and Sport.* London, England: Routledge and Kegan Paul.

Wilson, M., Warren, J. M., & Abbott, L. (1965). Infantile stimulation, activity, and learning by cats. *Child Development, 36,* 843–853.

Zelazo, P. R. (1976). From reflexive to instrumental behavior. In L. P. Lipsitt (Ed.), *Developmental Psychobiology: The Significance of Infancy.* Hillsdale, NJ: Erlbaum.

Zelazo, P. R., Konner, M., Kolb, S., & Zelazo, N. A. (1974). Newborn walking: A reply to Pontius. *Perceptual and Motor Skills, 39,* 423–428.

Zelazo, P. R., Zelazo, N. A., & Kolb, S. (1972). Newborn walking. *Science, 177,* 1058, 1060.

Zelazo, P. R., Zelazo, N. A., & Kolb, S. (1972). "Walking" in the newborn. *Science, 176,* 314–315.

Ziv, A. (1975). *Psychological Aspects of Education.* Tel Aviv, Israel: Niv. (In Hebrew).

Author Index

Italics indicate bibliographic citations.

A

Abbott, L., 198, *211*
Achenbach, T. M., *127*
Ackerman, P., 92, *128*
Ainsworth, M., 147, 148, 154, *166*
Akiyama, M., 206, *210*
Almy, M., 32, *88*
Ambron, S., 134, 142, 143, 145, 147, *169*
Anderson, C., 132, 155, 156, *166*
Anderson, L. W., 26, *90*
Arend, R., 155, *166*
Atkinson, R. C., 171, *210*
Atkinson, R. L., 171, *210*
Attanucci, J., 154, *170*
Auerbach, S., 139, 158, 160, 162, *166*
Ausubel, D. P., 179, 208, *209*
Axelrad, S., 147, *166*

B

Balow, B. J., 92, 117, 125, 126, *127*
Banta, T. J., 44, *88*
Barnett, I., 147, 152, 154, *170*
Barthel, J., 5, *23*
Baumrind, D., 154, *166*
Bayley, N., 181, 190, 207, *209*
Bell, S., 147, *166*
Beller, E. K., 59, *88*
Belmont, I., 91, 92, *127, 128*

Belsky, J., 131, 132, 136, 138, 139, 141, 149, 151, 165, *166, 168*
Benn, J., 131, 140, *168*
Bennell, J., 26, *89*
Bereiter, C., 44
Biber, H., 31, 84, *88*
Biehler, R. F., 192, *209*
Bierman, J., 138, *170*
Bizzell, R. P., 27, 88, *89*
Blank, M., 49, *90*
Blehar, M., 136, 157, *166*
Blishen, B., 101, 102, *127*
Blomquist, M., 92, 117, 125, 126, *127*
Bloom, B., 152, *166*
Bond, J. T., 26, 27, *90*
Bradley, R., 152, *166*
Broberg, K., 16, *23*
Broder, P. K., 120, *128*
Brody, S., 147, *166*
Broman, S. H., 207, 208, *209*
Bronfenbrenner, U., 136, 138, *166*
Brophy, J. E., 123, *127, 172, 210*
Brown, J. D., 1, *24*
Brownlee, M., 142, 152, *167*
Bruck, M., 95, 99, *127*
Bryan, J. H., 94, *128*
Bryan, T. M., 94, 123, *128*
Bugbee, M., 30–32, 62, *89*

Subject Index